# LOST IN SPACE

# LOST IN SPACE

## GEOGRAPHIES OF SCIENCE FICTION

EDITED BY

# ROB KITCHIN AND JAMES KNEALE

continuum
LONDON • NEW YORK

Continuum
The Tower Building, 11 York Road, London, SE1 7NX
370 Lexington Avenue, New York, NY 10017–6503

First published 2002

**British Library Cataloguing in Publication Data**
A catalogue record for this book is available from the British Library.

ISBN 0-8264-5730-4 (hardback)
0-8264-5731-2 (paperback)

**Library of Congress Cataloging-in-Publication Data**
Lost in space : geographies of science fiction / edited by Rob Kitchin
and James Kneale.
    p.   cm.
    Includes bibliographical references and index.
    ISBN 0-8264-5730-4—ISBN 0-8264-5731-2 (pbk.)
    1. Science fiction—History and criticism. 2. Space and time in literature.
I. Kitchin, Rob. II. Kneale, James.

PN3433.6.L67 2001
809.3'8762'09384—dc21                                    2001032309

Typeset by Refinecatch Ltd, Bungay, Suffolk
Printed and bound in Great Britain by
The Cromwell Press, Trowbridge, Wilts

# CONTENTS

# THE CONTRIBUTORS

**Stuart C. Aitken** is a Professor of Geography at San Diego State University. His past books include *Place, Power, Situation and Spectacle: A Geography of Film* (co-editor with Leo Zonn; Rowman and Littlefield, 1994), *Family Fantasies and Community Space* (Rutgers University Press, 1998), *Geographies of Young People* (Routledge, 2001) and *Putting Children in Their Place* (Washington, DC: Association of American Geographers, 1994). Professor Aitken is also published widely in academic journals and has edited collections on film and the social constructions of masculinity.

**Nick Bingham** is a Lecturer in Human Geography at the Open University, UK. Current research on the GM controversy and the patenting of lifeforms explores the challenging geographies that emerge when we are forced to think the natural and the social at the same time. Such work is informed by an ongoing engagement with the 'cosmopolitical' thought of anthropologists of science and technology Michel Serres, Bruno Latour and Isabelle Stengers.

**David B. Clarke** is Senior Lecturer in Human Geography at the University of Leeds and an affiliate member of the Institute of Communications Studies. His research interests centre on the geographies of consumerism and the media. In addition to a number of journal articles, he has edited *The Cinematic City* (Routledge, 1997) and is currently conducting research on early cinema and working on a number of books on the consumer society.

**Marcus A. Doel** is Professor of Human Geography at the University of Wales Swansea. His research centres on social and spatial theory, with particular reference to subjectivity, technology and consumption. He is the author of *Poststructuralist Geographies* (Edinburgh University Press, 1999).

**Sheila Hones** is an Associate Professor in the Department of Area Studies of the Graduate School of Arts and Sciences at the University of Tokyo. Her major field is North American studies, within which she focuses on written texts and cultural geography.

**Shaun Huston** is an adjunct instructor of geography at Portland State University and Portland Community College. His work on environmental philosophy and social theory has been published in *Anarchist Studies, Capitalism, Nature, Socialism* and *Society and Nature.*

**Michelle Kendrick** is Assistant Professor of English at Washington State University, Vancouver, where she teaches in the Electronic Media and Culture programme. She is author of many articles on technology and culture, co-editor of the collection *Eloquent Images: Writing Visually in New Media* (forthcoming, MIT Press) and co-author of the forthcoming DVD *Red Planet: A Scientific and Cultural History* (University of Pennsylvania Press).

**Paul Kingsbury** is a PhD student in the Department of Geography at the University of Kentucky. He is writing a dissertation that uses psychoanalytical and poststructuralist approaches to examine tourism and community development in Jamaica. He recently edited *disClosure: A Journal of Social Theory.*

**Rob Kitchin** is a Senior Lecturer in Human Geography at the National University of Ireland, Maynooth. His research interests centre on the geographies of cyberspace and disability. He is the author of *Cyberspace* (Wiley, 1998) and *Mapping Cyberspace* (with Martin Dodge; Routledge, 2000), and the Managing Editor of the journal *Social and Cultural Geography.*

**James Kneale** is a Senior Lecturer in Human Geography at University College London. His interests in cultural and historical geography include popular fiction, the media, and cultures of drink. He has contributed chapters on William Gibson and SF to *Virtual Geographies* (ed. M. Crang, P. Crang and J. May; Routledge, 1999) and *Impossibility Fiction* (ed. D. Littlewood and P. Stockwell; Rodopi, 1996).

**Michael Longan** is a Visiting Professor at Gustavus Adolphus College in St Peter, Minnesota. He has research interests in geographies of cyberspace as well as in cultural and urban geography. He is currently studying the geography of the community networking movement in the United States.

**Barbara J. Morehouse,** Associate Research Scientist, is affiliated with the Institute for the Study of Planet Earth, The University of Arizona, USA. She also holds the title of Adjunct Assistant Professor in the University of Arizona, Department of Geography and Regional Development. Her research interests include nature–society interactions and border studies. Her publication credits include *A Place Called Grand Canyon: Contested Geographies* (University of Arizona Press, 1996), charting the history of boundary-drawing at Grand Canyon.

**Tim Oakes** teaches geography at the University of Colorado at Boulder. He is the author of *Tourism and Modernity in China* (Routledge, 1998) as well as numerous articles and chapters on Chinese culture, tourism development, place and subjectivity.

**Michael Marshall Smith** is a science fiction author and scriptwriter who has published several SF novels and numerous short stories. He received the prestigious Philip K. Dick Award for his novel *Only Forward.*

**Jonathan S. Taylor** is an Assistant Professor in Geography at California State University, Fullerton. He is interested in geographies of the Internet, geographies of music and geographic education, as well as in human–environmental issues. He has published on virtual reality and Internet education issues.

**Barney Warf** is Professor and Chair of Geography at Florida State University, Tallahassee. He is intrigued by social theory and political economy at the regional and global scales, and studies the economic geography of services and telecommunications. He has co-authored or edited two books, 20 book chapters, and 60 refereed articles.

# ACKNOWLEDGEMENTS

James would like to thank the following people for advice and encouragement in the initial stages of his investigation of science fiction: Lucie Armitt, Mark Bould, Jacquie Burgess and (particularly) Andy Butler. Thanks also to Rob, for getting this off the ground and keeping it there, and to Siobhán.

Rob would like to thank Cora for allowing him the time to indulge in his 'projects', James for signposting an interesting topic, and the various members of the crit-geog-forum mailing list who suggested readings.

We would both like to thank the contributing authors for generally sticking to deadlines and responding so positively to our critical reviews. We are grateful to Michael Marshall Smith for his Foreword, David M. Smith for making it possible, Martin Dodge and CASA for providing meeting space, and Tristan Palmer for editorial support and his enthusiasm for the project.

# FOREWORD

## Michael Marshall Smith

The two things for which science fiction is best known are these: the creation of new environments, and the evocation of a sense of wonder. New places are wrought and telling futures conjured, and within both we hold up a mirror to ourselves. Whether in the guise of traditional space opera or slick 1990s cyber-noir, the lyricism of Ray Bradbury's Mars stories, the gnostic unrealities of Philip K. Dick or the head-swirling complexity of Greg Egan's new conceptual worlds, much of the genre's sense of possibility comes from this revitalized consideration of where we live now, and what we think we know about it.

I understood this intellectually, but it was only recently, and with a degree of surprise, that I realized just how key both geographical and architectural concerns are to the fiction that I myself write. Certainly, I was aware that one novel concerned a compartmentalized city, in which cultural and social division were exaggeratedly concretized; and that another was centred on a flying expression of socio-economic difference, and featured a further, darker space, the environment of strangers. But I realized this largely in retrospect, and believe these features arose primarily out of the simple activity of trying to tell human stories, within a genre which is open to the imagined and unreal. Perhaps to a degree I was predestined to interpret the world in this way. My father is a geographer, and his fascination and enthusiasm for these matters has permeated his own life and those of the people warmed by him. My mother has long worked at the spiky, jagged coalface of inner space: social work and bereavement counselling – a zone where the constructed environments of safety and security are prone to collapse in the face of the reality of life and death, and to feel all the more real and important for this fragility.

But it is also a framework which is intrinsic to this type of fiction. Science fiction has traditionally been about space – outer space, the space of distant planets and imagined landscapes. It goes without saying, however, that any good fiction is also about inner space – about the character of humankind as manifest in the past, the present, the future. In our capacity as the creatures most prone to shape the outside world, out of this inner environment comes an undeniable and unstoppable influence on an intermediate space, that place which starts immediately outside our heads and continues to the visible horizon – in which the dialogue between mind and matter is expressed in the creation and re-arrangement of objects and environments. I can think of no place which is more worthy of our concern, for it is the one in which we are all born, live, work, love and die, in widely varying degrees of comfort and good fortune. It is, in every sense, where we live – and it behoves us to understand it.

In the absence of any notable recent progress to the stars, and as a function of a cyclical refocusing of its core concerns, modern science fiction can now be seen turning its attention once again to this closer space: the geographical space, the space of cities and landscapes, and the lives and relationships of the people within them. Perhaps then it is time for the traditional alliance between science fiction writers and the hard, physical scientists to be augmented and enriched with a further liaison, one between those who – through either invention or interpreta-tion – are concerned with the human space in both its most general and specific senses. Just as the existing landscape records our past, these future worlds and environments are an expression of our internal present. The better our maps of these lands, whether real or virtual, the keener will be our understanding of who we are, where we are, and why.

# 1

## LOST IN SPACE

### James Kneale and Rob Kitchin

Are there geographies of science fiction? William Gibson, one of the best-known SF writers of recent years, seems to suggest not. His descriptions of cyberspace, the virtual information realm introduced in his first novel *Neuromancer*, place it in the 'nonspace of the mind' (1984: 67); in his third, *Mona Lisa Overdrive*, a character recalls '*There's no there, there*. They taught that to children, explaining cyberspace' (1989: 55, emphasis in original). This is, of course, an echo of the argument that computer-mediated communications have 'conquered' space (see Kitchin 1998). In his latest novel Gibson goes one further: 'He had been taught, of course, that history, along with geography, was dead' (Gibson 1999: 165).

What Gibson means, however, is that conventional senses of geography and history are 'dead' – geography as a jigsaw puzzle made up out of discrete, bounded spaces, and history as truth rather than narrative. He continues the quote above by concluding: 'History was plastic, was a matter of interpretation. The digital had not so much changed that as made it too obvious to ignore. History was stored data, subject to manipulation and interpretation' (p. 165). Gibson's sense of the importance of space is equally significant. In the San Francisco trilogy (*Virtual Light*, 1992; *Idoru*, 1996; *All Tomorrow's Parties*, 1999), the Bay Bridge is clearly offered as an iconic representation of post- (or late) modernity. The Bridge is home to those squeezed out of a near-future San Francisco dominated by libertarian capitalism, and has been transformed into a kind of squatter settlement, ramshackle shops and houses built around its structure and on top of each other. This space of bricoleurs seems to represent a positive interstice for survival in an otherwise hostile world. But, returning to the Bridge in *All Tomorrow's Parties*, it seems that even this space is not immune from the touch of global capital:

> And emerged again into that wet light, but here it ran not across the stalls and vendors of memory, but across the red-and-white front of a modular convenience store, chunked down front and center across the entrance to the bridge's two levels, LUCKY DRAGON and the shudder of video up across the trademark tower of screens.

'Fucking hell,' said Tessa, 'how interstitial is that?'

Chevette stopped, stunned. 'How could they do that?'

'It's what they do,' Tessa said. 'Prime location.'

'But it's like . . . like Nissan County or something.'

' "Gated attraction." The community's a tourist draw, right?'

'Lots of people won't go where there's no police.'

'Autonomous zones are their own draw,' Tessa said. 'This one's been here long enough to become the city's number-one postcard.'

(Gibson 1999: 67)

Apart from the irony of a Singaporean multinational colonizing a First World space, implying that globalization does not necessarily flow one way, Gibson's recognition of the attraction that 'autonomous zones' hold for tourists, gentrifiers and other travellers suggests that some kinds of science fiction are highly geographical in their concerns.

Not all science fictional geographies are, however, as concrete as Gibson's Bridge; the space in SF is just as likely to be a metaphorical one. In some ways this is inevitable, given some of the concerns of these fictions:

References to borders and frontiers have always been the staple discourse of outer-space fiction. If fantasy is about being absent from home (the abandoned child or assertive voyager of the fairy tale, the science-fiction traveller or pioneer, and the inhabitant of the gothic mansion who finds her space invaded from within by the presence of the uncanny) then the inhabitant of the fantastic is always the stranger.

(Armitt 1996: 8)

This book sets out to explore the potential of geographical readings of science fiction.

### TEXTUAL GEOGRAPHIES

Over the last twenty years, as part of what has been described as a 'cultural turn' in the humanities and social sciences, geography has re-evaluated the importance of culture to its traditional concerns. Studies of the experience of place, representations of space, and issues of identity and cultural politics have gone hand in hand with a valuable re-theorizing of the nature of the discipline itself. Drawing upon a wide range of ideas – including poststructuralist and post-colonial theory, ideas of postmodernity, psychoanalysis, and post-Marxist approaches – recent work has emphasized that space is not a neutral backdrop for human action but is charged with meaning through discourse and practice. These developments have led, amongst other things, to an interest in spatial representations in popular texts: cultural productions like writing, film and landscape.

Geographers have long been interested in literature, from studies which used novels as sources of geographical 'data' (Darby 1948; Jay 1975) to humanistic interest in literature's apparent success in capturing the subjective experience of place in print (Tuan 1976, 1978; Pocock 1979, 1981). Following criticism of both approaches (Thrift 1978; Gregory 1981), and a closer engagement with literary theory (Brosseau 1994), representations of space in novels and non-fictional forms like travel writing are once again being interrogated. Attention is now given to the sociological and geographical imaginations of writers (Daniels and Rycroft 1993; Foster 1994; Schmid 1995); the textualization of movement, routes and other spatial narratives (Carter 1987; Cresswell 1993; Brosseau 1995); and the place of literature in the production and consumption of geographical knowledges and cultural differences (Sharp 1994; Phillips 1997). At the same time, increasing attention is being given to space by those working in cultural studies, anthropology, literary theory and elsewhere, and this has also emphasized the spatiality of literature (Davis 1987; Moretti 1998).

Geographers have also asked similar questions of other media, principally film (Aitken and Zonn 1993, 1994; Clarke 1997) and television (Burgess 1987; Higson 1987) as part of a wider interest in the production and consumption of mediated meanings (Burgess and Gold 1985; Burgess 1990). Key strands of research on the spatiality of film have examined the relationship between cinematic space and urban space, and how understandings of each inform each other (see Clarke 1997); how film through its various genres, such as road movies or the Western, and cinematic techniques, such as cut-aways and special effects, have shaped geographical imaginations and senses of place (Eyerman and Lofgren 1995; Short 1991); and how the relationships between space, identity and difference are (re)produced and challenged through film (for example Aitken and Lukinbeal 1998).

Much of this interest in the geographies of popular texts has been to some extent influenced by a wider interest in the aesthetics and politics of representation and a poststructuralist questioning of the idea of mimesis or realism (Barnes and Duncan 1992; Duncan and Ley 1993). It is this suspicion of mimesis which makes science fiction such an interesting set of fictions for geographers.

## WHAT IS SCIENCE FICTION?

The starting point for this book is the belief that science fiction opens up a space in which authors and readers or viewers can reflect upon the nature of a wide variety of things (including space, nature, and material things themselves). This potential is there, we would argue, because science fiction is a form of non-realist fiction; it is this relationship with the 'real' that gives it its nature as 'fiction squared' (Suvin 1979: 117). Defining SF, then, requires attention to its status as fiction, rather than its content. The latter strategy – listing all those tropes deemed to be science fictional – leads into 'a critical quagmire' (Shippey 1991: 1), not least because this kind of classification requires a prior definition of SF.

Instead we want to concentrate on a variety of ways in which SF can be seen as a privileged site for critical thought. What connects many of the arguments made for the value of this space is the sense that what drives SF is actually less a thing than a gap: between science and fiction, between the reader's reality and the world of the fiction, between the possible and the impossible. This gap sometimes seems like a weak link, broken easily with a little deconstruction; at other times it seems like a zone of tension between two opposed tendencies: science *and* fiction. It is entirely appropriate that it is possible to read the term 'science fiction' itself as an oxymoron.

While much of the following work develops theories of the fantastic through the analysis of written texts, it is possible to extend these ideas to film through a shared interest in the fragile fabrication of mimesis in both literature and film and the critical application of theories derived from poststructuralism and psychoanalysis. However, it should be noted that we are not trying to produce a synthesis of previous work on science fiction literature and film, nor are we suggesting that these critics are always entirely successful in attempting to 'fit' together some of these theories (particularly poststructuralism and psychoanalysis). Rather we are trying to draw out some of the most significant points from an extremely heterogeneous field of study.

One of the most influential accounts of the nature of SF has considered it as a literature of 'cognitive estrangement': 'SF is distinguished by the narrative dominance or hegemony of a fictional "novum" (novelty, innovation) validated by cognitive logic' (Suvin 1979: 63). By this Suvin means that SF discusses impossible or unknown things (intelligent life beyond earth, 'terraforming') in rational, usually scientific, ways. It is therefore different from fantasy, which is estranging but noncognitive, and from 'realistic' fiction (cognitive but naturalistic). The novum has since been discussed as part of the experience of reading SF (Shippey 1991) or as a way into thinking about the tensions between rational cognition and fantastic estrangement.

Other critics who have seen SF as related in some way to the broader mode of the fantastic[1] – which also embraces horror, the gothic and utopian or dystopian fiction, as well as fantasy – argue that it shares with these other genres an uneasy mixing of the real and the unreal.

> Literary fantasies have appeared to be 'free' from many of the conventions and restraints of more realistic texts: they have refused to observe unities of time, space and character, doing away with chronology, three-dimensionality and with rigid distinctions between animate and inanimate objects, self and other, life and death.
>
> (Jackson 1981: 1–2)

However, the fantastic is more than a simple *negation* of realism and rationality. Rosemary Jackson argues that the discourse of the fantastic attempts to discuss what lies beyond language: 'Structured upon contradiction and ambivalence, the fantastic traces in that which cannot be said, that which evades articulation or that which is represented as "untrue" and "unreal"' (p. 37). The fantastic is therefore a literature of desire which seeks to expose absences, indicating a culture's particular fears and taboos. It is located in the space between the real and unreal, and the two elements must co-exist together, allowing a text to move between the poles of mimesis and the fantastic. From this talk of desire and fear it should be clear that Jackson, like many other writers on the fantastic, is convinced that it expresses the workings of the unconscious. Lucie Armitt's *Theorising the Fantastic* (1996) critically explores the writings of Freud, Lacan and Kristeva for insights into the relationship between fiction and fantasy, and the troubling or comforting significance of dreams, the uncanny, mirrors, and the abject (see also Burgin *et al.*, 1989). Critical interest in psychoanalytical readings of the fantastic is strongly developed in studies of SF film, for example Constance Penley's discussion of time-travel and the primal scene in James Cameron's 1984 film *The Terminator* (Penley 1990) and Barbara Creed's influential analysis of the 'monstrous-feminine' in Ridley Scott's 1979 film *Alien* (1993). This tradition of criticism sees SF as a 'return of the repressed', as 'the strangeness, the fantastic nature, of the fictional worlds of science fiction films may endow them with some of the qualities of unconscious productions' (Kuhn 1990: 92).

The work of Tzvetan Todorov (1973) is enormously helpful in showing how the relationship between the real and the unreal takes textual form. Todorov argued that the blurring of the line between 'real' and 'unreal' depends upon two things: the reader's uncertainty over the truth of the narrative and the resistance of the text to narrative closure. The fantastic is therefore defined in terms of the inscription within the text of hesitation or anxiety. Three conditions must be met:

> . . . the text must oblige the reader to consider the world of the characters as a world of living persons and to hesitate between a natural and a supernatural explanation of the events described . . . this hesitation may also be experienced by a character . . . [and] the reader must adopt a certain attitude with regard to the text; he will reject allegorical as well as poetic interpretations.
>
> (Todorov 1973: 33)

Thus the reader is constantly encouraged to attempt to understand and make sense of an ambiguous text rather than dismissing it all as a 'mere fairy tale' or as an allegory of the real. Having identified this hesitation as the key textual embodiment of the fantastic, we can now begin to examine the conventions by which it is produced. Firstly, the fantastic recognizes and makes explicit the impossibility of literary realism, of mimesis. Simple explanations are deferred and narrative closure resisted; nonsense words, invisibility and incoherence are central concerns. Secondly, Jackson writes that this kind of text is antinomical; it holds contradictions together to create semantic impossibilities, chiefly through the oxymoron; it is polysemic. Finally, one of the most effective of the many ways of producing a hesitation within the text is 'a confusion of pronouns and of pronoun functions' (Jackson 1981: 29), conflating the subject positions of the narrator and the protagonist, problematizing vision and objectivity.

Todorov located the fantastic in a gap between his two categories of non-realist fiction, the uncanny and the marvellous, and Armitt reads his structuralism as straining and failing to contain the fantastic:[2]

> Thus, precisely because the fantastic comes to the fore at the point of interaction between two conflicting worlds/zones/modes, the resulting narrative is always to a greater or lesser extent on the edge between the two, simultaneously acknowledging both, simultaneously cutting across both . . .
>
> (Armitt 1996: 32)

This brings us to the question of mimesis in SF. One of the most important ways in which realism is created in SF is through the application of a particular form of scientific rationality. As a result, science fiction is generally *plausible* and *consistent with scientific principles*. The question of scientific realism has been most usefully developed by critics of 'hard SF', that part of the genre which foregrounds science and technology as content and organizing discourse (see for example Huntingdon 1989; Malmgren 1991; Samuelson 1993; Westfahl 1993). The principles involved in writing this kind of SF are well illustrated by this statement from the SF author Robert Heinlein:

> A man who provides Mars with a dense atmosphere and an agreeable climate, a man whose writing shows that he knows nothing of ballistics nor of astronomy nor of any modern technology would do better not to attempt science fiction . . . The obligation of the writer to his reader to know what he is talking about is even stronger in science fiction than elsewhere, because the ordinary reader has less chance to catch him out.
>
> (cited in Huntingdon 1989: 71)

Westfahl suggests that 'hard SF is committed to *avoiding scientific errors in stories*' (1993: 162, emphasis in original). This is complicated by the genre's place between realist and fantastic fiction, as David Samuelson points out: 'In SF . . . scientific accuracy is also limited by the competing demand for fantasy. Even hard SF requires an element of the unknown, into which writers cast a net fashioned of reigning theory' (1993: 193).

> Regardless of its setting in time and space, SF depends on transgressions of what its readers think of as reality. To justify those transgressions, it establishes images of reality on grounds essentially theoretical.
>
> (Samuelson 1993: 198)

Yet this fictional science can *never* be exactly right. Samuelson goes on to argue that 'all SF writers "cheat" on known science', but whereas most SF authors ignore these problems or cover them up with 'verbal legerdemain', 'the trick in hard SF is to *minimize* cheating, not just disguise it with fancy footwork' (1993: 193, emphasis in original).

Several SF critics have distinguished between *extrapolative* and *speculative* SF in terms which are clearly derived from consideration of this tension between the fantastic and mimetic (Westfahl 1993; Samuelson 1993; Malmgren 1991, 1993):

> The author may proceed either by extrapolation, creating a fictional novum by logical projection or extension from existing actualities, or by speculation, making a quantum leap of the imagination toward an *other* state of affairs.
>
> (Malmgren 1993: 17)

The distinction rests upon the *distance* between the world of the reader and the world of the fiction.[3] Samuelson notes that while speculation is freer than extrapolation, 'many SF writers feel an obligation to rationalize even outrageous speculations after the fact' (1993: 199). Speculation is 'a high-risk strategy' because it is more vulnerable to readers' criticisms (Westfahl 1993: 163). The further we get from the real, the weaker the scientific legitimation becomes.

Carl Malmgren's work on SF (1991, 1993) is enormously useful in developing this insight. The central premise of 'Self and Other in SF' (1993) is taken from SF author Gregory Benford's acute observation that 'rendering the alien, making the reader experience it, is the crucial contribution of SF' (cited p. 15). What Benford calls 'effing the ineffable' – making the strange understandable – represents the chief strategy employed by authors and readers in the transformation of the impossible into the plausible. 'SF rigorously and systematically "naturalizes" or "domesticates" its displacements and discontinuities' (Malmgren 1991: 6). It is possible, therefore, to suggest that SF depends upon impossibility, since it breaks with the realist novel in discussing spaces and times which are unknown and even unknowable. The fantastic is allowed into the text to give the author and reader room for their 'thought experiments' but is ordered and contained. In other words, scientific realism replaces hesitation with consistency within the text, and allows the reader to make sense of the impossible and fantastic elements of SF, though more 'speculative' works and readers' transformations may open up space for the fantastic.

This brings us to the important political question of the ways in which different producers and consumers of science-fictional texts occupy the critical space between realism and fantasy. Many of the most interesting worlds of SF have been created by women, people of colour, gay men and lesbians, who have made power visible through their estranging fictions. For similar reasons, the most engaging criticisms of SF have been centrally concerned with difference. The title of Sarah Lefanu's *In the Chinks of the World Machine* (1988) points to the marginalization of women not simply as subjects but as authors of SF; one of Jenny Wolmark's key concerns is the extent to which SF constructs its own *Aliens and Others* (1993); and the essays in Lucie Armitt's collection *Where No Man Has Gone Before* make a similar point (1991). Nothing could make this clearer than the case of James Tiptree Jr; he was discovered to be a woman named Alice Sheldon after an eight-year-long career in SF.[4] The space of SF is a place to speak from, a site for reflection, criticism and pleasure – but it should not be simply celebrated, because it contains its own Others.

Similarly, we should not assume that readers are always critically estranged from the taken-for-granted world. Armitt suggests that our familiarity with fantastic fictions acts to close off their transgressive potential:

> Largely constrained by formulaic constructs, those modes which we might refer to as science fiction, ghost stories, horror fiction and fairy tales offer readers, albeit paradoxically, the consolation of gratified desires.
>
> (Armitt 1996: 35)

As we have seen, SF contains the transgressive by an appeal not to mimesis but to plausibility; other forms of the fantastic are ordered in different ways. What Todorov called 'marvellous' fictions, for example, have no inherently fantastic potential because they invite a reading which makes sense of the text by reference to coherent religious or mythical belief systems (Brooke-Rose 1981: 243). Yet Armitt leaves room for this transgression by reminding us that the text may still hold incoherencies, which may be worked on by the reader:

> If we end up being disturbed because what we took to be a ghost story suddenly seems to be opening up to the hesitant possibility of a hallucination or madness, it ceases simultaneously to *be* a ghost story and to fulfil our expectant desires.
>
> (Armitt 1996: 35)

One final question needs to be asked: to what extent is this estrangement unique to fantastic fictions? Since mimesis is itself a fiction, all texts represent the 'unreal', and they are read by readers working between the world of their experience and the world of the text. This point might seem to invalidate a study of SF or related fictions as texts apart, but it is worth repeating Suvin's assertion that SF is 'fiction squared' – it, like other fantastic fictions, is far more ready to encourage a self-conscious questioning of mimesis than realist texts (Broderick 1995). This is particularly obvious in SF cinema, as special effects simultaneously present the unreal as real *and* draw attention to its nature as fiction (Neale 1990b). The critical appeal of SF, then, lies in its ability to de-naturalize mimesis and commonsensical understandings.

## SPACE AND SCIENCE FICTION

We have argued that SF offers a space in which readers and writers may re-view fiction and the world beyond it. Its texts offer us, just as they offered James Blaylock's web-fingered protagonist Giles Peach, 'windows into alternate worlds . . . he quickly saw a way to boost himself over the sill and clamber through' (1988: 17). In many ways SF's estrangement can be considered through spatial metaphors: it constructs spatial realms (new worlds, inner and outer spaces), concerns itself with borders and transgressions (alien invaders and invasive cyborgization). SF is therefore open to analyses that identify and trace out these geographies.

Such analyses in and of themselves are however fairly limited. Where they become particularly useful, however, is when they are used as a foil for thinking about present-day geographies, their construction, reproduction and contingency, and thinking through how we theorize and comprehend a range of concepts such as space, nature, subjectivity and reality. Here, SF becomes a useful cognitive space, opening up sites from which to contemplate material and discursive geographies and the production of geographical knowledges and imaginations. Given the centrality of space to the narratives of SF, and their potential utility as cognitive spaces, it is perhaps a little surprising that to date the imaginative geographies of SF have been little explored by geographers or other spatial theorists. That said, the work of theorists like Jean Baudrillard (1991a, 1991b), Donna Haraway (1985), Fredric Jameson (1991), David Harvey (1989) and Mike Davis (1990) all offers fascinating insights into the value of SF as a device to open up and illustrate particular concepts and ideas. For example, Donna Haraway (1985) has utilized films such as *The Terminator* and *Robocop* to examine and unsettle the relationships between nature, technology and culture. From this analysis she has developed an influential manifesto around the notion of a 'cyborg politics', detailing critical, resistive practices aimed at challenging patriarchal relations. Mike Davis (1992) takes a different perspective, using the writings of William Gibson and the film *Blade Runner* to explore the urban development and social problems of modern-day Los Angeles, and to extrapolate possible urban futures. We want to discuss a number of science fictional geographies here to illustrate this potential.

It should hopefully already be clear that SF represents space in ways which generally 'eff' the ineffable. While the 'topography of the modern fantastic' (Jackson 1981: 42–8) is made up of tropes – empty spaces, places of fog and mirrors, labyrinths – which lead the reader into 'a realm of non-signification, towards a zero point of non-meaning' (p. 42), in SF the reader is constantly encouraged to make sense of space through a variety of forms of mapping. If we adopt, just for the moment, the distinction between speculative and extrapolative SF, we can compare a few science fictional geographies to see how this is done.

The subgenre of 'cyberpunk', exemplified by William Gibson's fictions, was widely hailed as 'postmodernist SF' (Bukatman 1993; Csicsery-Ronay Jr 1991; Jameson 1991; McCaffery 1991). Yet the near-future, extrapolated worlds described by these writers were intended as realistic transformations of the present, descriptions of postmodern*ity*.

> The triumph of [Gibson's short stories] was their brilliant, self-consistent evocation of a credible future . . . These stories paint an instantly recogniz-able portrait of the modern predicament. Gibson's extrapolations show, with exaggerated clarity, the hidden bulk of an iceberg of social change.
>
> (Sterling 1988: 10–11)

The geographies of cyberpunk are therefore 'this world re-placed and dis-located' (Jackson 1981: 19); like the settings of fantasy fictions, they are made 'realistic' through careful extrapolation which rarely steps far from the plausible. This is not to say that they are not of interest, however; these representations have been read as critical expositions of the workings of contemporary capitalism in a globalized world. Through these fictions academics and ordinary readers can make sense of this world of cyberspace, simulation, cyborgs and privatized urban space (Dodge and Kitchin 2000; Kitchin and Kneale 2001; Kneale 1999). Ross suggested that 'cyberpunk sketched out the contours of the new maps of power and wealth with which the information economy was colonising the global landscape' (1991: 147). In doing so it produced a recursive relationship between authors, technologists and academic theorists. Gibson's representations of cyber-space are held to have 'provided . . . the imaginal public sphere and reconfigured discursive community that established the grounding for the possibility of a new kind of interaction' and thus the development of 'real' cyberspace and virtual reality environments (Stone 1991: 95, and see Tomas 1991). Similarly, Mike Davis (1992: 3) writes that:

> William Gibson . . . has provided stunning examples of how realist, 'extrapolative' science fiction can operate as prefigurative social theory, as well as an anticipatory opposition politics to the cyber-fascism lurking over the horizon.

Gibson acknowledged the influence of Davis's *City of Quartz* (1990) in shap-ing his representation of the privatization of public space in Los Angeles in his novel *Virtual Light* (1992), while Klein (1991) suggests that planners are actively seeking to remake Los Angeles in the image of *Blade Runner*. The gap between the worlds of cyberpunk and of the reader may not be very wide, but this simultaneous difference and similarity has proved to be extremely productive in developing new imagined and 'real' geographies, much as the political influence of utopian or dystopian fiction draws its strengths from its movement between the known and the unknown.

Brian Aldiss's Helliconia trilogy (1982, 1983, 1985) provides an example of a more risky extrapolation. The planet of Helliconia orbits (rather irregularly) around two suns, and consequently its seasons are longer than our centuries; in this way it is so different from Earth that it becomes virtually unthinkable. However, by accepting the principles of astronomy, and applying them to the situation that Aldiss presents us with, we can begin to imagine that the existence of Helliconia is *theoretically* possible after all. Aldiss took advice from academics, including Jack Cohen, a reproductive biologist who has acted as a 'consultant' to several SF authors who wanted plausible extraterrestrial life-forms.[5] Writing in *New Scientist*, Cohen observes that inventing new planets requires 'building a new world ecology with a detailed evolutionary history so that the plot does not have any obvious contradictions' (1991: 20). This evolutionary history pays attention to both contingent evolutionary solutions to particular challenges and 'universal' solutions:

> Although every detail must be different, there are patterns of general prob-lems, and common solutions to those problems, that would apply to life anywhere in the Universe.
>
> (p. 18)

While Cohen's aliens are certainly stranger than many SF extraterrestrials, his belief that the problems which would face life are all variants on those found on Earth means that these new worlds would only be distorted echoes of our own. Similarly the rules of ecology are often used as a conceptual map for the writing of fictions like Frank Herbert's *Dune* series. These geographies present the critic with a series of textual strategies for opening up and closing off new ways of thinking about space.

These strategies can be compared with what Malmgren calls 'an extreme example of speculative Otherness' (1991: 42). Stanislaw Lem's *Solaris* (1970) is a planet which is a cipher to the scientists who investigate it. The nature of this world cannot easily be described here, since none of the protagonists can do more than guess at its nature; throughout the novel there is a suggestion that the planet, or at least its surface, might be a conscious entity. Solaris, with its wilful and disorienting refusal to be understood, is indeed an excellent example of the fantastic place. This is in deliberate contrast to the extrapolated geographies of most SF; one of the themes of Lem's novel is the arrogance of human science in assuming that the ineffable can be 'effed'. This 'geocentrism' leads us to map the Earth onto the planets that we might find beyond our own solar system.

> We don't want to conquer the cosmos, we simply want to extend the boundaries of the Earth to the frontiers of the cosmos. For us, such and such a planet is as arid as the Sahara, another as frozen as the North Pole, yet another as lush as the Amazon basin . . . We are only seeking Man. We have no need of other worlds. We need mirrors.
>
> (Lem 1987: 72)

This is in itself a metaphor for world-building in SF: in imagining other worlds we have used our own (scientific and commonsensical) understandings of Earth to reproduce images of this planet throughout an imagined cosmos.

These geographies of SF, like other aspects of the genre, are situated uneasily within a mimetic or scientifically plausible framework of explanation. Some writers, like Lem, seek to criticize the representation of science fictional spaces and in doing so open up different ways of thinking about these 'new worlds'. Others invite the reader to make sense of these worlds through comparisons with our own. Readers, of course, may make their own senses of these representations.

## THE CHAPTERS

The chapters which follow address a number of different geographies of science fiction. Because of the variety of ways in which the authors weave together geography and science fiction, and the wide field of authors and ideas surveyed, we have not tried to organize the chapters into sections. Three of the papers are concerned with cinema, the rest with literature; some of the authors have chosen to concentrate on particular authors or texts while others have chosen a broader set of themes or ideas. Many of the authors have chosen to use some aspect of SF as a map to explore wider issues in the theorizing of space or nature, while some have read SF against theories drawn from elsewhere. However, there are a number of connections between many of them, and here we draw out some of these points of contact as well as suggest where there are tensions and conflicting interpretations.

In Chapter 2 Barney Warf utilizes a particular sub-genre of SF, alternative histories, to examine the contingency of present-day geographies. In his analysis he uses a number of examples, such as 'what if Germany had won the Second World War?', to argue against teleological views of history and geography. Warf argues that such teleological accounts still underlie much geographical analysis, and his reading of alternative histories draws on poststructuralism, realism and structuration theory to emphasize the contingency of geographical relations. His central thesis is that alternative histories can be utilized as critical tools, freeing us from the tyranny of teleology and allowing a re-interpretation of past and present geographies. By implication, reflecting on what might have been might also allows us to imagine how tomorrow's geographies might be very different; being suspicious about extrapolations of our present world might play a part in letting us 'get the future we deserve' (Ross 1991).

Michael Longan and Tim Oakes are also interested in ideas of history and contingency. Their reading of Neal Stephenson's fiction allows them to think through the complex relationships between space, history, power, culture and subjectivity. More importantly, they offer an important critique of his representation of China which is extended to wider (Western *and* Chinese) culturalist constructions of 'an ultrastable spatial identity of "Chineseness"'. *The Diamond Age* (1995) invokes a 'timeless cultural geography' which, Longan and Oakes point out, denies history; China is condemned to rehearse the violent upheavals of the past. The new technologies which are at the centre of the novel also offer West and East different prospects: for China they represent a chance to further strengthen a culturalist, spatially bound and historically stable identity; for the characters Nell and Hackworth they offer ways to achieve an emancipatory consciousness and freedom from scarcity. While they are highly critical of Stephenson's representation of China, they also argue that it mirrors culturalist tendencies in some post-colonial writing.

Michelle Kendrick also examines Stephenson's work in relation to space and subjectivity but, in contrast to Longan and Oakes, focuses her analysis on the construction and reproduction of the relationships between space, technology and gender. She argues that Stephenson's novels *Snow Crash* (1992) and *The Diamond Age* reveal a moment of cultural anxiety about space, technology and their relationship to the physical body. In *Snow Crash*, Stephenson acknowledges the role played by technology and text (cyberspace) in constructing subjectivity but also sees this inscription as threatening individuality and agency. *The Diamond Age* also considers the problems of the interface; bodies and technologies fuse or take on the character of each other. Again Stephenson represents technology as both 'prosthesis' and 'implosion'; it is both outside the subject, under its control, and inside, constituting the subject. This 'uneasy balance between being a subject and – through the technology – creating and projecting a subject out from the natural body' slides into a reassertion of bodily integrity against technological invasion. Significantly, this body is gendered, and Kendrick concludes that for Stephenson, 'At some level, the marker that tells the human from the computer is gender'.

Barbara Morehouse's analysis of Marge Piercy's *He, She and It* (1991) similarly reflects upon the possibilities of SF to engage critically with patriarchy as a form of feminist politics. In her chapter, Morehouse examines Piercy's novel as a feminist utopian text that explores the possibilities of inclusionary politics, the nature of difference, and geographies of power. She argues that in *He, She and It* Piercy explores a number of themes – relationships between technology and the body, the ambiguous freedoms of cyberspace, and the gendering of space – in ways which allow her to critique patriarchal socio-spatial relations. While recognizing the importance of this critical space for re-imagining society, Morehouse goes on to question the effectiveness of these critiques. She suggests that while Piercy's celebrated novel has much to praise, it valorizes some aspects of feminist politics while reproducing other geographies of difference through notions of borderlands and margins, and through a highly exclusive feminist utopia which is defined by contrast to a dystopian, racialized and 'impure' space.

Jonathan Taylor's contribution continues the exploration of the spatial subjectivities of SF, but from a different perspective, introducing the question of surrealism and the 'interior space' of consciousness (a theme developed, in different ways, in subsequent chapters). His chapter concerns the work of J. G. Ballard, a writer with an awkward relationship with SF and criticism. Rather than consider Ballard as an author of 'postmodernist SF', Taylor discusses his work in terms of surrealism, where objects (including landscapes) are taken as manifestations of the unconscious and mirror radical shifts in subjectivity. In Ballard's transformed worlds of crystal and water, as well as in ordinary spaces like motorway intersections and high-rises and in his 'leisure utopia', the desires and obsessions of his protagonists blossom in apparently pathological ways. Yet in these spaces they will have reached some kind of new understanding of themselves and of their surroundings, and Taylor takes care to stress Ballard's insistence that while 'the environment makes possible the . . . unfolding logics' of transformation, these possibilities are enthusiastically welcomed.

Stuart Aitken is also interested in the workings of the unconscious, but uses a psychoanalytical approach to examine patriarchal relations in SF horror movies. He argues that the persistence of this genre and its repetition of specific images and tropes is due to the way that it speaks to persistent fears and desires – and particularly those associated with feminine sexuality. Working through three of these cine-psychoanalytic repetitions: the Medusa's head, the monstrous womb, and the stalker/slasher in films such as *Dark City* and *Blade Runner*, Aitken considers their significance in expressing fears of castration and the abject feminine. This type of analysis, he suggests, allows us to 'tap into the grammar of man-made spaces' and to examine the relationship between the sphere of the social and that of the psyche in the creation and reproduction of everyday geographies. Aitken concludes by examining the importance of narrative closure in these films and their 'disturbingly happy endings': resolving the shaken certainties of the spectator through a flight from the city to a space where masculinity, capitalism, and the family can be restored and reproduced.

The next chapter, by Paul Kingsbury, also concentrates on the unsettling and the unexpected in SF film. Kingsbury mobilizes Alfred Jarry's notion of a 'pataphysics of absence' to show how SF texts use, disrupt and estrange space-time through staging a tension between presence and absence, possible and impossible. For Kingsbury, these elements of SF films are not simply *opposed* to reason but trace its limits. His examples – which concern scale, invisibility, and the cyborg – demonstrate the ways in which these tactics of estrangement are used in SF to unsettle the viewer, to make them question their understandings of space-time. It is also worth noting that Kingsbury differs from Aitken in his reading of the consequences of these ruptures and oscillations. Whereas Aitken sees SF films as bound by narrative conventions of closure, reproducing socio-spatial relations through the 'happy ending', Kingsbury highlights the value of SF to estrange and defamiliarize the taken-for-granted, opening it up for critical consideration.

The last of the three chapters which concern SF and the cinema takes a different tack from Aitken and Kingsbury. David Clarke and Marcus Doel go back to the period between 1895 and 1913, when cinema shifted from being 'an invention without a future' to the dominance of the feature film and the fixing of conventions that are still largely used today. The practices which most interest them are those developed as ways of representing space and time; some, such as agreed projection speeds or continuity filming, tied filmic time to 'real' time, while others, the 'special effects' of their day, like flashbacks or mounting cameras on trolleys, allowed the cinema to produce new experiences of time and space. Doel and Clarke point out that while modern SF and cinema appear at the same time, it was a while before (British) SF films were made. Instead they consider Robert W. Paul's plans for a 'Time Machine' which would involve film and other media to create the sensation of travelling through time and space. This and other examples provide valuable demonstrations of the ways in which film is (or became) a form of science fiction, a machine for making space and time.

Sheila Hones also explores the space-time grammar of SF through a comparison between the writings of popular physics, particularly those that aim to explain quantum physics, and those of SF writers, in particular Frank Herbert. Hones argues that the geographies of SF are grounded in the 'real' and that its mimetic and narrative conventions 'renders the unimagined imaginable'. Popular physics texts occupy a more ambiguous position. They need to describe, to non-specialists, a world which is indescribable in ordinary language; yet the rhetorical strategies (e.g. metaphors) and the conventions of fictional genres (e.g. adventure stories) which are capable of translating this mathematical world can do so only by reproducing conventional understandings of space. Herbert's novel *Dune* (1965) is read as an example of a coherent textual world which can safely stage the implosion of fictional time and space without bewildering the reader. Hones concludes by considering the ways in which the two kinds of text function as narratives which construct, rather than present, reality.

Developing the theme of nature into a discussion of human–environment relations, Shaun Huston's chapter examines the ways in which Kim Stanley Robinson's Mars trilogy, which charts the transformation of Mars into a habitable planet, incorporates the ideas of social ecologist Murray Bookchin. Critics have argued that Bookchin does not really detail the character of his 'third nature', and Huston offers Robinson's Mars trilogy as an imaginative exploration of this idea. The trilogy is built around the unfolding debates about what to do with Mars, and in the changing positions taken by the characters Robinson sets out a number of different ecological and social philosophies. The novels therefore stage a working-out of the dialectic between first and second natures to produce an image of third nature; Mars is not simply terraformed because it simultaneously 'areoforms' its human settlers. Huston concludes that Robinson's trilogy provides a useful cognitive space in which to consider and critique Bookchin's theory.

Finally, Nick Bingham also considers the relationships between society and nature, drawing on the work of Bruno Latour, Michel Serres and others to present a reading of Mary Shelley's *Frankenstein* as a cautionary tale. Unlike other readings of this canonical text, Bingham's warning concerns not the misuse of technology or nature but the dangers of treating the two as distinct categories. Noting that SF is particularly concerned with the non-human, Bingham argues that *Frankenstein* has long been used as a resource for making sense of the relationships between the two 'realms', as it is in contemporary discussions of genetically-modified organisms. However, many of these interpretations are relatively conservative because they take a number of 'shortcuts' through complex theoretical terrain; in working through these shortcuts Bingham demonstrates alternative ways of reading *Frankenstein* and other, 'non-fictional', narratives of the natural and cultural. In this way Bingham provides re-interpretations of both Shelley's novel, and wider questions about the social and the technical, the cultural and the scientific, and the nature of ourselves and our artefacts.

## FUTURE GEOGRAPHIES OF SF

These eleven chapters provide numerous points of departure from which to begin further explorations of the geographies of science fiction. We believe that they throw new light on both SF and geography, and that they raise important questions for the imagination and representation of space. However, there is still a great deal of work to be done in this area, concerning, perhaps, extended investigations of the place of non-humans (objects and aliens) in SF, the consumption and circulation of textual SF meanings throughout popular cultures, and the widening of what might almost be described as a canon of 'approved' authors, novels and films. Hopefully this collection will provide a starting point for further criticism.

### NOTES

1 Throughout this discussion we will distinguish between 'fantasy as genre fiction and the fantastic as a far more resistant, anti-generic mode' (Armitt 1996: 6).
2 Armitt goes on to note the similarity between Todorov's point between uncanny and marvellous, and Michel Foucault's famous description of transgression: 'Transgression is an action which involves the limit, that narrow zone of a line where it displays the flash of its passage . . . it is likely that transgression has its entire space in the line it crosses . . .' (Foucault 1977: 33–4).
3 See Malmgren (1991: 11–15) for a more extensive treatment of these ideas. In hard SF the plausibility of the fiction may be judged on scientific rather than mimetic grounds: 'we judge hard-core SF, not by an appeal to our experience of the world, but by the scientific language it uses' (Huntingdon 1989: 72).
4 See Lefanu (1988: 105–29) on this case of a woman writing as a man writing about women.
5 However, Cohen does describe Helliconia's climatic extremes as 'impossible' (p. 20).

# 2

# THE WAY IT WASN'T

## ALTERNATIVE HISTORIES, CONTINGENT GEOGRAPHIES

*Barney Warf*

When the Persians defeated the Greeks in Salamis in 480 BC, the necklace of polises along the shores was brought under Xerxes' control. Visiting satraps, amusing themselves amidst the ruins of Athens, speculated with curiosity about this odd rumour about something called 'democracy'.

Shortly after the Moors annihilated the Franks in the eighth century, they plunged northwards into the misty lands of England and Germany. Edward Gibbon, in the magisterial *Decline and Fall of the Roman Empire* (1776), noted that it was not unlikely that the Saracens could have reached Scotland: 'the Rhine is not more impassable than the Nile or Euphrates, and the Arabian fleet might have sailed without a naval combat into the mouth of the Thames.' He goes on to point, wryly, that the Koran might have been taught in Oxford.

Shortly after the Nazi conquest of Russia, following the seizure of Moscow in 1942, German troops quickly occupied the oil-rich fields of the Middle East, which they used as a springboard into Africa and India. Gandhi, employing the tactics of nonviolence that worked so well earlier against the British, was quickly crushed. With most of the Old World secured, and the atomic bomb in its hands, the Third Reich turned its attention to the New World.

Now, why should we bother asking about events that never took place? How could something that wasn't real be significant? Why concern ourselves over what did *not* happen, when we work so hard to comprehend what did? The answer lies in an exploration of how we understand historical change and the ways in which geographies are created. The future is always open for speculation, but the past is rarely considered in this light. Yet the past inevitably was once someone's future. To address this issue, I turn to alternative history, a genre of science fiction that has long been dismissed by historians as mere 'fluff' but has recently enjoyed a resurgence of popularity. Alternative history can be serious scholarship, not simply entertainment, and holds important implications for social and spatial analysis.

This chapter opens with a review of the costs of teleological interpretations of the past, which have invariably led to views that the present could not have been otherwise. Second, it reviews alternative history as a field of literature, offering several examples. Third, it turns to the philosophical dimensions of alternative history, including the role of plausibility, possible worlds, structuration theory and realism, and discourse analysis. The emphasis is upon alternative forms of social organization that could have emerged had history taken a different path, the social, political and cultural landscapes that never were constructed but might have been within reasonable parameters of understanding. Fourth, it explores alternative geographies, for alternative history is always alternative geography, noting its similarities to post-colonialism, cultural landscape analysis, and poststructural economic geography. Throughout, the goal is to shed light on the politics of contingency and to open a space for a new ontology of possibility. Alternative history and counterfactual analysis are, therefore, far more important than idle speculation, they lie at the core of how we explain social and spatial reality. Seen this way, geographies of science fiction are deadly serious business.

## HISTORY AND THE SINS OF TELEOLOGY

Western historical scholarship reflects deeply embedded assumptions about time, with far-reaching analytical consequences. In Western history since the Enlightenment, the idea of progress became so firmly entrenched that time became equated with change, and change became synonymous with improvement (Nisbet 1980). In the process, time became linearized; indeed, Western conceptions of history are the only ones that rely upon a linear, rather than cyclical, conception of time. Others have pointed out that the assumption of naturalism – that the social sciences and natural sciences are epistemological cousins – made the explanatory and predictive powers of the natural sciences a model that social sciences have long, if erroneously, emulated.

Causation and determination in history have frequently been attributed to teleological forces. Teleology may be defined as 'A theory that events can only be accounted for as stages in the movement towards a pre-ordained end' (Johnston et al. 1994: 617), and traditionally assumed eschatological or Marxist forms, which portray history as having a purpose or final end-point. Teleology has a long history in social analysis; indeed, until the modern age, fate was taken as a given in the course of human affairs (Giddens 1991). Hegel saw history as the unfolding of the spirit of progress, moving from Asia to Europe and culminating in the nineteenth-century Prussian state. Marxism adopted an evolutionary determinism with its modes of production marching in succession throughout the ages. Weberian sociology – idealist and pessimistic compared to Marx – saw the 'iron cage' of rationalism inevitably descending over the West, squeezing religion into the domain of the irrational. Braudel and the structuralists in the Annales school advocated a 'long duree' that shaped the course of historical events regardless of the daily life of the people who inhabited it. The social ecology of the Chicago School, borrowing from Darwinian social biology, stressed suburbanization as the final product of invasion and succession in urban housing markets. Modernization theory, wedded to Parsonian functionalism, likewise embodied an ethnocentric teleology that culminated in the twentieth-century West as the final product of world history, a view stated most explicitly in Rostow's famous stages of development or the Fisher–Clark thesis of transition from agriculture to manufacturing to services-based economies. Contemporary teleological interpretations continue to assume that the present is the end-point of history, and, implicitly, the only end-point: the present is as it is precisely because it could be no other way. As Fukuyama (1992) so famously argued, the triumph of liberal Western democracies at the end of the Cold War was a historical inevitability.

In all of these cases, contingency is made subservient to a predetermined end, which in hindsight appears inevitable. *Yet only in retrospect do we find inevitability.* By conferring inevitability, hindsight can be as destructive as it is useful. Frequently, the conceptual logic deployed in teleological accounts is functionalist, as in 'capitalism needs' a reserve army of labour. Teleological views elevate social structures above events, emphasize long-run over short-run processes, and fetishize social relations, giving them a power they otherwise could not, and do not, have. Determinism in history assumes that each set of causes has one and only one outcome (Carr 1961); for an outcome to be different, its causes must therefore necessarily be different. Determinism is closely associated epistemologically with the search for laws of explanation, in which explanation consists of showing the unique to be an outcome of the general (Sayer 1992). In the denial of the significance of human agency and its creative capacities, teleological interpretations draw a sharp line between the potential and the real, the possible and the impossible, the contingent and the necessary, what was and what might have been, between what occurred empirically and what *could* have occurred theoretically. Yet these distinctions are not nearly as clear-cut as they have been made out to seem. For example, every nationalist or secessionist movement, successful or not, is fuelled by dreams of an alternative political geography (Anderson 1983).

By obscuring the contingent nature of social life, such accounts present space and time as external to human action, as containers that 'hold' society but are not produced by it. Although time and space appear as 'natural' pre-social categories, they are in fact social constructs (Harvey 1990). Alternative history demonstrates the social construction of time, a common theme in postmodern narratives (Alkon 1994). Thompson (1966) and Thrift (1981) showed how the ascendancy of capitalist time-consciousness entailed the triumph of *chronos* time – abstract, rational, standardized, measurable, predictable, easily divided, frequently commodified – over *kairos*, the unmeasured, seasonal, personal, unconscious, continuous, organic, sensuous time of daily life widely characteristic of pre-industrial society. Time, like space, then, is formulated and experienced under varying social and historical conditions, a product of memory, perception and expectation, themselves deeply tied to social relations of wealth, knowledge and power.

But there is an important political as well as analytical repercussion to teleology. The real problem with teleological interpretations is not that they are
simplistic or wrong, but that they are reactionary. By reifying history, teleological
accounts deny the importance of human actors in the construction of space and
time, reducing people to finders of a world already made (Duncan and Ley
1982). To deny human agency is to deny contingency, and vice versa; to
dethrone teleology is to accept the bounded flow of agency through time and
space as the motor of historical and spatial change. Debates about teleology,
therefore, are important because they have ramifications in the present; they
shape the ways in which we come to understand how societies are reproduced
and transformed. As discourses, they do not simply mirror the world, they help
to constitute it.

Not all historical writing, of course, is so resolutely teleological. Good history
demonstrates the contingency inherent in the circumstances it describes. E. P.
Thompson's (1966) influential *Making of the English Working Class* revealed that
there was no inevitability about the construction of the proletariat by transforming
'culture' from a static superstructure to a shifting formation of attitudes and practices in everyday life that continually intersect with power relations, a common
theme in Western Marxism. Yet most of the discipline of history, as well as other
social sciences, remains imprisoned in implicitly teleological views of the world.

## ODDLY FAMILIAR YET DISTURBINGLY DIFFERENT: ALTERNATIVE HISTORIES

Alternative, or counterfactual, histories examine the world as if it had experienced plausible changes in the past, changes that in fact did not occur in reality
for one reason or another. Alternative history differs from 'real' history in that it
is concerned with past events that never materialized in actuality, but could have
done so. For historians, the dominoes fall backward; in alternative history, they
fall forward. Altering the past at any point means that it never reaches the present
in which we live today. Alternative history may consist of imaginative treatises
that simply entertain, or serious speculations may aid to test hypotheses. Fogel
(1964), for example, explored the contributions of railroads to American economic growth by constructing a model of the nation's economic history (and
thus geography) without them. Properly done, alternative history reads as if the
events it describes really happened. Improperly done, it toboggans off into idle
fantasy, entertaining perhaps but analytically worthless.

Alternative history differs from 'normal' fiction in the sense that it begins with
non-fictional events that occurred and real people who lived in the past, but goes
on to explore the multiple trajectories that their decisions and actions could have
taken, but did not. Alternative history differs from other types of science fiction
in that it is exclusively concerned with the past, not the future. Just as science
fiction differs from fantasy in that the former is obliged to conform to the known
laws of nature, i.e. its stories occur within plausible technological and physical

constraints, alternative history must occur within the plausible boundaries of real historical contexts. Alternative history has no aliens or time-travellers; its stories reflect the actual constellations of cultural, political, economic and technological forces in operation at different moments and places, and how they unfolded along different possible avenues. In this way, alternative history 'pushes the envelope' of our sense of how histories and geographies are made, examining the ways in which multiple potential temporal and spatial trajectories of change exist simultaneously at different conjunctures. To abolish inevitability is to open up counterfactuals for analysis; by speculating on what might have been, we learn what was, and is.

Alternative histories include ruminations about Roman Empires that never fell, victorious Spanish Armadas and failed American revolutions.[1] Essentially, the genre examines the world through a series of 'what if?' statements, thought experiments that alter the past at a given point of divergence to examine the subsequent impacts over time and space. What if the Romans had *not* been defeated in the Teutoburg Forest of Germany in AD 9 (Lapham 1999)? How would a Romanized Germany have shaped the subsequent political geography of Europe (Figure 2.1)? What if the Franks had *not* turned back the Moors in the battle of Poitiers in 732 (Strauss 1999)? Would the Arab empire have stretched to Scandinavia, as Gibbon suggested, and the Mediterranean become a Muslim lake (Figure 2.2)? Would Christianity have survived, or would Europe have become the centre of the modern world system? What if Napoleon had won at Waterloo? Would France have become the dominant power of the nineteenth century, precluding the Pax Britannica? 'Such riddles frame our own deep suspicions that perhaps even the currently high-and-mighty are but flotsam carried on the river of time, revealing the current's passing but unable to deflect the stream of events in the slightest' (Benford and Greenberg 1989a: 240).

The literature in alternative history has concentrated primarily on political events and turning points, particularly critical military conflicts. Perhaps precisely because politics is the struggle for power, the 'art of the possible', it lends itself well to this sort of interpretation. In the best examples of the genre, political, cultural and technological speculation fuse: Sterling and Gibson (1991)'s novel *The Difference Engine*, for example, portrays a Victorian London into which are introduced mechanical computers based on Charles Babbage's calculating machines.

The most common theme among alternative histories is 'What if Nazi Germany had won the Second World War?' (cf. Tsouras 1994; Macksey 1995; Benford and Greenberg 1998), including scenarios of a disastrous D-day invasion, a German conquest of Britain, Hitler's decision not to invade the Soviet Union or, conversely, a victory there, and a Nazi nuclear bomb. Dick's (1962) *The Man in the High Castle* examined a North America divided between the Germans and Japanese. In Harris's (1992) *Fatherland*, the German final solution was successful, and the postwar Nazi government erased all knowledge of the death camps. Fry (1996) described a world in which Adolf Hitler was never born.

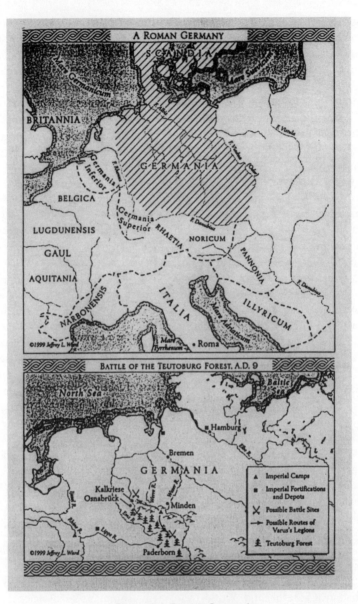

*Figure 2.1* Roman Germania.
(*Source:* L. Lapham, Furor Teutonicus: the Teutoburg forest, A.D. 9. In R. Cowley (ed.) *What If?*
New York: G. P. Putnam (1999), p. 67)

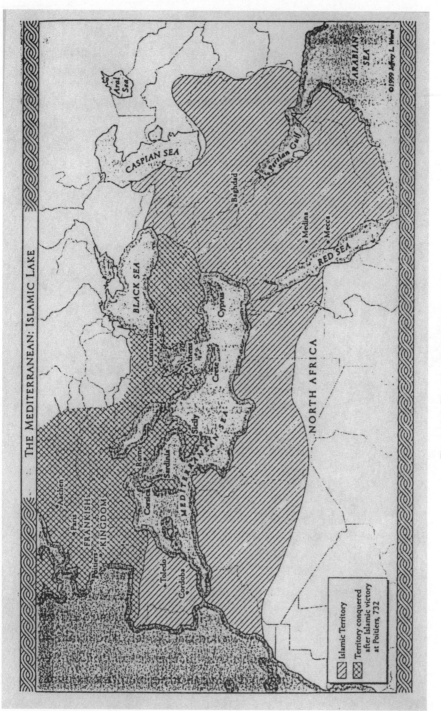

*Figure 2.2* The Muslim Mediterranean.

(*Source:* B. Strauss, 'The Dark Ages made lighter'. In R. Cowley (ed.) *What If?* New York: G. P. Putnam (1999), p. 82)

*Figure 2.3* Alternative Iwo Jima.
(*Source:* F. Smoler, Past tense. *American Heritage* (September 1999). Reproduced by permission of the artist, Les Jorgensen.)

Hayden (1997) wrote of a world in which Japan did not lose the war and established a circum-Pacific empire; in such a case, it is not difficult to imagine an alternative Iwo Jima (Figure 2.3), with Japanese troops hoisting the flag of the Rising Sun.

Another favourite theme is 'What if the South had won the Civil War?' What if Lincoln had become a Confederate prisoner? What if Lee had won at Gettysburg? In Moore's (1953) *Bring the Jubilee*, the USA, having never recovered from the Southern victory, lapses into Third World status. Turtledove wrote a series of novels (1992, 1997, 1998a) about the Civil War in which North and South continue to fight on and off into the twentieth century. Harrison (1998) pointed to an attack on the United States by Britain, struggling to insure a constant supply of cotton, which forces North and South to join against a common enemy.

To illustrate how alternative history can be used for serious scholarship, consider two examples in more detail. First, what if Charles I had averted the English Civil War of the seventeenth century (Adamson 1999)? Had Charles won the first conflict against the Puritan Scottish Covenanters in 1639, as appeared likely to observers at the time, he would have preserved personal rule and monarchical authority to dissolve Parliament at will, perhaps indefinitely. Yet instead of a military victory, Charles opted to open negotiations, leading to the Second Bishops' War in 1640 and the loss of his power (as well as his head). Had Charles stayed on the throne, the course of English (and perhaps Anglo-American) constitutional and political history would have been quite different. Without Charles's defeat, the Cromwellian revolt might well never have taken place, the Stuart dynasty would have taken quite a different trajectory, and the bloody resolution of Catholic–Protestant differences might have occurred more amicably. Might the 1789 Revolution in France have occurred in England instead?

Successful societies, such as the USA, generally snuff out consideration of paths not taken; after all, once they become wealthy and powerful, it is inconceivable for the past to have unfolded any other way. As Clark (1999: 125) notes, 'History labours under a major handicap in societies suffused with a sense of their own rightness or inevitability'. Yet had the Hanoverian monarchs exhibited more political sensitivity to the American colonies, say by not passing the Stamp Tax, things would have turned out quite differently. Without the tea duty, there would have been no Boston Tea Party. Even when revolt broke out, the likelihood of American success was by no means guaranteed. Exhausted by the Seven Years War, London, with only 3,000 soldiers in New England, scarcely committed the necessary troops to preserve its North American colonies (estimated to be 20,000). Sobel's (1973) *For Want of a Nail* begins with the British victory at the battle of Saratoga, which leads to a Canada-like Confederation of North America. Had there been no Revolution, or had it failed, the result might have fatally gutted the ideas and principles on which Americans resisted the British in the 1760s and 1770s. Clark (1999: 158) notes that 'Without war, the jealousies, rivalries and diversities of the North American colonies would probably have produced only a much weaker association, if any'. Democracy – the peculiarly American version of the Enlightenment – would likely not have emerged through the Constitution and Bill of Rights. Deprived of the influence of the American experience, the French Revolution would also have been quite different. Similarly, Seymour Martin Lipset (1990) advocated comparative politics as a means of discerning the differing national trajectories of societies, a form of applied alternative history in which he argued that Canada, which to a large extent resembles Western European social democracies, represents the 'road not taken' by the USA in terms of its political constitution, perhaps had the Revolution of 1776–83 never occurred or failed (cf. Fearon 1991).

The first alternative history novel was Geoffroy-Chateau's *Napoleon and the Conquest of the World, 1812–1823*, published in 1836, a nationalist tract in which the French conqueror did not tarry in Moscow as winter drew near, saved his forces, and established the first world empire (Benford and Greenberg 1989a: 5). The early twentieth century saw a number of speculative counterfactual histories (Hearnshaw 1929; Squire 1931). Conventional historians soon abandoned the practice, leaving alternative history to science fiction writers, many of whom engaged in simplistic speculation. Most historians regard the genre as frivolous speculation: what never became has no significance, could never be ascertained in any case, and detracts from the more important task of understanding the 'real' past. Carr (1961: 97) called it 'parlour games with might-have-beens'. Oakeshott (1933) called the genre 'an extravagance of the imagination'. Less charitably, E. P. Thompson (1978: 300) dismissed it as '*geschichtswissenschlopff*, unhistorical shit'.

Recently, however, alternative history has enjoyed a resurgence among historians. In part, this manoeuvre reflects the growing impacts of social constructivism in various forms and the general retreat from determinism (cf. Schmidt 1983). Rather than be relegated to the sidelines as a pointless flight of fancy, counterfactual history has been taken seriously as a tool to examine not only the past, but the present, which is, after all, nothing but the culmination of past events and processes. Hawthorn (1991) was the first to move the genre out of the world of fun and into social science. Ferguson (1999) and Cowley (1999) edited collections of essays that deploy alternative history not as a fiction but as serious historical scholarship.

## PHILOSOPHICAL DIMENSIONS OF COUNTERFACTUAL HISTORY

The significance of alternative history becomes apparent when one explores its philosophical implications. I offer four applications, including plausibility, possible worlds theory, contingency and its theorization in structuration and realist theory, and, finally, discourse analysis. Each has much to offer and gain from the study of alternative pasts.

### Plausibility and alternative history

At what point does alternative history degenerate into idle speculation? What separates good counterfactual analysis from bad is *plausibility*. It is useless, for example, to speculate on what would have happened if the Roman Empire had the atomic bomb. Frivolous alternative histories have given the genre a bad name. At times the line between plausibility and implausibility is difficult to draw. Could the American Indians have repelled the European conquest, for example? 'It probably did not matter whether Columbus or some other southern European sailed westward at the historically ripe moment. But were the extraordinary victories of Cortez inevitable?' (Benford and Greenberg 1989a: 240). And yet, as Louis L'Amour noted, 'The history of the United States would have been very different if there had been an Indian Genghis Khan' (cited in Sargent 1998). Does 'plausible' mean that which departs the least from known historical reality? After all, the number of possibilities increases exponentially with distance from the plausible. Perhaps only minor departures from what 'really' happened can be considered realistic; we may have the most faith in counterfactual scenarios that most closely mimic the known past, yet they are also the least interesting. Demandt (1993: 48) notes that the most plausible alternative histories are those in which events are negated: 'It is always easier to imagine the absence of something that happened than to invent something that never happened.' Other plausible options include interrupted developments that continue, roles played by different persons, the realization of unfulfilled plans, changes in the balance of forces, and the rise of defeated competitors:

> If the ravages of the plague in Athens in 429 B.C. had been more severe and had compelled the making of a peace treaty, the mightiest state in Greece would have been Sparta, not Corinth, Argos, or Thebes. If an epidemic had swallowed Rome's remaining strength in 216 B.C., the hegemony would have fallen to Hannibal and the Carthaginians, not to the Gauls, the Macedonians, or the Illyrians.
>
> (Demandt 1993: 49–50)

In any case, what we take to be plausible, like what we assume to be normal or abnormal, proper or improper, important or unimportant, is a value judgement, a statement about our culture's understanding of how the past – and the present – is constructed. By focusing on historical alternatives that are plausible, we resolve the dilemma of choosing between a single deterministic past and an infinite number of pasts. As early as 1913, Goldenweiser (1913) proposed the 'principle of limited possibilities'.[2] As Demandt (1993: 40) puts it, 'The historically possible occupies the space between the unimaginable and the actual'. Unrealized possibilities can be theorized based on our understanding of the past and of how social relations behave over time and space. To understand an event is to know the probability that it took place, as well as the probability that it might not have taken place. Thus, the distinction between what did happen and what could have happened is not so clear-cut after all. Social science becomes as concerned with possibilities that seemed probable in the past as it is with possibilities in the future. History – and geography – are the understanding not only of why things happen, but of why they do not.

Implausibility and simplistic social analysis often plague alternative history through an exaggerated emphasis on the capacities of individuals to change social processes single-handedly, the so-called 'Great Man' theory of history that fails to account for social relations or contexts. Resnick (1992, 1993, 1994, 1997) and Benford and Greenberg (1989b), for example, offer stories of alternate outlaws, presidents, warriors and tyrants, all of whom are interesting, few of whom would, simply by themselves, be capable of changing the course of world events. This error concerns the belief that big effects are always the result of single, small causes. Can small tweaks and tunings wrench history onto different tracks? As Ferguson (1999: 12) notes, 'while there is no logical reason why trivial things should *not* have momentous consequences, it is important to beware of the reductive inference that therefore a trivial thing is *the* cause of a great event'. Stated this way, counterfactual analyses aid in making social investigations more explicit, clarifying the range of 'possible worlds' to which a theory applies, and guiding the choice of empirical case studies. Put differently, not all counterfactuals are equally absurd because they are equally hypothetical.

### Possible pasts and possible worlds theory

Alternative history bears a striking resemblance to a rich philosophical tradition concerned with 'plausible worlds' (cf. Bennett 1974; Nute 1975; Nozick 1981; Kvart 1986). Leibniz, who started this train of thought, argued that of all the possible worlds that might exist, God chose to create only the one we inhabit. Lewis (1973, 1986) is the most famous and ardent modern advocate of 'modal realism', the thesis that our world is but one among an infinite number, unique only in that we happen to inhabit it. The ontology of *possibilia*, as Lewis calls the universe of alternative worlds, is unimaginably vast, filled with unactualized possibilities. He argues (1986: 2): 'There are so many other worlds, in fact, that absolutely *every* way that a world could possibly be is a way that some world *is*.' Possible worlds are not parts of the actual one we inhabit, but alternatives to it. Which worlds are real and which are ersatz is a matter of actualization; *all* worlds are actualized somewhere, i.e., within different spatio-temporal co-ordinates. Lewis notes (1986: 81): 'I would be the last to denounce decent science fiction as philosophically unsound. No; tales of viewing or visiting "other worlds" are perfectly consistent. They come true at countless possible worlds.'

### Contingency, structuration, realism, and alternative history

The utility of alternative history as social commentary relies heavily upon how we view the ontology of chance, i.e., the relative weights we assign to serendipity as opposed to predetermination, contingency as opposed to necessity – simplistic dichotomies that thwart their integration. As Demandt (1993: 24) puts it,

> Anyone who irons out the various contingencies from the sequence of events by declaring that everything that happens is the product of chaotic chance or immutable laws comes to the conclusion that everything is feasible or that nothing is. One of these views is as senseless as the other.

Jones and Hanham (1995: 187) offer a plethora of definitions of contingency, all of which signal 'the possibility of multiple outcomes derived from similar causal processes due to the complexity of social relations embedded in spatially differentiated contexts'. Contingency can denote accident or chance, simple indeterminacy and unpredictability, or opposition to all-determining forces that dictate the course of human affairs. Contingency in whatever form is a vital antidote to teleological readings that hold history rolls along a single track of possibility. To ignore contingency is to assume that historical outcomes are also logical necessities. Collingwood (1965) was the best-known advocate of an idealist 'history from the inside', an approach sensitive to the thoughts, ideologies and motivations of historical actors (see Guelke 1977). Phenomenology and existentialism over-emphasized contingency through a celebration of consciousness and experience, but at the cost of any conception of social relations or causation, collapsing social life into the ahistorical individual and yielding a naively idealist view of reality devoid of social relations, power, or struggle.

Of course, reconciling determinism and voluntarism has long been one of the most intractable problems of social science. Giddens's (1981, 1984) structuration theory has become the most popular resolution to this dilemma. In this view, people are always conscious, acting subjects, capable of 'doing otherwise'. If we hold someone responsible for an action, we presume that s/he had alternatives; responsibility is measured by the degree of risk one takes (Demandt 1993). However, the human subject is a social product, as individuals live through a life-long process of socialization. In forming their biographies every day, people unintentionally reproduce and transform their social worlds; the counterpart to the unacknowledged preconditions to action is the unintended consequences, which means that social relations continually escape the intentions of their creators. In this way, structuration theory sutured the macrostructures of social relations to the microstructures of everyday life (Thrift 1983; Pred 1990). Unlike the epic conflicts that preoccupy alternative history, contingency in this view is produced continuously through daily life, not simply through decisive military battles.

Applied to the past, this perspective reveals that the way in which the present is constructed historically may be likely, arbitrary, accidental or serendipitous, but it is never pre-ordained. As Giddens (1984: 220) notes, 'History is not "unmastered human practices." It is the temporality of human practices.' Gregory (1976, 1978, 1982) argued for reorienting historical geography along the lines suggested by structuration theory. This view has important epistemological implications: *to know a society and a geography is to know how it could be different*, a key foundation for any critical social science. Indeed, criticality is impossible without a sense of how a society or landscape could be different; in this sense, alternative histories are far more important than they appear at first sight.

Even in the natural sciences, in which the social construction of reality is generally not an issue, contingency has become an increasingly widely accepted part of how the world works. While the Darwinian revolution led to the wide-spread view that nature inevitably evolves from simple to ever more complex, and hence 'better', lifeforms, many contemporary biologists stress the role of environmental catastrophes and accidents that disrupt the process of natural selection. Gould (1989), for example, in his famous study of Canada's Burgess Shale, sketched seven alternative possible evolutionary worlds and concluded that the eighth, the only one to include humans, arose only from the unlikely success of one phylum. In physics, Einstein argued that 'God does not play dice with the universe', but he was wrong: Heisenberg's uncertainty principle of quantum mechanics holds that there are multiple outcomes for any particular observation, introducing an element of unpredictability at the most fundamental subatomic level (Hawking 1988; Prignogine 1996). Contemporary chaos theory reveals much the same conclusion: that the 'arrow of time' is not unidirectional, that causality can never be separated from context. Chaos, or complexity theory, applies stochastic forms of mathematics to demonstrate that the impacts of small, seemingly trivial events can become magnified over time, creating ripples and eddies with large, unpredictable consequences. In this context, chaos does not mean anarchy, it means indeterminacy. These issues have important reper-cussions for social analysts, who should never lose sight of their own uncertainty principle.

This view resembles philosophical realism (Putnam 1987). As with structural-ism, realism holds that the interrelations among observations are ontologically real, even if they cannot be measured directly; social relations are thus 'real' even if they are not directly 'observed'. Explanation in realism centres on the distinc-tion between necessary and contingent relations (Sayer 1992). Necessary rela-tions, identified through theoretical abstraction, concern the mechanisms that produce change, not events or observations *per se*; contingent relations, in con-trast, are specified in concrete empirical contexts. Whereas necessary conditions must exist in every social explanation, whether the causal properties they describe are activated or not empirically is contingent and indeterminate. Thus, under realism, causal properties are detached from empirical regularities. As Sayer (1992: 108) notes, 'Not surprisingly then, depending on conditions, the opera-tion of the same mechanism can produce quite different results and, altern-atively, different mechanisms may produce the same empirical result'. Only if causal laws are equated with empirical regularities does necessity triumph over contingency. In the open, contingent systems of the social sciences, causation concerns necessity, not universality; explanations do not concern events, but what produces them, and the same causal mechanism may produce many different events, or not produce them, as the case may be.

What exactly do we mean by the 'real'? If reality consists only of what we observe, as in the positivist and empiricist conceptions, we deprive ourselves of any understanding of that which is not directly observable, yet still very real, which includes causal properties. Yet empirical outcomes are only contingently related to their causes. *If, however, the 'real' is not simply equated with the observed, we broaden the definition of 'reality' to include not only what is, but what might have been,* then the lines between the real and the might-have-been become blurred in productive and imaginative ways. Realism thus elevates unmaterialized possibilities to the level of ontology, i.e. what is taken to be 'real' is not simply what is observable or actual but forms one island surrounded by a sea of possibilities. Thus reality includes events that never happened in fact, but *could* have happened. The task of social theory is to identify those outcomes that are realistic and plausible – and thus real – but never actually materialized empirically; the task of alternative history is to examine these same questions empirically.

### Alternative history and discourse analysis

We all know that 'history is written by the winners', but modernist discourse has tended to imbue the past, and the present, with a coherence it does not deserve, and in the process, delegitimize alternative constructions of the present. In contrast, poststructuralists celebrate the diversity and complexity of the past, for reality, past or present, is more complex than language allows us to admit; as Mann (1986: 6) notes, 'Societies are always messier than our theories of them'. Poststructural and postmodern theorists have problematized history as discourse (White 1973, 1987, 1999), revealing it to be an interpretive act constructed in the present by authors, for a purpose, to an audience, rather than an objective record of the past (Price 2000). In the view of poststructuralists, history is inevitably a narration, filled with silences, including silences about what did not transpire, linked to interests in the present. The past never exists independently of our interpretation of it; indeed, the past *only* exists by virtue of our interpretation of it. The idea that the past is a social construction is not an easy one for many to accept; yet societies, like individuals, construct a 'usable past' to make sense of their origins and development over time in ways that are expedient in the present.

When our past is viewed as one possible path among many, there is no privileged past, but an infinitude of pasts. The selection of one history over its alternatives is not a purely intellectual choice, but one grounded in the politics of knowledge. Discourse analysis sheds light on why some interpretations gain legitimacy and others do not. The contingency of social life is thus partly a function of the discourses that we employ to understand it. If the past, and the present, is truly, essentially, chaotic and random, then the probability of every alternative history is, by definition, equal. If we define history and geography as stories we tell about the world, we can always tell different stories with the same set of facts; whatever coherence the past has is a function of the discourses we employ to make sense of it. Contingency is inherent not just in the social construction of the world, but in its interpretation as well.

Hutcheon (1988) provocatively explores the intersection of history and fiction. History's referents, unlike those of fiction, are presumed to be real. Yet what is taken to be historical 'truth' and what is dismissed as idle fiction often blend into one another: both history and fictional narratives are representations, always textualized and filled with silences. She notes (1988: 143) that 'only by narrativizing the past will we accept it as "true"'. Both history and fiction are ideologically-laden narrative mediators of meaning: neither exists independent of observers, as both are actively constructed through interpretation. She cites (1988: 101) Angela Carter's scene of a puzzled hero gazing at paintings in a diabolical doctor's home:

> When I read the titles engraved on metal plaques at the bottom of each frame, I saw they depicted such scenes as 'Leon Trotsky Composing the Eroica Symphony' . . . Van Gogh was shown writing 'Wuthering Heights' . . . with bandaged ear, all complete. I was especially struck by a gigantic canvas of Milton blindly executing divine frescos upon the walls of the Sistine Chapel.

The doctor's daughter explains:

> 'when my father rewrites the history books, these are some of the things that everyone will suddenly perceive to have always been true.'

The lines between history and fiction are thus often blurry, just as the lines between the real and the potential are blurry in the world that people make through everyday life.

## CARTOGRAPHIES OF THE PLAUSIBLE: CONTINGENT GEOGRAPHIES

Counterfactual analysis has much to offer geography. Alternative histories are inherently geographical, just as all histories, 'real' or otherwise, unfold spatially, for different temporal trajectories produce different maps of human behaviour. Demandt (1993: 57) notes that the spatial context of events is fundamental to their temporal outcomes:

> The East Germani could have permanently germanized the area around the Black Sea and the Danube if the Hunnish onslaught had not taken place and the Roman frontier on the Danube had held firm. The Arabs, if Byzantium had fallen to their attack in 675, would presumably have settled in Asia Minor.

Geographers have rarely explored alternative territorial configurations, although Meinig (1993: 214) offers two 'might-have-beens' of the greater and lesser nineteenth-century United States (Figure 2.4), noting that 'such a speculation underscores the point that the actual southern limits of the United States are no more 'natural' or 'logical' or 'appropriate' than other boundaries might have

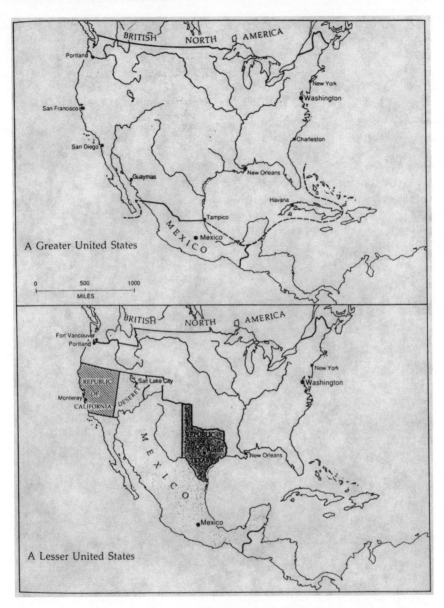

*Figure 2.4* Two 'might-have-beens' in North America.
(*Source:* D. Meinig, *The Shaping of America*, Volume 2: *Continental America, 1800–1867*. New Haven, CT: Yale University Press (1993), p. 215)

been'. Both literally and figuratively, 'the road not taken belongs on the map' (Cowley 1999: xii).

In the language of realism, the relations between necessary and contingent events are inescapably geographically specific: 'Whether an object's causal mechanisms are activated and with what effect depends on the presence of certain contingently-related conditions; this in turn depends on the spatial form' (Sayer 1992: 148). Thus, to understand how alternative geographies are constructed is to identify, theoretically, the specific causal properties involved, their contingent manifestations in particular places and times, and the plausible alternatives that never materialized empirically but are nonetheless 'real'. If maps reify some versions of spatiality and not others (Wood 1992), alternative histories help to demythologize those same representations of space. To illustrate this theme, I offer three domains of contemporary geography for further exploration: post-colonialism, cultural landscape analysis, and economic geography.

### Post-colonialism and alternative history

Geography's engagement with post-colonialism has forced a widespread re-examination of the inevitability of the West's hegemony. Abu-Lughod (1989) notes that there was a thriving world system long before the emergence of capitalism, and Chirot (1985) points out the unique conjuncture of circumstances that favoured Europe's rise. Blaut (1993) goes farther, arguing that Western domination was simply the product of a fortuitous discovery of the New World; in his reading, Eurocentric history is inescapably teleological, celebrating a mythical 'Orient Express' that lodges the locus of innovation and power to progressively more northern and western parts of the Continent. Attempts to rectify the pervasive functionalism of world-systems analysis have made it more amenable to the role of human agents and, as a result, to the contingencies inherent at the global level (Wendt 1987).

Alternative histories also speak to recent works on representations of geographic space. Lewis and Wigen (1997) offer a compelling overview of the arbitrary nature of spatial nomenclature, denaturalizing the terms and concepts that regionalize the world in various ways. The 'Orient', for example, has moved east over time, from the Aegean Sea to China, as Europe's awareness and penetration of various social formations led it to redefine that region, in succession, as the Middle East, the Indian subcontinent, or Pacific Asia. Similarly, 'as the continental system was thus formalized in the nineteenth century, its categories were increasingly naturalized, coming to be regarded, not as products of a fallible human imagination, but as real geographical entities that had been "discovered" through empirical inquiry' (1997: 30). Counterfactual histories point to alternative schemas for categorizing the world, demonstrating that received categories of structuring space are no more 'real' or proper than are the arbitrary lenses that we use to make sense of our past.

Gregory (1994, 1995), building on the seminal work of Said (1978), explored the implications of Eurocentricism in spatial thought as a long-lasting remnant of the teleological, mechanistic views of geography that accompanied the West's domination of non-Western peoples. In this light, the Western conquest was natural and inevitable (cf. Rogers 1992; Simon 1998). The cultural construction of imperialism, inevitably justified by teleology, was as destructive as the economic and political conquest of non-Western peoples. Post-colonialism denaturalizes Western supremacy by revealing that it might never have taken place; to argue the social construction of the West, and the East, is to presuppose they could have formed alternatively, without the power relations that accompanied them historically. In this sense, alternative history uncouples truth from power, difference from Othering.

### Alternative cultural landscapes

Much recent cultural geography owes a great deal to Lefebvre (1991), who famously refused to collapse geography into the realm of the material, insisting instead on the autonomy of representational spaces in which imagined mental spaces blur into the lived ontologies of daily life and historical time. Numerous authors (e.g. Barnes and Duncan 1992; Duncan and Sharp 1993; Smith 1996) have explored the constitutive role of discourse in the representation and construction of landscapes. Kenney (1995), for example, examined British hill stations in colonial India to unearth the power of discourses that conflate 'tropicality' with disease, poverty, and non-white skins. Warf (1993) wrote of a postmodern geography centred on the themes of complexity, contingency, contextuality, and criticality that is necessarily sensitive to the uniqueness of localities. In all these views, a serious concern for human agency, language and metaphor has rendered teleological views obsolete; throughout, contingency emerges as fundamental to understanding the construction of space, demonstrating that it always can be made 'otherwise'.

Soja (1989, 1993) argued that a postmodern geography overcomes the legacy of historicism by putting space on a par with time. Historicism, the doctrine that holds time is important in social explanation, yet space is not, triumphed in the nineteenth century, when time became intimately associated with dialectics and change while space was relegated to the fixed and unchanging. In the postmodern age, he claims, 'it is not time but space that hides consequences from us', i.e. geographies appear to freeze the contradictions of advanced capitalism by reifying and naturalizing them via teleology. In this light, alternative geographies expose the contingent, politically pregnant construction of space that lay hidden under the patina of commodity fetishism, the 'geohistory of otherness'. As an alternative to historicism, Soja's *Thirdspace* (1996) advocates 'journeys to real-and-imagined places', a trip through what Jorge Luis Borges (1970) calls the 'garden of forking paths', a dizzying net of divergent, convergent and parallel times in which all possibilities are examined synchronically.

## Alternative economic landscapes

Within economic geography, too, contingency and unpredictability have enjoyed a recent surge of popularity that has brought this field into alignment with the contours of alternative history as discussed here. The literature on flexible production, for example, has emphasized the constitutive roles of inter-personal networks, trust, tacit knowledge, milieu, untraded dependencies, 'insti-tutional thickness', etc. as much more than simple epiphenomena, but at the core of how economies are structured, changed and stretched over space and time (Grannovetter 1985; Gertler 1995). Storper (1988, 1997) pioneered the inter-pretation of territorial production complexes as path-dependent, reliant upon the interpersonal relations of actors to disclose regions' 'paths taken' and 'paths foreclosed'. Barnes (1996) pointed to the role of discourse and metaphor in economic geography, while Gibson-Graham (1996) used a feminist critique to reveal capitalism to be only as strong as our discourses allow it to be. Economic landscapes are thus always capable of being produced in ways that have not taken shape empirically, rephrasing the central theme of alternative history in analytically meaningful ways.

While far from constituting a homogeneous whole, these works share in common an appreciation for the complexity and heterogeneity of social life, the critically important roles of culture and ideology, an emphasis on the actions of living human beings, and the profound contingency of landscape construction. As such, they present the future, and the past, as more open-ended than has most earlier human geography, much of which was mired in economic and techno-logical determinism. There is never one path to economic and political develop-ment, for history never rolls along a single track, but a multiplicity of paths, each of which leads to different spatial configurations. Indeed, alternative histories and alternative geographies shape one another inescapably. If geographers have come to appreciate the contingency of the future, then the contingency of the past is open for examination as well; indeed, one presages the other.

### CONCLUDING THOUGHTS

Why do we analytically privilege that which has occurred over that which has not? The answer to this seemingly simple question is far more complex than it first appears, and takes us into the nature of historical explanation and the intersections of determinism, chance and contingency. Teleology is the language of domination, of views that justify the status quo by presenting it as the only possible outcome of the past. The rise of social constructivism has exposed historical time as a historical product, linked to the power relations of the pres-ent. As critiques of our historical imaginations, alternative histories have power-ful philosophical and political potentials. Science fiction is no mere plaything, it can be a tool of critical social analysis.

Alternative histories teach us how our own world came to be by illuminating how it did not become. Such a view tends to challenge the widespread tendency to take the past, and hence the present, for granted. After all, to understand who we are, we must also understand who we are not. Thus, alternative histories and geographies are wormholes into parallel universes in which we do not live, but might have. The study of 'plausible worlds' allows us to speculate creatively but realistically about alternative consequences to actions as they reverberate over time and space. Every alteration of the past is inescapably a 'postdiction' of the subsequent cascade of events that follow in its wake; such an exercise forces us to clarify our assumptions and lines of causality. In doing so, alternative histories and geographies blur the boundaries between the possible and the impossible, fiction and nonfiction, the real and the imagined, and bring these dualities into a creative tension with one another. By demonstrating that history and geography could always 'be otherwise', they reveal our world as anything but the culmination of inevitabilities, but as a palimpsest of unintended consequences. Every set of actions is path-dependent, open-ended, and creatively negotiated over time and space by human beings through unacknowledged preconditions and unintended consequences to action. Anything less than this is reactionary reification; anything more is naive idealism.

Once we rid ourselves of teleology, we can acknowledge that collective histories and geographies are no more certain in their formation than are our own lives. Structuration theory allows us to appreciate the contingency inherent in social structure and change, and realism provides powerful tools for theorizing the relations between causal laws and contingent contexts. If we take 'reality' to be simply that which we can observe empirically through the historical record – a highly suspect notion – then the world as it appears to us could have been no other way. To appreciate the real as something more than that which is observed – to blur the artificial line between the empirical and the possible – is to recognize its deeply contingent nature. 'Reality' includes the alternative trajectories that never actually occurred, but plausibly might have. In this sense, alternative histories are just as 'real' as the history we believe to have actually happened.

All of these lines of thought share with alternative history the deep appreciation that the present did not have to be the way it is. Alternative histories and geographies force us to appreciate the importance of turning points, critical conjunctures, accidents, wars, crises and sudden disruptions that interrupt the reproduction of social systems across time and space. In this light, social structures seem less structural, less cohesive, stable or deterministic. Every trajectory can pursue a finite number of paths, none of which leads inevitably to the present. Alternative history has the salutary effect of forcing a keener appreciation of the impacts that choices have on destinies. In this sense, alternative history as discourse helps to create the freedom that it projects intellectually. By blurring the boundaries between the observed and the possible, the genre sheds light on the politics of the contemporary, forcing us to clarify our assumptions and lines of causation, our 'ways of worldmaking' (Goodman 1978). When we acknowledge the past and the present to be mutable, plastic products of human effort, even if largely unintended ones, the future too is up for grabs. Confident eras tend to project a future that seems a logical extrapolation of their present, much as they depict a past that could have led only to the present they enjoy (Smoler 1999). These perspectives can serve as a wonderful teaching tool and means to spark lively political debate. Yet alternative history has more than purely academic implications: after all, we are all products of a future that might not have been.

## NOTES

1  An extensive bibliography of such works may be found at www.uchronia.net.
2  I am grateful to Peter Hugill for pointing this out.

# 3

# GEOGRAPHY'S CONQUEST OF HISTORY IN *THE DIAMOND AGE*

*Michael Longan and Tim Oakes*

Most of my geography I have learned as a byproduct of reading about history.

Neal Stephenson (1996b)

In *The Diamond Age* Neal Stephenson envisions a post-nation-state world of the future, where countless fragmentations of cultural identity differentiate humanity into spatially discrete tribal zones. Identity has become entirely spatialized, rendering its historical basis – that is, the experiences that generate a 'collective memory' for a community – into a de-contextualized montage of nostalgia. Stephenson writes a world where history has been conquered by geography. In the absence of a historical narrative from which to derive one's subjectivity, identity is instead self-consciously constructed by adopting the ready-made form of a particular cultural group. Indeed, one can join the cultural group of one's choice simply by taking an oath, acquiring the selected dress and manners of the group, and living in the space they have carved out as their own. History, then, becomes little more than a resource for borrowed cultural traits that are mapped onto discrete territories.

Yet there is a dramatic unevenness to Stephenson's future world. Three 'first-tier phyles' ('New Atlantis', 'Nippon' and 'Han') and hundreds of lesser tribes have taken the place of the defunct nation-states, but differential control of information technology, and more specifically microscopic 'nanotechnology', among the phyles and tribes has resulted in striking social differences. For those who control technology, time has been mastered and history reduced to heritage. Indeed, history becomes a toy to be played with by the members of New Atlantis, who call themselves Victorians and adopt the trappings of nineteenth-century elite English society. Those who do not control technology continue to struggle over history as they endeavour to arrest the ever-widening techno-gap between rich and poor. A more sinister history continues to haunt the less fortunate parts of the world, like China (the Han phyle), where the events of the novel actually take place. Here, historical ruptures and revolutions have a habit of reappearing like apparitions that have not yet been laid to rest. Thus, many of the key experiences that defined China's violent nineteenth- and twentieth-century struggles to reinvent itself as a modern nation-state in the face of Western hegemony find themselves oddly echoed in the future China conceived by Stephenson. In China, then, history appears 'trapped' in a seemingly endless pattern of recycling – a recycling driven by the deep structure of China's timeless cultural geography.

Thus, history is conquered by geography not only in terms of identity and subjectivity, but also in broader social and cultural terms. China's history is trapped by a highly mobile geography of power, expressed in the form of nanotech-wielding phyles. The relationship of technological dependency that exists between the bulk of the Han and the Atlanteans and Nipponese is mirrored by their relationships to time and space. Whereas the most powerful phyles have freed themselves from the modernist teleology of history, and are no longer territorially bound (being able to simply create new utopian offshore islands on which to live), most of the Chinese remain territorially bound and weighted down by their cultural geography, living in an impoverished 'Celestial Kingdom'. Their continuing struggle with foreign power recycles a familiar discourse in China's encounter with modernity: the contradiction between the need for technology and the need for cultural authenticity.

Into such a world, Stephenson introduces an interloping story-teller in the form of an interactive cyberbook – *The Young Lady's Illustrated Primer* – an agent of narrative which allows its readers to (story)tell themselves into subjectness. While the Primer serves to mobilize an alternative process of subject-formation in the novel's protagonist, Nell, it also proves subversive to larger social conditions as well. For the Primer is the prototype for the Seed, a new kind of technology with the potential to profoundly destabilize the unevenness that dominates Stephenson's world. Yet although the Primer represents a kind of liberating technology for those who have invested themselves in its creation and acquisition, the subjectivity narrated for Nell – its chief user – is ultimately a subversive force that disrupts even the intentions of those who seek to use the Primer for liberating purposes. Stephenson thus ends the novel not by affirming the liberating potential of new forms of technology, but by reaffirming the importance of recognizing the subject that strives for freedom and subverts all forms of instrumental rationality towards which technological 'liberation' so often leads.

Stephenson's immensely creative novel offers a story about the disequilibrium between space and time, about reconstituting subjectivity in a world where geography has conquered history, and about the importance of narrative in the creation of subject positions. In this chapter, we argue that geography's conquest of history defines the struggles over culture, identity, subjectivity and power that drive the events in *The Diamond Age*. There is an intriguing parallel between the future Stephenson imagines and the direction of current intellectual debates over culture, identity politics, and the subject in postmodern society. We doubt Stephenson himself is particularly concerned with these debates; indeed, we *hope* he's not. But *The Diamond Age* can be read as a cautionary tale, revealing the excesses of postmodern culturalism, and the dangers of denying history its role in shaping revolutionary and liberating subjectivities in the face of a global techno-power that has marshalled geography in its conquest of history. The chapter proceeds with a brief discussion of the 'spatial turn' in social and cultural theory, before turning to a more detailed recounting of the novel itself. Engaging the text, we hope to show the problematic aspects of Stephenson's hyper-spatialized world – in terms of both individual subjectivity and social relations – and the events in the novel whereby struggles with power, and struggles over subjectivity, lead to ruptures in the spatial logic that secures the control of technology, opening the way for a freedom-seeking subject.

## THE SPATIALIZED SUBJECT

As defined by Judith Butler (1997: 10), the subject is not the individual, or the person, but a linguistic category.[1] 'The subject is the linguistic occasion for the individual to achieve and reproduce intelligibility, the linguistic condition of its existence and agency' (Butler 1997: 11). While we often use the term as if it were an equivalent to the individual, Butler's definition reveals the importance of language in subject formation. This is particularly significant in Stephenson's novel when considering the role of the Primer in generating a new subjectivity for its readers. In 'reading' the Primer, the subject 'speaks' itself into existence, makes itself intelligible and develops the capacity for action. Through an accumulation of virtual experiences, it helps to create a personalized historical narrative that becomes the basis for action. We will return to the role of the Primer later in the chapter. For now, we want to focus on the questions of history and narrative as sources of the 'linguistic occasion' that is the subject.

Much of the debate surrounding the subject has been generated by assumptions about the role played by history and narrative in subject-formation. A great deal of modern intellectual thought – radical critiques, like Marxism, in particular – has centred on raising consciousness about the historical conditioning of subject positions. Revolutionary action, for instance, is presupposed by a consciousness of one's historically situated subjectivity (i.e. 'class consciousness'). Narrative, then, provides a language by which such consciousness becomes intelligible. Of course, all modern social institutions depend upon narratives of one form or another in attempts to forge common subject positions that are, say, loyal (patriotism), hard-working (capitalist work ethic), governable (citizenship), and so on. Modern radicalism simply tries to unify subjectivity around counter-narratives and alternative histories.

Many postmodern critics have claimed that this historical-narrative-based model of subjectivity – whether radical or conservative – is hegemonic and oppressive. They criticize narrative as a 'master text' that elides difference, and deride history for its teleological disposition (Lyotard 1979; Baudrillard 1983). Much of the impulse for this postmodern critique has come from the rising voices in the marginal peripheries and borderlands of global power, insisting that modernity has *not* narrated their subjectivities out of existence and that the modern subject is *not* unified by historical consciousness, but *fragmented* and hybridized (Bhabha 1986; Anzaldúa 1987; Hall 1991; Chakrabarty 1992; Prakash 1992). The same impulse has resulted in a popular discourse of multiculturalism in advanced capitalist societies. Significantly, this has been accompanied by the fall of state socialism as a viable alternative to capitalism, and the celebratory (if not profoundly ironic) pronouncement of 'the end of history' (Fukuyama 1992).

Some postmodern criticism has gone so far as to eulogize the subject as the now deceased vestige of a defeated modernity (Lyotard 1979). It is more than coincidence that such radical pronouncements ('the death of the subject') have occurred simultaneously with the self-congratulatory conservatism heralding 'the end of history'. Both impulses indicate a new privileging of space over time in social theory (Soja 1989). Even those who seek not the death of the subject but its non-hegemonic reconstitution must look towards spatial metaphors for articulating subjectivity in non-linear, open-ended and pluralistic ways. As one radical historian put it, 'the reconstitution of the subject, under the circumstances, can only be local and conditional' (Dirlik 1994: 90), resulting in a strategy of action termed 'critical localism'. This is not a call for a dehistoricized subject. But gone from this reconstituted subject is any kind of universal narrative as well as any focus on diachronic time; they have been replaced by localized and contingent narratives, synchronicity, and *difference across space* (Pile and Thrift 1995). Indeed, it is the question of difference that now drives all efforts toward reconstituting subjectivity, and difference has come to be expressed primarily in spatial, rather than historical, terms (Kirby 1996).

Of course, a celebration of difference lies at the heart of postmodern multiculturalism. In these terms, difference means *cultural* difference, yet such difference implies a privileging of space over time. The ideology of culturalism that is the basis for multicultural discourse dehistoricizes culture as it creates an essential and timeless representation of symbols and markers around which identity can be mobilized (Dirlik 1997: 23–51). Though cultural change over time remains a significant topic of discussion, it has become less important in popular cultural discourse than cultural difference across space. Experiences of diaspora, of migration, travel and exile, of borderland and periphery and of cosmopolitan mixture have become the focal topics in critical theory, cultural studies and, indeed, of the humanities and social sciences more generally.

In *The Diamond Age*, it is as if Stephenson has taken each of these trends to their extreme, if not logical, conclusions. For those in the powerful New Atlantis phyle, subject positions are articulated in the borrowed and dehistoricized discourse of Victorian England. This produces a great deal of discipline, loyalty, and complacency among the 'Vickys'. Devoid of a real historical narrative, most of the subjects of New Atlantis seem to display little, if any, capacity for critical thought. But Stephenson does not delve deeply into this issue, save for leaving us with the impression of New Atlantis as something of a nineteenth-century rendition of Seaside, Florida (the planned community of *The Truman Show* fame).[2] What he does reveal with striking clarity, however, is the fragmentation of cultural identity into smaller and smaller groupings ('tribes' or 'phyles') and the spatial expression of this fragmentation, with each group occupying its own space or 'clave'. It is as if today's discourse of (multi)culturalism has ultimately sorted itself out according to the spatial logic of difference that has always supported it.[3] The result is a landscape of pure cultural segregation, except that the lack of history and narrative in the constitution of subject positions has made possible individual mobility between such culture spaces: within some racial limitations, perhaps, one can easily join whichever tribe one likes.

This culturalist and spatialized subject, we would argue, becomes a premise upon which Stephenson's imagination thrives. It drives his ability to envision a world where space and time are in disequilibrium with one another. But the space–time disequilibrium in *The Diamond Age* is also unstable, just as the spatialized subject cannot be sustained. The impulse for liberation is never far from the fantastically rendered surface of Stephenson's social landscape. It is to that landscape, and the struggles for freedom that ultimately disrupt it, that we now turn.

### ATLANTIS/SHANGHAI AND NELL'S UPBRINGING

The central irony of *The Diamond Age* – and, one could argue, of our own age – is that despite the ubiquity of resources, gaping inequalities persist in their distribution. In the Shanghai of the future, struggles over the control of resources continue. The key resource, in this regard, is the Feed: the source of all artificial matter compilation. The Feed originates at Source Victoria in the Diamond Palace at the centre of Atlantis/Shanghai, a New Atlantis colony occupying the artificial island of New Chusan just offshore from Shanghai and Pudong (see Figure 3.1). Controlled by the neo-Victorians, the Source is a 'molecular disassembly line' and mines water and air for their constituent molecules and trace elements. The main line of the Feed extends from the Source, on New Chusan, across a causeway to the mainland, where it branches off to supply raw matter for home matter compilers (MCs for short) in Shanghai and throughout China. Like a new form of opium, the Feed has maintained a relationship of dependency between China and the West. As Dr X, an enigmatic agent of the Celestial Kingdom, explains, 'When the Feed came in from Atlantis, from Nippon, we no longer had to plant, because the rice now came from the matter compiler. It was the destruction of our society' (Stephenson 1996a: 457).

One of those MCs is located in the apartment where Nell lives with her mother Tequila and her brother Harv, a streetwise kid and petty thief. Though the family is poor, their basic needs are met through the MC, but it is slow with an output of only 'a few grams per second'. Each day Nell's mother travels from their home in New Chusan's Leased Territories (or LT), a zone of claves

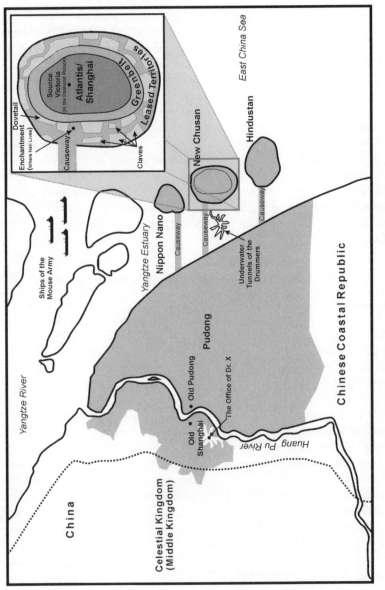

Figure 3.1 The geography of *The Diamond Age*.

sandwiched between Atlantis/Shanghai and the ocean, to work as a maid in a 'Vicky' home. Unlike most of the other characters in the novel, Nell and her family lack a tribal affiliation and literally live in the spaces between claves.

The story of how the Primer gets into Nell's hands is a complex one and a simplified telling will have to suffice for now. Lord Finkle-McGraw, one of the leaders of the New Atlantis phyle, hired Atlantean engineer John Percival Hackworth to create the Primer for his daughter Elizabeth. Hoping to create an unauthorized copy for his own daughter Fiona, Hackworth ventures on a rare trip across the causeway, plans for compiling the Primer in hand (so to speak). His destination is the office of the mysterious Dr X, where he compiles a copy of the Primer from an MC hooked up to the doctor's private source (making this illegal copying undetectable). On his way back, a gang of ruffians, one of whom happens to be Harv, steals the book from Hackworth. Harv salvages the book from the other boys and brings it home as a present for Nell.

At its core, the Primer is subversive. The Primer bonds with its owner and sees 'all events and persons in relation to that girl, using her as a datum from which to chart a psychological terrain, as it were. Maintenance of that terrain is one of the book's primary processes. Whenever the child uses the book, then, it will perform a sort of dynamic mapping from the database onto her particular terrain' (Stephenson 1996a: 106). The database, Hackworth explains, is 'a catalogue of the collective unconscious' and the book functions as a system 'for mapping the universals onto the unique psychological terrain of one child – even as that terrain changes over time'. The effect, 'like Beatrix Potter mapping the Trickster onto Peter Rabbit', is that while each Primer tells a story unique to each child's circumstances it also communicates universal ideas (1996a: 107). Thus the fairy-tale story of Nell's Primer mirrors her own life, but casts that life as a series of encounters with a variety of trickster characters, including King Coyote, whom she must trick into defeat in order to achieve her life's quest.

The bond between Nell and the Primer is strengthened through the fact that the Primer is 'read' to Nell by a critically acclaimed ractor (or remote actor) named Miranda. Ractives are a type of interactive virtual theatre where professional ractors perform with and for their amateur clients. Because even in this highly technologically advanced era, a computerized voice still cannot match a human voice, Hackworth has designed the Primer to be read by a ractor. Soon Miranda, working from a booth in the Theatre Parnasse in mainland Shanghai, is deriving most of her income from reading the Primer to Nell. Over time Miranda essentially becomes a mother to Nell, teaching her to read, write, and think for herself, though neither mother or daughter had ever seen each other. Though the chances of Miranda and Nell ever meeting each other in the flesh, we are told, are 'astronomically improbable', this human touch makes all the difference.

A single mother, Tequila brings home a succession of abusive boyfriends who make life difficult for Nell and Harv. Eventually, one of those boyfriends forces Nell and Harv to flee for their lives into the dangerous streets of the LT. Hovering robots called aerostats patrol the mediatronic, billboard-lined streets of the LT, making sure that no one pauses long enough to loiter or rest on the sidewalk or in the swathe of greenbelt that separates the LT from Atlantis/Shanghai. Nell and Harv retrieve a pair of space blankets from a public matter compiler and settle down for the night on the beach of New Chusan with the rest of the home- and clave-less people who lack an identity of their own and who therefore lack either a history or a geography.

Meanwhile Hackworth returns to the Celestial Kingdom, where he is convicted in a show trial – orchestrated by Dr X – for the crime of trafficking in stolen property. He is sentenced to ten years' imprisonment and charged with the task of adjusting the Primer to meet the needs of Dr X, whose plan is to make hundreds of thousands of copies of the book to help raise young orphan girls saved from infanticide and housed by the hundreds in cargo ships off the coast of China. Yet Hackworth tricks Dr X when reprogramming the Primer. The result is one of the Primer's many subversions, for the orphan girls – all dressed in pyjamas with mouse ears – will later become a 'mouse army' serving none other than Nell herself, rather than the needs of Dr X and China. Meanwhile, Hackworth's imprisonment is to be served as a member of the society of the Drummers, where another kind of subversion begins to take shape.

Living in underwater warrens, the collective bodies of the Drummers constitute a global-scale computer. Nanosites – microscopic capsules containing a 'rod logic system' and 'a tape drive containing some few gigabytes of data' (Stephenson 1996a: 495) – flow through the Drummers' blood. In this 'wet Net' data are exchanged through sexual intercourse. When two different nanosites come into close proximity they lock onto each other, exchange data, and perform a computation that throws off waste heat. Collectively these nanosites 'formed a vast system of communication, parallel to and probably linked to the dry Net of optical lines and copper wires' (ibid.). Acting as cogs in a machine, the Drummers exist in a constant dreamlike state where individual subjectivity is lost to the collective whole. Occasionally the heat of computation will consume the bodies of Drummers who sacrifice themselves. It is in the warren of the Drummers that, Dr X hopes, Hackworth will ultimately help to create the Seed, a utopian counter-technology to the Feed (more about which will be said below).

Frustrated by the limited lens of the Primer, Miranda takes a leave of absence from the Theatre Parnasse, in order to locate Nell. Eventually her search takes her to the society of the Drummers. Miranda's hope is that the 'unconscious, non-rational processes' at work in the wet Net will help her find her adopted daughter Nell.

While Harv continues to make his life in the streets of the LT, Nell finds her way to Dovetail, a clave adjacent to Atlantis/Shanghai filled with people who make things by hand. The residents of Dovetail export their wares to Atlantis/Shanghai, whose residents prefer to write on hand-made paper rather than mediatronic paper and to ride real horses rather than robot chevallines. A stream of labourers from the LT arrives each morning to clean the Atlanteans' houses, cook their food and tend to their gardens. Soon Nell too finds herself commuting to Atlantis/Shanghai to attend Miss Matheson's Academy, which accepts non-Atlanteans on occasion to prevent stagnation in neo-Victorian culture. Having learned the fine points of neo-Victorian society and culture, Nell, still an outsider, leaves the lofty heights of Atlantis/Shanghai and heads across the causeway towards the Chinese metropolis of Pudong to seek her fortune.

## CULTURAL CHINA, THE SEED, AND NELL'S SUBVERSIONS

The China into which Nell ventures offers a landscape upon which geography's conquest of history is played out. Echoing the cultural critiques of 1980s Chinese intellectuals who sought to articulate the 'deep structure' of Chinese society, and explain its 'super-stable' systemic qualities, Stephenson's China is more an organic cultural system than a historically progressing nation; it is, in a way, its own kind of 'wet Net'. This idea mirrors those of intellectuals such as Jing Guantao and Sun Longji, who, finding in cybernetics and systems theory alternatives to the orthodox historical materialism of Chinese Marxism, argued that China, as a cultural system, displayed an 'internal resilience' and a 'capacity for adjustment' so that revolutionary upheavals and disruptions were recurrently absorbed into an 'ultrastable' system (see Barmé and Minford 1988: 131–6). Similarly, events in Stephenson's China unfold in a cyclic rather than diachronic pattern, forcing China to continuously relive the past. It is not simply that history repeats itself in Stephenson's China, but that 'China' marks a more general condition of history trapped by geography. More specifically, China's history is trapped by a *cultural* geography, an ultrastable spatial identity of 'Chineseness'.[4]

Entrapment is most explicitly rendered by China's technological dependency on the Feed. The Feed flows into China like opium, and this comparison with China's nineteenth-century entrapment by British control of global trade is only one of many intriguing parallels that suggest to us China's role as the ultrastable landscape of spatialized subjection. But cultural China is in fact a splintered landscape, and this adds considerable nuance to Stephenson's portrayal. Splitting off from the old Communist China, the 'Coastal Republic' emerged when the export-processing elite and their slave-wage earning minions rebelled, sparking a civil war that brought an end to Marxist rule and the beginning of the neo-Confucian 'Celestial Kingdom' (or CK). Stephenson's account of the rebellion offers an interesting study in recycled history:

> Trouble had been brewing [in South China] since Zhang Han Hua had gone on his Long Ride and forced the merchants to kowtow. Zhang had personally liberated several lao gai camps, where slave laborers were hard at work making trinkets for export to the West, smashing computer display screens with the massive dragon's-head grip of his cane, beating the overseers into bloody heaps on the ground. Zhang's 'investigations' of various

thriving businesses, mostly in the south, had thrown millions of people out of work. They had gone into the streets and raised hell and been joined by sympathetic units of the People's Liberation Army. The rebellion was eventually put down by PLA units from the north, but the leaders had vanished into the 'concrete countryside' of the Pearl River Delta, and so Zhang had been forced to set up a permanent garrison state in the south. The northern troops had kept order crudely but effectively for a few years, until, one night, an entire division of them, some 15,000 men, was wiped out by an infestation of nanosites.

(Stephenson 1996a: 279–80)

This passage reveals a China with such a deep cultural structure that events never seem to break away from their continuous recycling within the system. Past events have become synchronically jumbled together, out of place and time. Much in the passage recycles the communist revolution of the twentieth century. Zhang's 'long ride' is an implicit reference to Mao Zedong's Long March of 1934, and Stephenson's use of the term 'investigations' invokes the title of Mao's famous 1926 report on peasant uprisings in Hunan. Yet these terms are simultaneously cast with *lao gai* ('labour reform') camps of a later, post-revolution period, and the free trade zones of the late twentieth century.

The violent formation of the Coastal Republic also has its antecedents in China's past. It bears resemblance to the various rebellions that indirectly contributed to the establishment of Shanghai as China's major *extraterritorial* city (Lu 1999: 25–36). Indeed, Shanghai under international control became a haven for the Western-oriented business elite of the entire Yangtze river delta region during the violence of the 1850s, just as much as the Coastal Republic becomes a haven for China's outward-looking coastal elites in *The Diamond Age*. The rebellion of the Small Swords in 1853 is also recycled later in the novel as the rebellion of the 'Fists of Righteous Harmony', which wins the Coastal Republic back for the CK, and against which Nell emerges late in the novel as a powerful freedom fighter. The Coastal Republic, like colonial Shanghai before it, serves to emphasize the very culturalist basis for the CK, the still-trapped home of true, cultural China. For the Coastal Republic is a Western place, a very non-Chinese place, born from free trade zones, Western individualism, investment and technology. The Coastal Republic is a place where people are comfortable, and where the Feed rules. It is home not just to Chinese, but to people of cultural groups from around the world, all making money.

Contrasting this, the Celestial Kingdom represents 'true' China not only as a deeply structured cultural geography, but as a site where an alternative to the global power of the Feed can be imagined. This alternative is expressed in the yet-to-be-realized technology of the Seed. The Seed is a utopian technology with the potential to supplant the Feed, such that 'one day, instead of Feeds terminating in matter compilers, we will have Seeds that, sown on the earth, will sprout up into houses, hamburgers, spaceships and books', thus founding a 'more highly evolved society' (Stephenson 1996a: 384). While a number of phyles have apparently toyed with developing and acquiring Seed technology, only China can link its development with cultural destiny. We might presume that the Seed's proponents in the CK believe that it will set China's trapped history free from geography's grip, will allow it to break loose from a cyclic pattern of revolution and violence that only confirms the control of the West (Marxism, we are reminded, was little more than an 'imperialist plot' that only took China further from its cultural core). When Dr X explains to Hackworth why the Seed is important to China, it is significant that he repeats precisely the same terms that nineteenth-century Chinese intellectuals used when confronted with the power of Western technology: the so-called *ti-yong* (essence-appearance) construction.

'For centuries, since the time of the Opium Wars, we have struggled to absorb the *yong* of technology without importing the Western *ti*. But it has been impossible. Just as our ancestors could not open our ports to the West without accepting the poison of opium, we could not open our lives to Western technology without taking in the Western ideas, which have been as a plague on our society. The result has been centuries of chaos. We ask you to end that by giving us the Seed . . . The Seed is technology rooted in Chinese *ti*. We have lived by the Seed for five thousand years.'

(Stephenson 1996a: 478)

However, the Seed is metaphorically extended here to represent the agrarian heart of China's super-stable culture. In unshackling its dependence on the Feed, Dr X envisions a China that will, in fact, *return* to its cultural roots, only *intensifying* a Han subjectivity determined by cultural geography. It was precisely the spectre of this cultural geography that haunted many 1980s cultural critics in China: China had for too long been an agrarian, inward-looking 'yellow' culture. In the 1988 television series *Heshang* (Su and Wang 1991), for example, it was argued that China's geography explained its resistance to change, its lack of democracy, its xenophobic tendencies. China was contrasted with Europe, a 'blue' civilization of openness and seafaring traders rather than farmers. Stephenson's Celestial Kingdom recapitulates this idea, only now inwardness, cultural purity, and suspicion of outsiders are regarded as the only means by which an alternative to Western power can be envisioned. Geography is destiny in this rendering, for China's cultural qualities, and indeed its significance for the novel as a whole, are geographically determined, just as the qualities of China and Europe in *Heshang* were geographically determined (Europe's long coastline versus China's vast interior).

We have, then, a regressive kind of liberation being revealed in the struggles of the Celestial Kingdom. The CK's attempt to acquire the Seed – an attempt supported by the rebellion of the Fists – echoes the kind of civilizational thinking reinforced by 1980s culturalist scholars like Jin and Sun. However, rather than seeking to escape the trap of geography (as modernists Jin and Sun would have it), Stephenson's Celestial Kingdom pursues the ultimate fruition of its conquest, a completely spatialized subjectivity, where culture and geography are all that matter, and where the Seed will enable a final return to a Middle Kingdom cut off from, and independent of, the rest of the world. As we shall see below, the regressive nature of a Seed-based liberation in the CK is perhaps offered by Stephenson to reveal the more generally dark underside to the utopian potential of the Seed. This dark underside, buried deep within the novel – as deep as the warren of Drummers who live deep beneath the ocean waves, and who collectively process the data needed to develop the Seed – does not escape Nell and her subversions. The struggle for freedom inspired in Nell by the Primer will be something quite different from the utopian dreams of Seed technology. Rather than seeking to realize the spatialized subject completely, the Primer reintroduces history and narrative into subject-formation. The result is not a subject seeking liberation through rationalized programmes, but a subject that embraces paradox and ambiguity in the name of freedom. Thus we return to Nell and her journey into China and further into the world of the Primer.

Arriving in downtown Pudong, Nell quickly finds a job as a scriptwriter for Madame Ping's, an emporium offering a variety of personalized entertainments for men. Living in a dormitory with the young girls who perform the fantasy scenarios that she writes, Nell continues to read the Primer, whose story is nearing conclusion. In the story Nell finally meets up with the mouse army, the hundreds of thousands of young girls who – thanks to Hackworth's trick – share in Nell's virtual world via their own Primers. Using a magic spell, Nell (who, in the Primer, is Princess Nell) turns them from enchanted mice back into young girls. We discover here that King Coyote, it just so happens, is none other than Hackworth himself, who gives Princess Nell access to King Coyote's library. She easily opens the 'Book of the Book', instructions for creating the Primer, and realizes that there has been another person – Miranda – accompanying her through her life's journey. But among the other books in the library is one she cannot open, the 'Book of the Seed', containing the instructions for the Seed technology on which Hackworth had been working during his confinement with the Drummers. Unlocking this book would take more computation by the Drummers, and ultimately the sacrifice of a human being to the heat of computation. The human being chosen by the Drummers is none other than Miranda.

Nell's life at Madame Ping's is disrupted by the arrival in Shanghai of the Fists of Righteous Harmony who in their invasion of the city destroy the causeways and Feed lines between New Chusan and mainland China. Nell, being a foreigner in Shanghai, is imprisoned by the Fists. She is soon liberated, however, by the mouse army, which she then instructs to protect the refugees as they seek passage across the water to New Chusan to escape the Fists. Inoculated against the nanotechnological devices in the Drummers' bloodstreams, Nell enters the world of the Drummers, where she finds Miranda about to be sacrificed, against her will, in the heat of the final computation required to produce the Seed.

Nell cradled Miranda's head in her arms, bent down, and kissed her, not a soft brush of the lips but a savage kiss with open mouth, and she bit down hard as she did it, biting through her own lips and Miranda's so that their blood mingled. The light shining from Miranda's body diminished and slowly went out as the nanosites were hunted down and destroyed by the hunter-killers that had crossed into her blood from Nell's.

(Stephenson 1996a: 499)

With that kiss Nell subverts both Hackworth's and the Celestial Kingdom's efforts to create the Seed. The relationship between mother and daughter and their common humanity, Stephenson seems to say, is more important than the Seed.

## CONCLUSION: THE STORIES OUR MOTHERS TOLD US

The narrative of the Primer can be read as a call to action for Nell, an enabling force for the formation of a freedom-seeking subject that subverts the culturalist, spatialized subjectivities constituted through Stephenson's post-national landscape of claves, tribes and phyles. But, by the end of the novel, it is clear that the Primer by itself is not a sufficient agent in developing Nell's powerfully emancipated consciousness. The Primer alone cannot account for the woman Nell turns out to be. For the Primer has been read by two other Vicky girls – Fiona Hackworth and Elizabeth Finkle-McGraw – with totally different results. Fiona ends up seduced by the Drummers' warren, and Elizabeth checks out of public society altogether, with unclear consequences. In all three girls the Primer has introduced its profoundly destabilizing forces, but only Nell is able to channel these forces into meaningful and emancipatory action. Additionally, the Primer has been read by the thousands of abandoned Chinese girls, the 'mouse army' that eventually embraces Nell as its queen and paramount leader. In this case, the Primer seems to have merely generated an army of devoted followers. Although the mouse army is composed of exceptionally well-trained fighting girls, there is nothing particularly emancipated about their subjectivities, at least not on the individual level that we find in Nell.

The difference for Nell is Miranda, who, in becoming the mother that Nell never really had, fills the Primer's stories with love and meaning, and establishes an unbreakable bond that neither she nor Nell really understands until very late in the novel. Thus, Nell's most significant act of freedom is not her valiant struggle to save the residents of Pudong and the Coastal Republic from the onslaught of the Fists – for which she is crowned a princess by none other than Queen Victoria herself.[5] Rather, it is her search for her mother, for Miranda, that expresses Nell's truly free subjectivity. It is Miranda, then, who enables Nell to articulate the truly subversive subjectivity inherent in the narrative of the Primer.

Nell's subversion can most broadly be expressed as one that emerges within the novel's disequilibrium between space and time. Geography's conquest of history is subverted by a subject position invested with narrative, and imbued with a recognition of the role that paradox, contradiction, tricks and deception play in intersubjective relations. Embracing paradox becomes an emancipation from the culturalist conformity of spatialized subjectivity. Indeed, Nell expresses such sentiments on the eve of her departure for Pudong, as revealed in an exchange with the Constable. Nell tells him that while the neo-Victorians believe in their elaborate code of morals and conduct because experience has taught them its benefits, their children believe it because they are indoctrinated to believe it. The result, Nell says, is that:

'Some of them never challenge it – they grow up to be small-minded people, who can tell you what they believe but not why they believe it. Others become disillusioned by the hypocrisy of the society and rebel – as did Elizabeth Finkle-McGraw.'

'Which path do you intend to take, Nell?' said the Constable, sounding very interested. 'Conformity or rebellion?'

'Neither one. Both ways are simple-minded – they are only for people who cannot cope with contradiction and ambiguity.'

'Ah! Excellent!' the Constable exclaimed. As punctuation, he slapped the ground with his free hand, sending up a shower of sparks and transmitting a powerful shock through the ground to Nell's feet.

'I suspect that Lord Finkle-McGraw, being an intelligent man, sees through all of the hypocrisy in his society, but upholds its principles anyway, because that is what is best in the long run. And I suspect that he has been worrying about how best to inculcate this stance in young people who cannot understand, as he does, its historical antecedents – which might explain why he has taken an interest in me. The Primer may have been Finkle-McGraw's idea to begin with – a first attempt to go about this systematically.'

(Stephenson 1996a: 355–6)

Indeed, the Primer *was* 'Finkle-McGraw's idea to begin with'. But Nell's subversion in fact goes beyond the project envisioned by Finkle-McGraw. There appear to be three distinct levels of subversion inspired by the Primer. The culturalist, spatialized subjectivity of the Vickys is unstable, being threatened from within by conformity and a lack of critical thought. Finkle-McGraw realizes this and thus commissions Hackworth to create the Primer. Finkle-McGraw's commission represents the first level of subversion inherent in the Primer, that is, subverting the unthinking adoption of Victorian discipline in order to generate an authentic sense of why such discipline is needed. Thus, Nell herself appropriates and masters the outward manifestations of Victorian culturalist behaviour in language and interaction with others, and she ultimately becomes the heroine who revives what Finkle-McGraw fears is a decaying culture.

For John Hackworth, the Primer represents another level of subversion. While

Hackworth appears to accede Finkle-McGraw's commitment to the disciplinary shackles of neo-Victorianism, his actions belie a deeper rebelliousness. His rebellion, in fact, aims for the very heart that fuels the power of the Atlanteans and enables them to maintain a position of dominance in the world: the Feed. Using the warren of the Drummers, Hackworth aims to develop Seed technology – the utopian alternative to the Feed – and in fact uses the Primer as an intermediate step toward this goal. Having comprehended the truly subversive nature of the Primer, Dr X sees this deeper rebelliousness in Hackworth before Hackworth himself does, and this is why Dr X exiles him to the Drummers' warren. For, while the Primer reveals the possibility of and potential for Seed technology, King Coyote's Book of the Seed remains closed, indicating Hackworth's hope that readers of the Primer would have developed the faculties of thought to comprehend the nature of the Seed and develop it further.

Nell *does* comprehend the nature of the Seed, but sees in it only a new kind of oppression, a utopian promise that negates the freedom it aims to provide. Her recognition of this becomes the third level of subversion represented in the Primer. It is Nell's search for Miranda that reveals this darker underside of the Seed, an underside represented in the 'wet Net' of the Drummers' warren. The Drummers are the ultimate society of conformity, existing less as a group of people living beneath the oceans and more as a vast unitary mind. That the Seed requires such a level of conformity and loss of autonomous subjectivity reveals, finally, the problematic nature of the 'liberation' it promises. Developing the Seed, in effect, requires that everyone be running on the same operating system, so to speak – a pre-programmed system without options or preferences.

Thus Nell's ultimate act of freedom – in seeking out, finding and saving Miranda from the Drummers' warren – is a subversion of the Seed itself. Her ability to perform this act derives partly from Miranda's role as her 'mother', and partly from the Primer itself. For, although the Primer is a kind of Seed technology, it is also an agent of narrative in subject formation. The trickster embedded in the Primer (King Coyote – Hackworth himself) gives Nell the tools to see oppression and resist it, to think for herself as a freedom-seeking subject, a historical subject, rather than a spatialized, cultural subject. In the end, it is not so much that Nell embraces the neo-Victorianism of New Atlantis, but that she has maintained a place for freedom in her subject position. The keys to doing this lie embedded within the Primer (the 'twelve keys of King Coyote'), but it is Miranda who breathes life into it, energizing it with humanity. Technology itself is only oppressive when it lacks this human interface.

Such seems to be Stephenson's ultimate message in *The Diamond Age*. However, there remains a more troubling aspect to the novel that appears unresolved. While we choose to read *The Diamond Age* as a cautionary tale about the excesses of postmodern, spatialized (multi)cultural subjectivity, we remain disturbed by the culturalist assumptions about China that, ironically, go unchallenged in Stephenson's narrative. Nell's subversion of the Drummers' warren recapitulates a faith in the autonomous individual, and while the narrative-based subjectivity initiated by the Primer may inspire freedom, it comes perilously close to reviving a Cartesian sense of the autonomy of consciousness. While we maintain that Nell's embracing of paradox and ambiguity suggests a subject position that steers away from the Cartesian faith in transparent consciousness and instrumental rationality, we do find that the emancipatory nature of Nell's subjectivity is problematically revealed by Stephenson through its contrast with Chinese subjectivity.

In the end, Nell's triumphant return to Atlantis/Shanghai highlights the return of a real separation between China – newly liberated by the Fists as the 'Middle Kingdom' – and the West. The freedom Nell espouses seems to presuppose a Western individualism because it is so clearly separated from and opposed to China's 'liberation' and pursuit of the Seed. The contrast between Chinese and Western subjectivity is reified in the distinction between Nell as a powerful woman warrior and her loyal Primer-trained minions of battle, the abandoned Chinese daughters who constitute the mouse army. Why do the hundreds of thousands of abandoned Chinese girls who read the Primer under the tutelage of Dr X rise up as the machine-like mouse army, rather than as unique, free-thinking subjects of their own right? The immediate answer is that Hackworth adjusts the version of the Primer turned over to Dr X so that it enables just such an outcome. This adjustment is, in fact, one of King Coyote–Hackworth's tricks, for the result is a fighting force that displays loyalty to neither Dr X nor the CK, but to Nell. Yet Hackworth's trick passes unnoticed because of the culturalist disguise that he deploys to hide it. During his show trial in Shanghai, Hackworth says he can adjust the Primer 'so that it will be more suitable for the unique cultural requirements of the Han readership' (Stephenson 1996a: 179–80).

That such a statement is enough to fool his Chinese interrogators, 'who were better at noticing tricks than most people in the world', speaks to Stephenson's tendency throughout the novel to reaffirm the deep structure of Chinese culture. Cultural China becomes an inescapable feature of a broader civilizational discourse that underlies *The Diamond Age*. While the subjectivity displayed by Nell is emancipating on its own terms, it becomes problematic when seen as part of the Orientalizing duality that pervades Stephenson's novel. In his 1993 *Wired* article on China (Stephenson, 1993), Stephenson wrote that 'In China, culture wins over technology every time'. In this article, we find confirmation of his approach to Chinese culture as a deep structure that remains both resilient and adaptive to change. Indeed, he comes close to describing Chinese culture in similar terms to his portrayal of the Drummers' warren in *The Diamond Age*. Thus he points out in the *Wired* article that the Chinese have a 'collective' approach to technology: 'A billion of them jammed together have created the world's most efficient system for honing and assimilating new tech . . . As soon as someone comes up with a new idea, all the neighbors know about it, and through an exponential process that you don't have to be a math major to understand, a billion people know about it a week later.' This 'human net' of Chinese culture reads like a prototype of the 'wet Net' of the Drummers. Given his belief in the organic wholeness of Chinese culture, it makes sense that *The Diamond Age* would posit a China pursuing Seed technology by attempting to manipulate – via John Hackworth – the wet Net of the Drummers.[6]

Geography's conquest of history, then, remains powerfully embodied in cultural China, despite Nell's subversions. While her subjectivity may ultimately be viewed as an emancipating force for her adopted neo-Victorian culture, it does not begin to challenge the deep structure of Chinese culture. China, by the end of the novel, has closed itself off, shut its doors, burned the Feed lines and reclaimed itself as the Middle Kingdom. It remains a society conquered by a cultural geography that 'wins over technology every time'.

## NOTES

1 Our discussion of the subject begins with the assumption that the Cartesian subject of Enlightenment thought has been decentred and fragmented. We begin, then, by accepting the critique of the Enlightenment subject initiated in the mid-nineteenth century, and approach the subject as a contested field between those who have stressed its determined qualities and mistrust the autonomy of consciousness (for example, Marx and Freud), and those who have emphasized its reflexive qualities and emancipatory potential (see Berman 1970; Dirlik 1994; Touraine 1995).

2 According to the production notes from *The Truman Show*'s website (http://www.trumanshow.com/epk/b_scenes.html) it was Seaside's 'neo-Victorian architecture' that attracted director Peter Weir to the location. Production designer Dennis Gassner called Seaside 'a kind of neoclassical, postmodern retro world'. He could have just as easily been describing Stephenson's Atlantis/Shanghai.

3 A word on the position of the authors is, perhaps, in order. While we support the project of reconstituting the subject in spatial terms, we share a concern with privileging space over time in constituting subjectivity, and we remain suspicious of the culturalist tendencies that such privileging can entail. It is not, then, the subject constituted through difference or hybridity that we question, but rather the ideology of multiculturalism that can emerge from such subjectivity. *The Diamond Age* is read as a caution against such multiculturalism.

4 Of China's ultrastable cultural identity, Sun Longji writes 'This tendency toward stagnation is also evident in the personality of every Chinese individual. A Chinese is programmed by his culture to be "Chinese." In other words, in-bred cultural predispositions make the Chinese what they are and prevent them from being full-blown individuals. Dynamic human growth is an alien concept to the Chinese' (Barmé and Minford 1988: 136). While Stephenson may not go to such culturalist lengths in his portrayal of Chinese identity (though we think he comes close to this in his 1993 *Wired* article: Stephenson 1993), he is clearly drawing upon the same sentiments as have inspired Sun to reach such heights of self-flagellation. Of history's entrapment, Jin Guantao writes 'China has not yet freed itself from the control of history. Its only mode of existence is to relive the past. There is no accepted mechanism within the culture for the Chinese to confront the present without falling back on the inspiration and strength of tradition' (Barmé and Minford 1988: 133).

5 The fact that Nell appears in the Primer as Princess Nell offers yet another instance of the way the Primer anticipates the subject-formation of its reader. In (story)telling herself into 'existence' as a fully realized subject, Nell does indeed become a real-life princess, when she is honoured by Queen Victoria for saving Coastal Republic residents from the onslaught of

the Fists. While it appears that the Primer is magically predicting the future, it is simply providing the narrative-model through which Nell comes to realize her subjectivity.

6 Similarities between the Drummers' warren and China can also be found by comparing Stephenson's description of Old Shanghai with the undulating underwater tubes where the Drummers live. Old Shanghai is a 'living vestige of Imperial China', a 'small but anfractuous subregion whose tendrils were seemingly ramified through every block and building of the ancient city. On the map, this region looked like a root system of a thousand-year-old dwarf tree; its borders must have been a hundred kilometers long, even though it was contained within a couple of square miles' (Stephenson 1996a: 125–6). There is an organic, network-like quality to this description that resembles the hidden underwater maze of the Drummers.

# 4

# SPACE, TECHNOLOGY AND NEAL STEPHENSON'S SCIENCE FICTION

*Michelle Kendrick*

I hear the ruin of all space, shattered glass and toppling masonry, and time one livid final flame.

James Joyce

As philosophers since Hume have recognized, the concepts of space and time are critical in understanding our narratives of subjectivity. Elizabeth Grosz argues that space and time are represented and understood in ways that are irrevocably masculine, and such theories deny women social and political agency (Grosz 1994). Fredric Jameson attributes the shift to postmodernism to a crisis in our experience of space and time (Jameson 1992). It seems clear that cultural and historical shifts in conceptualizing space/time can lead to widespread anxieties that are expressed in our narratives regarding their subjectivity. In this chapter I suggest that technologies of communication, artificial intelligence and immersive environments – technologies that influence what Jameson terms 'hyperspace' – are radically redefining the relationship among space, time and subjectivity. Understanding both the nature of such shifts and the anxieties they provoke – that is, understanding that narratives of identity are always in the process of being reinscripted by technologies of communication – is fundamental to an ongoing critique of the subject.

In this regard, Stuart Moulthrop argues that narrative, rather than a given material or psychological identity, is crucial for understanding new networking technologies:

> Uploading or downloading people into information networks is the stuff of *Star Trek's* 24th Century (i.e., of television) not of the present era. What we transfer into the network, now or in the foreseeable future, is not our literal mind/body but some representation: some text . . . Questions about cyberculture thus lead away from 'edges' (new or otherwise) and back towards surfaces – or to scenes of writing.
>
> (Moulthrop 1994: 300)

In this essay I explore the concept of space (edges and surfaces) as it relates to scenes of writing. I question Moulthrop's distinction between the 'literal mind/ body' and the text and look instead at the connections that exist between them.[1] To do this I use one particular scene of writing – science fiction – to examine the ongoing interactions of space, technology and subjectivity.

In particular, I argue that Neal Stephenson's science fiction demonstrates a historically situated moment of cultural anxiety about space, technology and their relationship to the *gendered* physical body. Although much of what is called cyberpunk (or post-cyberpunk) is concerned with virtual geographies, Stephenson's work in the early 1990s marks an interesting moment in such fictional accounts because it charts the move away from the notion of cyberspace as a spatial geography that one enters, to a notion of virtual space unfolded within or mapped upon the material body of the subject. In his second novel *Snow Crash*, like other science fiction authors writing at that time (Gibson, Sterling, etc.), Stephenson creates a unique geography with a visual materiality that surrounds the user/hacker. Unlike other authors, however, Stephenson moves us – not completely and not comfortably – beyond cyberspace in *The Diamond Age* to trace the turning of the virtual space back to the gendered body. As technologies grow ever smaller, and finally disappear into an organism, the space of technology is troublingly like the space of the body and, in *The Diamond Age*, the overriding discursive issues centre on bodily integrity and the ramifications of bodily violations. In his turn from unique spatial geographies to a mapping of technology on the body, Stephenson marks a crucial moment in the early 1990s, offering an interesting – if temporary – corrective to other cyberliberationists who continued to see new technological spaces as frontiers to be colonized by the intact and independent subject.

Writing about the same time (1991), for example, Michael Benedikt writes, in celebratory terms, of the possibilities of cyberspace for the subject:

> Cyberspace: Through its myriad, unblinking video eyes, distant places and faces, real or unreal, *actual or long gone*, can be summoned to presence . . . Around every participant, this: a laboratory, an instrumented bridge; *taking no space*, a home presiding over a world.
> 
> (Benedikt 1991: 2, emphasis mine)

Benedikt's vision is of transcendence over history and temporality – everything imaginable is available and can be 'summoned to presence'. The laboratory in which to conduct these experiments takes up no space, thereby reversing the logical order and importance of traditionally demarcated spaces. Hence, the home (or home page) presides over the world, that is, the world in every way controllable. The terms of such celebration are cast in notions of human agency *over* such spaces and in controlling the effects of time. Humans – and in the discourse of 'control' the emphasis is on a traditionally male human – still 'summon' the past to the present; they still actively experiment in this new, space-less laboratory. These images are of satisfying desire, overcoming the Lacanian lack that seems fundamental to most postmodern descriptions of identity.

In Benedikt's vision the subject is transcendent and discursively positioned in a place separate from technology and in control of the effects of technologies on such basic organizational, perceptive and absolute categories as space and time. He argues, therefore, that the attraction of computer technologies lies in their ability to empower the user:

> A great deal of attraction of the networked personal computer in general . . . is due to its lightning fast enactment of special 'magical' words, instruments, and acts, including those of induction and mastery, and the instant connection they provide to distant realms and buried resources.
>
> (Benedikt 1991: 6)

Benedikt's celebration suggests that the move to cyberspace is the final 'shift': the human is no longer the effect of time, space and sensory experience (as, say, Hume would posit) but instead the demiurge presiding over such changes. Positioning the subject as distinct from these contexts creates a discursive position of distance from and control over technology. Note again the masculine character of the demiurge; positioned by Benedikt, he is an adventurer searching out exotic 'realms' from which to plunder resources.

Stephenson seems, at first, to replicate this dynamic in his first novel – his protagonist displays the mastery that Benedikt dreams – but on closer reading his representations of the similarities between the computer spaces and the space of the human brain/body make it hard for a discourse of separation and mastery to carry the day. Stephenson instead creates a shared space, a continuum between virtual spaces and bodily spaces – what Kate Hayles (1999: 246) has called the 'infoworld' – and in doing so collapses the boundaries and undercuts the discourses of separation and control promulgated by other proponents of cyberspace in the early 1990s. In *The Diamond Age*, Stephenson narrates a world in which the constructed nature of subjectivity, and the role of technologies in such construction, is acknowledged by his characters in a complicated mixture of celebration and condemnation.

Interestingly, however, although Stephenson's two novels offer an insightful representation of contemporary anxieties scripted to a technological future, ultimately Stephenson cannot seem to accept the miscegenation that he creates. Finally, his novels pull back from the implications of conflating the space of the machine and the space of the body. His narratives conclude by representing the 'intervention' of technology in the body and subjectivity as ultimately dangerous, and – in the end – his novels struggle to reassert masculine control and agency in terms of protecting a specifically gendered, romanticized human space of identity from technological impurities. Humans, he concludes, are machine-like, are infiltrated by the machine, are even 'constructed' by the machine, but ultimately their gendered bodies provide the 'line in the sand' that maintains a critical separation.

## ELECTRONIC TECHNOLOGIES IN *SNOW CRASH*

David Porush calls *Snow Crash* a second-generation cyberpunk novel, an essentially dystopian vision of a technological future (Porush 1996: 106). In this future, the space of 'America' is fractured and divided, no longer under the control of a central government. Instead the USA consists of huge 'franchises', which offer everything from speedy pizza delivery to covert investigations and assassinations. In this vision, Stephenson recreates a familiar science fiction scenario, a dystopian vision of capitalism as a force fracturing, commodifying and morphing all stable identities. The one coherent space is the 'Metaverse', Stephenson's version of cyberspace.[2] At the novel's beginning, Stephenson's cyberspace offers the same 'magic' of external control seen in Benedikt's vision. The Metaverse is a fictional, electronically created world in which users interact through representative figures called 'avatars'. Hiro Protagonist, the playfully named central character, is a hacker, freelance guerrilla and pizza deliveryman. Although Hiro can barely make ends meet in the 'real world', as one of the original programmers for the Metaverse, he has Benediktian powers within the computer-generated space. With a hacker's skill, he navigates through objects at will; he is a master swordsman, a celebrity who has access to inexhaustible data that allow him to uncover and decode conspiracies. His warrior skills allow him to 'kill' bad guys and to ride his virtual motorcycle away at impossible speeds.

And he has an attitude. In Hiro we see none of the postmodern angst that marked earlier cyber-cowboys, such as Gibson's Case in *Neuromancer* (Gibson 1984). Rather than relinquishing the devalued 'meat' of bodily experience, Hiro moves comfortably between real life and the Metaverse with a flip of his goggles. There is none of the ephemeral 'floating' or disorientation that marks Gibson's cyberspaces. Stephenson's Metaverse mimics the physics of the real world (importantly, exceptions can be made for talented hackers); and it mimics the 'meta'physics of reality as well. Unlike cyberspace in Gibson's novels, the Metaverse is a simulacrum of the real world, not the representation of a data-driven imaginary space of capital. In this space one walks about, or rides in specially designed vehicles.

Early in Stephenson's *Snow Crash*, his vision of technology and the space it creates is fairly traditional. Technology supplements and enhances the real world and enables access to interesting, but not radically different, computer-created spaces. Technology's relation to the physical body is essentially that of 'hardware'.

> [Hiro] is wearing shiny goggles that wrap halfway around his head; the bows of the goggles have little earphones that are plugged into his outer ears . . .

The goggles throw a light, smoky haze across his eyes and reflect a distorted wide-angle view of a brilliantly lit boulevard that stretches off into an infinite blackness. The boulevard does not really exist; it is a computer rendered view of an imaginary place.

(Stephenson 1992: 20)

The goggles, with their 'light, smoky haze', barely interfere with interaction in material reality. The user can choose to be fully immersed in cyberspace, or simply see a transparent overlay that does not obscure how he/she sees the 'real' world. *This* cyberspace is not a revolutionary new space; it is a 'hang out' where violent fantasies are contained and managed, where hackers go to bars, and suburban teenagers go on dates.

Stephenson's cyberspace is essentially a metaphor whose articulation is made possible through technology and which is made interpretable to users through its analogy to and continuity with 'real life'. For instance, Hiro tells us that avatars cannot simply 'pop' in and out of cyberspace at any point: 'You can't just materialize anywhere in the Metaverse, like Captain Kirk beaming down from on high. This would be confusing and irritating to the people around you. It would break the metaphor' (Stephenson 1992: 36). The coherence of the metaphor is maintained by the rules and protocols that mimic 'real' space.

Despite the technology that 'performs' cyberspace as a coherent locale, Stephenson's Metaverse is, at its foundation, textual. The audiovisual wonders it offers are enabled through an essential, precise, underlying mathematical code. Hiro reminds the readers, at one point, that:

Everything you see in the Metaverse, no matter how lifelike and beautiful and three-dimensional, reduces to a simple text file: a series of letters on an electronic page. It is a throwback to the days when people programmed computers through primitive teletypes and IBM punch cards.

(Stephenson 1992: 350)

To stress the 'basic' nature of such text files, likening them to teletypes and punch cards, is to demystify computer spaces and to promise that mastery is, indeed, possible once you understand the building blocks, which are, of course, strings of mathematical and alphabetic code. Hence Hiro, as one in the 'know', has no problem doing the impossible in cyberspace. A figure of masculine agency – wielding his sword – he creates and breaks rules at will.[3] It is perhaps important to note that Stephenson's version of knowledge = control = power, although here put in terms of programming, is analogous to the traditionally conceived notion of the literary author. Control the code and create the world.

Asserting the textual foundation of computer-mediated spaces seems guaranteed to reassure us that cyberspace consists of finite information. New spaces then are seen as fundamentally simple and stable, and thus offer the possibility of Benedikt's mastery for the masculine user.[4] In asserting his description of a 'write-able' cyberspace, Stephenson recounts a view of technology that is not uncommon in postmodern discourses. It is helpful, in situating his narrative in broader cultural contexts, to examine briefly the dilemma created by this view of technology. These same reassurances are offered in contemporary discourses on technology that seek to interpret new technological developments within traditional rhetorics that presuppose a fundamental difference between subjectivity and technology. For example, Richard Lanham, in 1993, praised the new 'common ground' that digitization gives the arts and sciences. Recognizing the 'base' of all information as that of text (or of a traditional view of mathematics as universal and true) – the ones and zeros of computer languages – Lanham argues, gives all disciplines 'a new common ground, a quasi-mathematical equivalency that recalls the great Platonic dream for a unity of all knowledge' (Lanham 1993: 11). This digital text, in its mathematical purity and accuracy, serves to unite all knowledge in a new space, renders all knowledge fundamentally coherent, and positions the user in control of access to this coherent info-space. The so-called democratic, utopian space that is cyberspace is again constructed paradoxically. It is simple, reverting back to a basic code, constructed primarily through texts and performed with technologies. In such simplicity, however, it offers a kind of transcendence.

Acknowledging the creation of space from such texts and technologies of inscription, however, is fraught with many of the same problems as recognizing the nature of subjectivity as a product of texts and technologies. On the one hand, such a theory does offer a 'common ground' that demystifies the construction of space/subjectivity. It promises a 'mathematical' (or 'quasi'-mathematical) certainty and fixity. That is, know the code and – so Stephenson seems to claim – you'll know how the space or the subject functions. On the other hand, such an acknowledgement shifts the focus to the *constructed nature* of space and to the ephemeral nature of such constructions.[5] If both the space and the subject that occupies such space are constructed by textuality and technologies – and language or code is a shifting, relational and constructed entity – then there can be no foundational 'real' to either space or the subject.

A contemporary example of this dilemma can be seen in recent debates surrounding the Human Genome Project. This project is an attempt to sequence the DNA of human beings, as R. C. Lewontin explains, 'to write down the complete ordered sequence of As, Ts, Cs, and Gs – the four nucleotides – that make up all the genes in the human genome' (Lewontin 1994: 107). Recently completed (a working 'draft' was announced in June 2000), this string of letters is three billion elements long.[6] The idea that the human being can be 'reduced' to a code, even such a complex code, has led some to proclaim that this project will solve the mystery of life. Lewontin quotes one of the world leaders in molecular biology, who claimed that with the complete DNA sequence of an organism, he could 'compute the organism, by which he meant totally describe its anatomy, physiology and behavior' (Lewontin 1994: 109). Lewontin cautions that 'knowing the code' will not bring us any closer to understanding the underpinnings of human subjectivity. Like all languages, the code of the DNA is shifting:

> A deep reason for the difficulty in devising casual information from DNA messages is that the same 'words' have different meanings in different contexts and multiple functions in a given context, as in many complex languages.
>
> (Lewontin 1994: 112)

Knowing the basic text of the subject gives some reassurance that the 'human' is fundamentally intelligible, a product of science. However, as Lewontin cautions, the code does not have that one-to-one, cause-to-effect certainty that researchers assume. The code's affects are context-dependent and demonstrate the constructed nature of the subject, its shifting and relational nature.

Stephenson's *Snow Crash* is a narrative impaled on the horns of this dilemma. By stressing the 'code' and text of the Metaverse, Stephenson is able to represent Hiro as masterful, a powerful hacker who knows how to manipulate the very building blocks of an alternative reality. But Stephenson does not end his fictional representation with the creation of virtual geographies and their external creators and controllers. Stephenson goes on to suggest that this 'basic' level of computer programming, on which all else is built, has its correlative with the human mind. Hiro explains:

> We've got two kinds of languages in our heads. The kind we're using now is acquired. It patterns our brains as we are learning it. But there's also a tongue that's based in the deep structures of the brain that everyone shares. These structures consist of basic neural circuits that have to exist in order to allow our brains to acquire higher languages – Linguistic infrastructure.
>
> (Stephenson 1992: 395)

Thus human brains are programmed with a kind of Ur-language that precedes and provides the structure for the more complicated languages (and the emerging subject), much like the creation of the Metaverse from a set of basic code.

The claim that subject and cyberspace are homologously structured, however, creates anxiety for the characters and tension in the plot. Stephenson's narrative soon shifts away from the isomorphic nature of technology and subjectivity to describe instead how subjects came to *differ* from machines. Where Hiro seems, at first, to celebrate the connections between the subject and technology, later, as he receives more information, he learns that the connections are insidious. Before the creation of individual consciousness, Hiro finds, there was a pre-historic man who was not self-aware: 'The Sumerian word for "mind," or "wisdom," is identical to the word for "ear"', he tells us, 'That's all those people were: ears with bodies attached. Passive receivers of information" (Stephenson 1992: 397). In the world prior to 'self-consciousness' an informational virus controlled human beings. Humans operated as machines, whose operating instructions came from a basic code. If humans and cyberspace are both the products of a basic text, then their connection is undeniable. Humans, when textually determined, are simply different kinds of information-processing technology.[7] The foundational subject, like other technologies, cannot be self-aware; he simply records, transmits, stores information, with no ability to discern useful information from 'bad' information. Without an ability to make such critical judgements, humans – like computer technologies – are susceptible to viruses, 'bad' information that self-replicates and affects the host system. In *Snow Crash* viruses can be informational, biological and psychological concurrently. Humans are a kind of organic machine and susceptible to biological and technological viruses that are considered – in the world of the novel – part and parcel of the bodily space.

In *Snow Crash* the 'common ground' that this linguistic infrastructure represents is not, as Lanham would see it, benevolent or beneficial. Rather than subjects reaching Platonic unity and mastery over knowledge on this common ground, the subject, in *Snow Crash*, can only come into being through radical differentiation. As Hiro tells readers, only with the growing development and divergence of language – the equivalent of the tower of Babel – could self-consciousness develop. He explains:

> No matter how smart we get, there is always this deep irrational part that makes us potential hosts for self-replicating information. But being physically infected with a virulent strain of the Asherah virus [the virus that causes us to revert back to our linguistic infrastructure] makes you a whole lot more susceptible. The only thing that keeps these things from taking over the world is the Babel factor – the walls of mutual incomprehension that compartmentalize the human race and stop the spread of viruses.
>
> (Stephenson 1992: 400)

What makes us different from our machines, then, is our suppression of our 'common ground'; language and hence individuality are viruses. What makes us different from machines is our heterogeneity: our 'compartmental' spaces and the 'walls of mutual incomprehension' which divide them. Thus, Stephenson's narrative veers towards an acknowledgement of the role of technologies in the construction of subjectivity (through technologies of inscription) and towards a parallel and complicated link of mind, body and machine. His descriptions of preliminary, historical subjectivity, however, finally categorize the human as nothing more than a 'soft' form of information-processing technology. He is unable, seemingly, to endorse such construction and intervention as positive, and his narrative reverts back to the myth of compartmentalized individuality as the core of subjectivity. Humans are only 'humans' when they suppress and diverge from the basic inscriptions and mechanized functions that are their foundation; they are humans only when they corrupt or break the code that constructs them. Lanham's dream of Platonic unity is in the end, Stephenson suggests, a nightmare that denies individuality and hence agency in *Snow Crash*.

Paradoxically, despite the resistance in the novel to acknowledging the relationship between subjectivity and technology, the blurring of the boundaries remains represented throughout *Snow Crash*, through the idea that the 'virus' can pass through any of these mediums – as if they are one and the same. The fact that the similarities are focused on contamination and disease (as viruses move through the body, the mind and the machine) fosters a deep ambivalence in the text for the very connections that it proposes.[8]

### THE DIAMOND AGE

Stephenson's next novel, *The Diamond Age or, A Young Lady's Illustrated Primer*, represents an age in which technology is thoroughly interwoven with the very fabric of society itself. Gone are controlling governments and rigid borders, and instead of franchises, ethnic tribes, called 'phyles', rule this rigidly divided future. The word 'phyle' evokes connection with 'file', as a technological container for information, and phylum, a method of natural categorization. Whereas *Snow Crash* represented text and technology as troublingly parallel to the human, *The Diamond Age* jumbles all such categories together.

The tale is a convoluted one that involves John Percival Hackworth, a creative engineer of nanotechnology, who steals the program for a 'smart book', an illustrated primer he developed for the daughter of a nobleman, Lord Alexander Chung-Sik Finkle-McGraw. In this aspect of the plot Stephenson draws on contemporary fears of literacy vanishing with the computer age. *The Diamond Age* is so far in the future that books are rare (having been replaced by visuals) and most of the population is functionally illiterate. This 'smart' book, therefore, is meant as an educational supplement, one that will encourage subversive thinking in a system that breeds only conformity.[9] Returning home from the illegal technology lab where he pays to have the copy created, Hackworth is mugged. One of the muggers, a young man named Harv, takes the book for his little sister Nell (Stephenson's nod to Charles Dickens). Nell and Harv are of the underclass, 'thetes', who subsist mainly through criminal activities. Stephenson's novel follows the adventures of Hackworth, as he tries, in vain, to recover the twice stolen Primer, Nell, as she interacts with the book and begins her 'educational' adventures, and Miranda, the 'ractor', the human actor behind the technology of the book, who narrates the interactive tales that Nell is following.

Early in this novel Stephenson reinscribes the careful separation of technology and subjectivity with which *Snow Crash* ends. Hackworth is a member of New Atlantis, the Victorian phyle created in reaction to the twentieth century, a time when people 'took no moral stances and lived by none'. Where *Snow Crash* images a future gone amok, *The Diamond Age* images a return to social order and hierarchies. Looking to the nineteenth century for their model, the neo-Victorians value work, education and a strict social hierarchy. In Stephenson's new world, the neo-Victorians are the most successful phyle because they have not given over to the chaos of blurred boundaries (among technologies and bodies and culture) and, instead, have returned to a community governed by strict social controls.

The neo-Victorians have strict rules controlling the use of technology, and within this phyle technology is seen as 'useful' rather than constitutive. Rather than allowing technology and the 'mediaglyphics' (images and figures that replace written language as a method of communication) to clutter their surroundings, as they do in other phyles, the neo-Victorians live in a world which is modelled on the nineteenth century, with the modern twist that technology is everywhere, but is politely unobtrusive. Stephenson, however, again demonstrates the difficulties in maintaining such rigid boundaries. Despite the success of this phyle, Stephenson explains, the rigidity and prosperity of the Victorians have led to a generation of children who lack an 'edge'. Paradoxically, they are taught correct social behaviour but are deprived of the wider, historical context that had demonstrated to the older generation the necessity for such behaviour. In *Snow Crash* Stephenson describes the construction of subjectivity as based on 'disorder' rather than order. In *The Diamond Age*, he seems to suggest something similar. The problem, Stephenson suggests, is that order – here reflected in the neo-Victorians – can only be defined in opposition to disorder. Or more precisely, fetishizing of the need to be distinct from technology is most prevalent in a world where the boundaries are always in danger of blurring.

## THE DISAPPEARANCE AND NATURALIZATION
## OF TECHNOLOGY

Scott Bukatman describes a paradox of contemporary culture and technology:

> The newly proliferating electronic technologies of the Information Age are invisible, circulating outside of the human experiences of space and time. That invisibility makes them less susceptible to representation and thus comprehension at the same time as the technological contours of existence become more difficult to ignore.
>
> (Bukatman 1993: 2)

Although it is clear that technology is ubiquitous in contemporary culture, technology seems to be growing ever smaller, rapidly approaching a time when technology itself will disappear, hidden in the body, or manifest in microscopic external technologies. In discourses of computer technology the disappearance of technology often gets narrated in specific terms that attempt to reassert control and agency. For example, the creation of electronic forums, and subsequent disappearance of most of the technologies which make such forums possible, supports a discourse, like Benedikt's, which projects cyberspace as inherently empty or passive, and thus ready to be shaped and navigated by the human as agent who enters that space at will. Furthermore, the shrinking of technology leads to the naturalization of technology as it collapses notions of outer 'space' altogether and turns inward towards the space of the gendered body. This disappearance of the material presence of technology, the hardware of technology, leads to discourses which focus on the disappearing of technology into the space of the body and to a narrative of technological problems in bodily terms of health: immune systems, disease and cures. Such metaphorizing in the terms of disease and health express the fear that the boundaries of the body are in danger of violation. At the same time, such discourse posits the body as *a priori* to technological 'invasion' and suggests that bodies ingest the technologies in such a way that a romanticized self persists – effectively unchanged – from its 'pre-technological', essential wholeness. Therefore, in *The Diamond Age*, the 'morality' of the nanotechnology is directly related to functions *vis-à-vis* the health of the human body. The attempt to equate technological and bodily functions, however, is only partially successful, as technology, no matter how 'bodily' and embedded, inevitably emerges as always, somehow, foreign and other than the body.

Stephenson fictionalizes such a disappearance of technology in *The Diamond Age* by creating a future world in which the dominant technology is nano-technology. Reduced to the size of 'mites', tiny robotic technologies perform certain cultural functions – security, entertainment, etc. – and operate, in many ways, like the bodily immune system. The security of the geographic region called Atlantis/Shanghai, for example, is provided by something called the 'dog pod grid – a swarm of quasi-independent aerostats' (Stephenson 1995: 56). These pods defend against microscopic technologies that seek to invade individual bodies. One example is 'Red Death, a.k.a. the Seven Minute Special, a tiny aerodynamic capsule that burst open after impact and released a thousand or so corpuscle-size bodies, known colloquially as cookie-cutters, into the victim's bloodstream' (Stephenson 1995: 58). These microscopic techno-weapons penetrate the body with ease. However, Stephenson (1995: 59) writes:

> What worked in the body could work elsewhere, which is why phyles had their own immune system now . . . A well-defended clave was surrounded by an aerial buffer zone infested by immunocules – microscopic aerostats designed to seek and destroy invaders.

The technology of this world is metaphorized in bodily terms. The city is a body and is susceptible to attack and capable of defence. In addition to the fairly familiar metaphor which posits the world (city, clave) as body, Stephenson gives us an alternate metaphor which posits a technology interior to the human body. As technology shrinks in size, it replicates, supplements and to some extent supplants natural functions. Stephenson opens this book with Bud – a caricature of masculinity and aggression – getting a new gun installed in his skull.

Incredibly muscular, Bud's body is not the result of working *with* technology, but rather, technology working within him:

> On a previous visit to the mod parlor . . . he paid to have a bunch of 'sites implanted in his muscles – little critters, too small to see or feel, that twitched Bud's muscle fibers electrically according to a program that was supposed to maximize bulk.
>
> (Stephenson 1995: 1)

The nanotechnology replicates the physical twitching of the muscles from within the muscle fibre itself. The bodily masculinity of Bud is a working of technology, an example that emphasizes the irrevocable constructedness of the body. In *The Diamond Age* Stephenson creates a strong version of what Anne Balsamo claims already exists, that is, a world where 'machines assume organic functions and the body is materially redesigned through the application of newly developed technologies' (Balsamo 1996: 3).

Often Stephenson's narration of the disappearance of technology, then, differs in interesting ways from theories of technology as prosthesis which describe technology as expanding the human body and allowing its natural functions to be amplified by technological assistance. In this novel, however, as often as technology is represented as prosthesis, it is alternatively represented as turning inwards, invading the material recesses of the flesh. Such disappearance into the space of the bodily may constitute the ultimate technological intervention in subjectivity: technology is no longer 'outside' of and affecting the way a body is constructed, rather, technology is within, an integral part of what is considered the organic. In both representations – as prosthesis and as 'implosion' – the underlying anxiety is the sanctity of the boundaries of the body and the effects on bodily integrity, which are translated into discourses of 'health' and purity.

Again, however, Stephenson ultimately shrinks from the ramifications of his own argument. The definition of the technological space as mapped onto the human body is undercut by Stephenson's narrative. The character of Miranda serves both as an illustration of the power of a naturalized technology, and as Stephenson's ultimate reassertion that the 'human' prevails despite these ever-increasing technological interventions. Miranda wants to be the future equivalent of an actor: a 'ractor'. These 'ractors' are linked technologically with the characters they play in the interactive movies. To accomplish this, the new theatre requires that thousands of pieces of nanotechnology be implanted in the body of the actor. Subsequently the technological sites are 'mapped' onto characters that appear in the ractive plots. The ractor thus becomes a kind of technological projector onto the space of the body. In fact, the more technological intervention, the better 'racting' ability a person will have. Ambitious Miranda saves up money and gets herself a 'Jodie', the most intensive set of implants available. Stephenson (1995: 87) describes the 'implants':

The tat machine worked on her for sixteen hours; they dripped Valium into her arm so she wouldn't whine . . . The grossest part was when the machine reached down her throat to plant a trail of nanophones from her vocal cords all the way up to her gums . . . The 'sites are implanted into a dermal grid . . . ten thousand of them in the face alone.

Thus implanted, Miranda seeks employment in the virtual reality theatres. The fact that Stephenson imagines a computerized theatre still needing the 'human' to participate suggests his narrative necessity for the naturalized body in virtual reality. The computer, despite being able to generate most material objects, is incapable of generating truly convincing characters; there is something, some essence of the 'human', still needed in these interactive performances to make them convincing.[10] Miranda's dermal grid allows her to adopt any character, and she can endow these characters with her natural bodily movements. The ghost of her body controls the computer-generated 'spirits':

Miranda was looking at a black wall speckled with twenty or thirty thousand individual pricks of white light. Taken together, they formed a sort of three-dimensional constellation of Miranda, moving as she moved. Each point of light marked one of the 'sites that had been poked into her skin by the tat machine during those sixteen hours. Not shown were the filaments that tied them all together into a network – a new bodily system overlaid and interlaced with the nervous, lymph, and vascular systems . . . for the first time ever, she was watching another person move exactly as she moved, as the stage mapped Miranda's grid onto this imaginary body. Miranda pressed her lips together as if she'd just put on lipstick, and the Spirit did the same.

(Stephenson 1995: 88–9)

The nanotechnology creates another 'bodily system' which interlaces with those of the natural body. In this manner, Miranda's body is both invaded and enhanced, thus creating the uneasy balance between being a subject and – through the technology – creating and projecting a subject out from the natural body. Stephenson suggests, then, that technology can, in complicated ways, 'interlace' with the material body and hence makes visible what is implicit: that technology is constitutive of the body and the subject. He also suggests, however, that something essentially 'human' can be projected outward as a controlling essence.

The visual representation of the technological implants in the body of Miranda suggests what Scott Bukatman has called 'terminal space'. 'Terminal space', he writes, 'becomes phenomenal in the discourse of science fiction, a *narrative* compensation for the loss of visibility in an electronically defined world' (Bukatman 1993: 201, italics his). That is to say, as technology 'disappears' it becomes necessary to create a substitution – a metonymy – for the technology no longer visible. In 1990s science fiction, as well as in broader cultural narratives, this metonymy was often the space of cyberspace. Crucial, however, for the space to function as metonymy for the disappearing technology is the insertion of the body – and a body endowed with agency – into such space. Bukatman writes 'For to dramatize the terminal realm means to somehow insert the figure of the human into that space to experience it *for us*, to affect it *for us*, and to be affected by it *for us*' (Bukatman 1993: 201). Miranda's dermal grid is a map of the human body, technologized, created by and creating the space of technology.

Despite emphasizing the necessity for the technological interventions in such 'acting', Stephenson again moves away from recognizing the implications and complications of his narrative and the role of technology in the construction of subjectivity and the body. In specifically gendered terms, he reasserts the primacy of the *natural, maternal* body as prior to and stronger than the technological interventions. Miranda is the 'ractor' narrator for little Nell's interactive Primer; as she spends time narrating, teaching and nurturing Nell via the interactive book, she develops an overwhelming maternal affection for her student. Once a rising star, a famous 'ractor', Miranda gives up her day job (for Nell reads primarily at night), loses her contacts and friends in the business and busies herself raising a child she has never met; the fact that such mothering is possible only through the technological implants is undercut by the fact that Miranda is not satisfied with a technologically mediated relationship and feels that she must find a way to mother 'bodily'. She then sets out on a quest to find Nell.

Miranda attempts to find a way to bypass the technological interventions that have made the relationship with Nell possible in the first place. As part of her quest she joins an orgiastic cult called the Drummers, whose bizarre sexual rites transmit information in the form of viruses. As in *Snow Crash*, the bodily, the technological and the common ground of information come together in the form of the physical, semantic, biological virus. The Drummers are the phyle that epitomizes the naturalization and disappearance of technology. Undoubtedly a jab at the men's movement and 'drumming' as a way of asserting a primal masculinity, Stephenson shows how the Drummers – like the victims of the virus Snow Crash – lose their sense of individuality through sharing a communal vision. They are a vast connected mind, created through biological nanotechnology which links them all in a 'wet' Net that is maintained through the exchange of bodily fluids. This would seem the ultimate vision of the naturalization of technology: technology is seamlessly, literally 'fluidly' at one with the human body. In his evocation of the AIDS virus, spread through the passing of bodily fluids, Stephenson represents the linking of human minds through technology as ultimately destructive. The distribution of this technology is destructive to individual bodies, and particularly, it is destructive to women's bodies. Hackworth, who, on his own mission, spent ten years with the Drummers, describes a ritual exchange of viruses and information. At the heart of the ceremony is the sacrifice of a woman, who has ritualistic sex with many of the men as they fill her with 'information' in the form of semen:

> The drumming and chanting explode to a new impossible level of intensity. The girl moves for the first time, tossing her bouquet up in the air ... The girl faints, or something, falling backward, arms out, and is caught by several of the dancers, who hoist her body over their heads and parade her around in a circle for a while. She ends up flat on her back on the ground, and one of the dancers is between her legs, and in a very few thrusts he has finished . . .
>
> (Stephenson 1995: 257)

This bodily exchange of information – like the AIDS virus itself – is fatal. In masculine 'community', Stephenson suggests, the woman is the sacrifice to the 'wet' information web. The overload of information in this bodily fluid causes her spontaneously to combust – she literally burns up, unable to accommodate in her body the 'information' from the men.

> Toward the end, smoke or steam or something begins to spiral up from the middle of the orgy ... Flames erupt from several locations, all over her body, at once, seams of lava splitting open along her veins and the heart itself erupting from her chest like ball lightning.
>
> (Stephenson 1995: 257)

In a world where the space of the body and the space of technology are one, the exchange of bodily fluids leads to an antithesis of 'normal' bodily reproduction. This attempt at the integration of technology and bodies leads, instead, to the ultimate destruction of the physical boundaries of the body. The internalized information technology still must claim its space in the body. There is no seamless integration. Here, the bodily space is represented as a place of invasion and Stephenson's primary concern is with bodily integrity. The 'invasion' of the sacrificial woman in the Drummers' rites destroys the 'space' of her body – she explodes.

The Drummers expose the basic paradox, in the novel, of bodies and technologies. Technology allows connection – the Drummers are more able to 'think' collectively, to generate more information and more complex thoughts – but technology also breaks down the physical barriers of the body – the female body.[11] The trade of connectivity and empowerment for bodily integrity, ultimately, is shown by Stephenson to be unacceptable. As Hackworth explains, 'They [the Drummers] believe that information has an almost mystical power of free flow and self-replication, as water seeks its own level or sparks fly upward – but lacking any moral code, they confuse inevitability with Right' (Stephenson 1995: 384). What is 'right' in Stephenson's new world is to maintain the separation of body, subjectivity and technology and therefore to maintain some human control over flows of techno-information.

*

Stephenson's two novels, then, point to the connections between our technologies and our constructions of selves. Cyberspace is shown to be a construct that
mirrors and ultimately morphs with the human. The spaces of technology and
the spaces of the body are contained within each other and are permeable to the
'viruses' that no longer discriminate between human and machine. Ultimately,
however, Stephenson denies the vision of 'Platonic unity'. He reasserts in *Snow
Crash* the masculine agent, whose individuality is maintained by 'walls of
incomprehension that maintain bodily integrity'. In *The Diamond Age* ultimately it is the naturalized, maternal woman who is asserted against the forces of
homogenization. Women's bodies reject the technological, reject the joining of
two 'uncommon' things.

In his complicated novels, Stephenson captures the ongoing cultural anxiety
regarding new technologies perfectly; he seems unable to represent the human
either as technologically created, or as natural and *a priori* to technological
interventions. His narratives oscillate between a celebration of technology as
'interlaced' and, in some cases, undifferentiated from bodily spaces, and a
reassertion of the primacy of the 'natural', the human who ultimately, and hero-
ically, must reject technology no matter how necessary or helpful. At some level,
the marker that tells the human from the computer is gender. Humans may be a
kind of information-processing machine, Stephenson suggests, but they are not
all or only machines – something bodily, and specifically gendered, overrides the
mechanical. As more and more of us go 'online', where bodies and gender can
seem irrelevant, Stephenson's struggles suggest that new spaces for the subject
complicate as often as they liberate.

### NOTES

1 In the age of the World Wide Web, in the proliferation of images and words existing side-
  by-side in all aspects of culture, in a time of 'avatars' and visual representations in MOOs
  and MUDs, Moulthrop's distinction is even more suspect.
2 Interestingly, the 'Metaverse' is now something of a reality. Like the term cyberspace,
  which entered the lexicon from science fiction, the Metaverse has materialized out of
  fiction and onto the World Wide Web. The founders of the virtual 'Alphaworld' created
  their two-dimensional visual space based loosely on the descriptions in *Snow Crash* of the
  Metaverse. See http://jaring.nmhu.edu/future/pages/alpha.htm.
3 In casting Stephenson as an author who relies on conventional gendered representations, I
  am doing him something of a disservice. Stephenson, in *Snow Crash*, includes characters
  that play with gender and break stereotypes, particularly Y.T. the skateboard-riding chick
  who ultimately succeeds in delivering the pizza that Hiro doesn't. As he does with his
  representations of technology, however, Stephenson ultimately turns his gender narratives
  back to traditional roles – perhaps ironically, but always predictably.
4 I use masculine here, of course, as culturally constructed.
5 This seems to me the basic paradox of postmodernism. Many postmodern critics attempt
  to undermine the myth of an *a priori*, 'natural' subject through theories of the 'constructed' nature of subjectivity. However, descriptions of the various factors that contrib-
  ute to such construction are often essentialist and teleological. Descriptions, say, of the
  way the subject is constructed through language suggest only one basic building block
  (however shifting and relational).

6 See http://www.ornl.gov/hgmis/ for more information on the Human Genome Project.
7 It is interesting that technology takes precedence. Technology is not seen as a different kind of human function.
8 David Porush, in his article on *Snow Crash*, suggests that the virus Snow Crash 'effects a transcendence of the categories *natural* and *artificial*, between the biological world and the simulated reality of cyberspace' (Porush 1996: 133). The transcendence is primarily physical, but Porush notes that Stephenson ultimately 'rewrites the history of the world' to make it metaphysical.
9 In Stephenson's representations of Nell and the Primer, the novel is quite conservative, advocating the power of print literacy and the advantage of liberal, individualized education. For arguments in contemporary culture concerning the "death of literacy" see Sanders (1995) and Birkerts (1994).
10 For an interesting, if somewhat dated, discussion of computers and/as theatre see Brenda Laurel's *Computers as Theatre* (Laurel, 1993).
11 This same fear can be seen in contemporary discourse on such 'technologizing' of the body as test-tube babies, cloning, even technological implants. See Balsamo (1996).

# 5

## GEOGRAPHIES OF POWER AND SOCIAL RELATIONS IN MARGE PIERCY'S *HE, SHE AND IT*

*Barbara J. Morehouse*

The year is 2059. The world is dominated by 23 multinational enclaves that are sequestered under protective domes. The enclaves are havens from a landscape, the 'Raw', that has been ravaged by nuclear war, global warming, plagues and profound economic and social disintegration. The 'multis' do not, however, possess complete control. Pockets of resistance exist among a scattering of Free Towns and Rural Zones, and in the gang structure of the 'Glop', the festering, decayed, dangerous remains of the megalopolises where most of the world's population struggles to survive. Huge artificial intelligence systems provide the essential framework for information management, communications, and maintenance of the bubble within which the remnants of the pre-apocalypse power structure survive and prosper. This is the world that forms the backdrop for Marge Piercy's 1991 feminist science fiction novel *He, She and It*.

Winner of the 1992 Arthur C. Clarke Award for best work of science fiction published in the United Kingdom – where it was published as *Body of Glass* – the novel reflects many of the attributes of a form of fiction known as feminist fabulation (Barr 1992). More specifically, *He, She and It* is a Jewish feminist fabulation (Doherty 1997). This sub-genre of science fiction constitutes a variation on the conjunction of feminism, utopian fiction and science fiction (Lefanu 1988). As defined by Lefanu, feminist science fiction is 'informed by the feminist, socialist, and radical politics that developed during the 1960s and 1970s' (Lefanu 1988: 3) as a part of, but struggling against, mainstream science fiction (Lefanu 1988: 5). The particular forms that feminist science fiction has taken have presented women with new ways of writing, and have freed them from the constraints of realism (Lefanu 1988: 5). As one of these innovative forms, feminist fabulation represents a particular sort of speculative fiction that 'theorizes about feminist futures' (Barr 1992: 13) and 'articulates woman's torment, brings to light woman's fate, and attempts to threaten the stability of patriarchal structures, the order of the world. It retells and rewrites patriarchal stories, points toward incalculable feminist futures, and thinks as yet unviable thoughts of effectively transforming patriarchal society' (Barr 1992: 15).

For example, much of the story of *He, She and It* occurs in the utopian free town of Tikva, where men and women are fully equal in status as well as in responsibility for defending the town's free status. As such, Tikva represents a compelling alternative to the kinds of gendered relations that dominate today's world. Piercy carries the fabulation deeply into the realm of feminist science fiction when she gives two of her main female characters, Shira and her grandmother Malkah, a cyborg to programme, thus providing the two women with an opportunity to rethink gendered constructions of human behaviour. Through Malkah's heuristic programming and Shira's patient efforts to socialize him as a 'human', Yod, a cyborg built by a man in the physical image of a male, develops thought patterns, behaviours and ways of communicating that mirror feminine desires. Through the unfolding of interactions among inhabitants of Tikva, between Tikvans and outsiders, and through the women's education of Yod, Piercy's narrative explores alternatives to patriarchal institutions and codes, and encourages readers to think innovatively about what alternative worlds might look like and how they might function. In its construction of one of many possible alternative worlds, the novel focuses sharply on the specific feminist values of community, home, motherhood and personal bonds, in combination with personal integrity, courage, intelligence and ingenuity.

*He, She and It* operates not only as a feminist fabulation, but also as a feminist spin on cyberfiction. As described by Wolmark (1993), cyberpunk focuses on how new technologies destabilize traditional spaces while at the same time responding to the collapse of traditional hierarchies and the decentring and fragmentation of the subject. Cyberpunk creates intriguing landscapes that appear to efface boundaries between inner and outer worlds. With its emphasis on style and with its focus on the sign itself rather than the referent of that sign, cyberpunk has 'reworked the spatial and temporal dislocation that is the most characteristic feature of [traditional] science fiction' and, as a postmodernist literary form, has erased the 'critical distance between appearance and reality' (Wolmark 1993: 112). Importantly, feminist science fiction 'has provided cyberpunk with a conceptual vocabulary' and has had 'an undeniable impact on cyberpunk, both in its refusal to accept the generic limitations of this traditionally masculine genre, and in its concern to reframe the relationship between technology and social and sexual relations' (Wolmark 1993: 110). In comparing cyberpunk with feminist science fiction, Wolmark goes on to note that:

> cyberpunk explores the interface between human and machine in order to focus on . . . what it means to be human; feminist science fiction has also explored that interface, but in order to challenge those universal and essentialist metaphors about 'humanity' which avoid confronting existing and unequal power relations. Cyberpunks and cyborgs can therefore be regarded as related responses to technology that are rooted in gender, and

in different ways both seem to gesture towards possibilities for self-definition that move beyond existing sets of social and political relations.
(1993: 110–11)

More nuanced than cyberfilms such as *The Matrix* or the cyberfictions of writers such as William Gibson, Piercy's novel embeds cyberspace within a rich tale of complex human relations occurring in and across material space. A comparison of Gibson's *Mona Lisa Overdrive*, widely considered to be a classic in the genre, with *He, She and It* reveals striking similarities on the surface, but profound underlying differences. Piercy borrows Gibson's vision of a world characterized by vast wastelands punctuated by hives of human activity. Thus Gibson's chaotic 'Sprawl' becomes, in Piercy's narrative, the more fully realized 'Glop', a place where human beings struggle against seemingly insuperable odds to survive and resist the depredations of the multinational corporations that now rule the world. In Gibson's world, the Sprawl remains separate from that of the cyberpunks who find their greatest rewards in the simulated spaces of artificial intelligence. In Piercy's world, citizens of the Glop and of Tikva begin to search for ways to co-operate in an organized resistance against the multis. Ultimately, the females in Gibson's novel are less fully developed as characters than are the women in Piercy's book. Gibson's world is ultimately male in its social relations, power structures, and systems of reward and punishment. At the same time, Gibson constructs a world in which, as Wolmark has noted (1993: 116), the female characters, including the prosthetically enhanced mercenary Molly Millions, derive from the character of Jael in Joanna Russ's *The Female Man* (Russ 1975), and inhabit contradictory territory with ease. 'In the borderless territory of the Sprawl, women have the liberty to act because cyberpunk narratives undermine the opposition between public and private spheres. The Sprawl is therefore a feminised spatial metaphor in a way that the other central metaphor of cyberpunk – cyberspace – is not' (Wolmark 1993: 116).

In cyberpunk novels, the virtual reality of cyberspace articulates a 'contradictory fear of and fascination for technologies which actively participate in the breakdown of the boundaries between . . . human and machine . . . [thus opening up] radical possibilities for the breakdown of gender and other identities as part of a transformative social and political process' (Wolmark 1993: 118). However, as Wolmark notes, these possibilities, ultimately, are not realized in cyberpunk novels 'because the social and temporal experience of cyberspace is centrally concerned with individual transcendence rather than transformation, with escape from social reality rather than engagement with it' (ibid.). By contrast, feminist cyberfiction directly addresses questions of identity, boundary transgression and transcendence, and self versus other. The female characters in *He, She and It* do not 'escape' their bodies or material spaces; rather, they enter cyberspace to enhance their physical powers and to achieve ends that have direct implications not only for their material lives but also for the geographies of power and social relations in which the characters are embedded. As discussed below, these geographies encompass the body, home, community and cyber-space, with each alternately enabling or constraining the possibilities of the story's characters. These geographies of scale also interact with each other to create a multidimensional mosaic of socio-spatial relations. In constructing this mosaic, Piercy empowers her readers to think through the social and geographical implications of her Jewish-feminist-cyborgian-utopian alternative to present-day life.

### THE BODY

Perhaps nowhere in *He, She and It* is the mark of patriarchy and its socio-spatial implications more evident than in the body itself. Patriarchy manifests itself particularly in the bodies, minds and actions of key male characters such as Avram, who built Yod. Thus, Avram responds to threats by becoming combative, and attempts to invoke his male dominance at key stress points in the novel. Most crucially, it is Avram who ultimately holds Yod's fate in his hands, for he has programmed Yod in such a way that he can destroy the cyborg at any time. Avram's son Gadi, by contrast, expresses patriarchy not through contentious aggressiveness, but through his sexuality, which is coded through his attire, his surgical 'enhancements' and his behaviour with the young women in his world, including Shira.

The women in the novel are more fully drawn, and represent a much wider array of embodied social relations. All of Piercy's women, for example, have been technologically enhanced in one way or another. Yet, even with certain enhancements such as retinal and computer plug implants, the novel's main female character, Shira, represents a traditional young, attractive heterosexual woman who comes to realize her own empowerment through her interactions in the multi-sexual and multi-gendered relations that she experiences as the story unfolds.

In comparison, Shira's mother Riva is a remote, decidedly un-motherly character whom Shira has seldom seen and about whom she knows very little. Riva is a data pirate who relies on her capacity to remain invisible and anonymous. Riva is anything but a helpless female, and certainly does not manifest her daughter's more feminine characteristics. Rather, she is an adventurer who has no inclinations toward domesticity; indeed, she long ago gave Shira to Malkah to raise. Body image means nothing to Riva, and in fact her readiness to assume the role of characters from society's margins allows her to remain unnoticed as she moves through the material world. Thus, she first appears before Shira as one of society's least powerful people: a querulous old woman accompanied by, to all appearances, a very ordinary nurse.

The nurse, however, is no more ordinary than Riva herself. In fact, she is not only Riva's lover, but a powerful, technologically enhanced woman and a self-professed assassin. Her name is Nili, and she comes from an area known as the Black Zone, which formerly encompassed Israel and the Muslim countries of the Middle East. She, like Riva and Shira, has a child, but embodies yet a third alternative for motherhood, in that she is a member of an all-female cave-dwelling society where the raising of children is shared among the women of the community. Of all the women in the book, Nili has the most direct lineage to other feminist science fiction characters, for Piercy has constructed Nili more or less in the image of Jael, one of the four women in Joanna Russ's feminist separatist science fiction novel *The Female Man*, published in 1975. Like Jael, Nili represents a border zone of possibilities created by futuristic advances in biological and cybernetic engineering. Also like Jael, Nili combines feminine and masculine features, as well as behaviours that strongly blur the boundary between male and female. Although Nili is not as well developed novelistically as Jael (Armitt 2000), both characters embody new possibilities for redefining and reoccupying the spaces constructed by patriarchy, for they now have the physical strength and socialization needed to move beyond entrenched notions of gendered relations and geographies. For these women, their 'place' is everywhere, and politics of the body, home and community are intimately and inextricably entwined. These are women who are eminently capable of defending their place, with or without male assistance.

Like Nili, the cyborg, Yod, also occupies a border zone, a place in between masculine and feminine, by virtue of embodying both male and female attributes. In his case, however, he began as an engineered machine endowed with human attributes, rather than, as in the case of Nili, originating as a biological being who is subsequently enhanced through advanced engineering techniques (see Armitt 2000).

Yod's skin is as smooth as a woman's, his sense of touch can be acutely sensitive and gentle, and his programming includes attributes that are distinctly feminine, such as his capacity to communicate with humans in 'feminine' ways. Thus, Yod manifests empathy, responsiveness, desire to please, gentleness and a willingness to reflexively examine his relations with his human companions. At the same time, his general appearance and body parts clearly mark him as male. Much of his fundamental programming is also male, for he is designed for the defence of Tikva and is programmed to initiate violence as well as to answer violence with violence. He responds to a stab from a thorn on a rose, for example, by yanking out the entire rose bush. His design as a woman's idea of the perfect male companion – sexual as well as social – frequently causes tensions for him and for his human companions, not least because he has entered the world as an adult, without the benefit of the gradual socializing into the codes of conduct and expectations that children receive from the day they are born. In this, his existential condition differs markedly from that of Nili, who, beginning life as a human child, possesses a much wider repertoire of alternative behaviours and responses. That she does not always behave appropriately is a function of her inexperience with the nuances of the local culture, rather than, as in the case of Yod, complete lack of foundation for how to behave in any culture.

Piercy's inspiration for Yod was Donna Haraway's speculations about the possibilities of cyborgs for redefining gender and gendered social relations. In her seminal 'manifesto for cyborgs' (1985), Haraway defines a cyborg as 'a cybernetic organism, a hybrid of machine and organism, a creature of social reality as well as a creature of fiction' (Haraway 1985: 65). The cyborg is a creature of social reality, an example of lived social relations and thus 'our most important political construction, a world-changing fiction' (ibid.). Cyborgs do not simply inhabit the future, however. According to Haraway, 'we are all chimeras, theorized and fabricated hybrids of machine and organism; in short, we are cyborgs. The cyborg is our ontology: it gives us our politics' (Haraway 1985: 66). Piercy reflects this viewpoint when Shira observes:

> we're all unnatural now. I have retinal implants. I have a plug set into my skull to interface with a computer. Malkah has a subcutaneous unit that monitors and corrects blood pressure. We can't go unaided into what we haven't yet destroyed of 'nature.' Without a wrap, without sec skins and filters, we'd perish. We're all cyborgs, Yod. You're just a purer form of what we're all tending toward.
>
> (Piercy 1991: 150)

Yet the transformation to cyborg is not without its challenges, for, according to Haraway, 'the relation between organism and machine has been a border war. The stakes in the border war have been the territories of production, reproduction, and imagination' (1985: 66). In *He, She and It*, this kind of border war rises to the surface, for example, in the relations between Malkah and Shira on one side, and Avram on the other, with Avram insisting that Yod be treated as a machine, and the two women asserting Yod's rights to be treated as a human. It also arises when Yod, upon meeting Nili for the first time, is offended when Nili refers to him as a machine. He counters her disparaging remark by noting that she is part machine also. Most crucially, the border war metaphor informs the ultimate dramatic tension in the book, the contest between Y-S and Tikva for control of Yod's body and all that it holds. Avram has built Yod in defiance of an interdiction on cyborgs promulgated in the wake of a cyborgian uprising, but has justified his experiment as necessary to assure the continued independence of Tikva, which has been under escalating pressure from external forces. Now Y-S wants Yod for its own nefarious purposes. Keeping Yod's existence secret ultimately proves to be impossible, and in the final showdown, it is Yod that must be sacrificed. Piercy opts to eliminate the possibility for future cyborgs when, at the end of the book, she has Shira destroy the last vestiges of information that would have made Yod's re-creation possible. It is interesting to note, however, that in so doing, Piercy also eliminates consideration of the radical possibilities of cyborgian transformation for women, as suggested by Haraway (Armitt 2000).

On the other hand, Haraway's argument in favour of 'pleasure in the confusion of boundaries and for responsibility for their construction' finds reflection in Nili who, as a cyborg, is the product of female birth and female engineering and thus holds promise for a more thoroughly empowered feminist future. Unfortunately, Nili's character lacks full development in the novel (Armitt 2000), while Yod's characterization and fate is given in great detail. In the end, Piercy does not fully develop the possibilities of the cyborg as a 'creature of the postgender world', though tantalizing possibilities lurk beneath her prose. These possibilities invite further speculation as to how a fully developed cyborgian politics might encompass Haraway's view of the creature as 'resolutely committed to partiality, irony, intimacy, and perversity', as well as being oppositional, utopian, and completely without innocence (Haraway 1985: 67). Perhaps most importantly for this narrative and others like it, the cyborg, 'no longer structured by the polarity of public and private', has potential to embody a 'technological polis based partly on a revolution of social relations in the oikos, the household' (ibid.).

## THE HOUSEHOLD

Depictions of households are richly detailed in Piercy's novel, suggesting the power of social geographical relations at the household level to structure life possibilities. Malkah's home is most memorable for its utopian and at the same time backward-looking attributes. The house is a welcoming structure with its feminine ambiance, its garden and its motherly house computer – complete with female voice – known simply as House. House defends the home and its inhabitants, thus creating a haven from the external world, a complex geography of inclusion and exclusion. As an agent of inclusion, House monitors environmental conditions, carries on conversations with the inhabitants, reads stories to Shira's son. As an agent of exclusion, it holds the power to disable or destroy threats from outside. It can even display its displeasure – but its ultimate directive is to obey its human controllers, as when it is ordered to allow a 'machine' that it dislikes and possibly even envies (i.e. Yod) to enter.

By contrast, Avram's dwelling is a rather cold, silent edifice, an old hotel, that has little household significance beyond providing shelter for Avram and for Gadi when he returns to Tikva. Significantly, this building also houses Avram's laboratory, where Yod and his since-destroyed, uncontrollably violent, predecessors were created. Here, geographies of home, linked to body and community, are obliterated in favour of masculinist spaces of asocial and aspatial science and technology. Significantly, when Avram's son moves 'home', the hotel also becomes the site of a series of artificial environments ('virons') Gadi creates to amuse himself and his young fans. The virons provide a means for escaping the quotidian world, in direct contrast to Malkah's home, which invites rootedness in the material and metaphorical spaces of family, community and the larger world.

In one of the few reflections of the kind of homelike qualities that permeate Malkah's home, Avram's dwelling retains echoes of a time now gone when Gadi's mother was still alive. It also holds memories of Shira's youthful relations – sexual as well as social – with Gadi, as well as of Gadi's betrayal of their relationship with another young woman. As long as Avram has his way, this is Yod's 'place' as well, his storage place when he is not required to perform the functions for which he was built.


## COMMUNITY

In the nested hierarchy of places in *He, She and It*, the community constitutes a crucial scale for the playing out of the novel's central drama. The political geography of Piercy's novel depicts a world of sharp contrast between Tikva, Y-S and the Glop, where the multis rule their enclaves, the free towns defend themselves as best they can, and the Glop rots under a 'poisonous sky, ruled by feuding gangs and overlords' (Piercy 1991: 33).

More specifically, Tikva is a utopian community that echoes the free cities that prospered in Europe five centuries earlier. Its independence is contingent upon its betweenness: the ability of its highly skilled citizens to continue providing essential services to competing corporate enclaves, none of whom want the community to be absorbed by any of its competitors. This 'middle person' role is, of course, one that Jews held for centuries, just as their ghettos historically represented in-between places walled off from, but intimately linked to, the dominant community in which they had to struggle for survival. In contrast, Piercy's construction of Tikva is that of a propertied community, and a privileged, if embattled, garden in the midst of a post-apocalypse world.

Politically, in Piercy's words, 'the foundation of Tikva was libertarian socialism with a strong admixture of anarcho-feminism, reconstructionist Judaism (although there were six temples, each representing a different Jewishness) and greeners' (Piercy 1991: 404). She contrasts Tikva with Y-S, noting that the corporate enclave is 'a hierarchy with a head', while Tikva is 'a town meeting, a full and active democracy' (Piercy 1991: 404).

The domed Y-S enclave presents a severe alternative world, one of strict enforcement of a corporately determined, strict social and spatial hierarchy in which everyone knows his/her place, both literally and figuratively. Here, individuals are relegated to living spaces and neighbourhoods based on their corporate-defined status. The amenities offered both within the home and in the neighbourhood are likewise determined by status. For example, access to day care, schools, parks, and so on, depends on status. Those at the top of the hierarchy, of course, have the best of everything, including the wealth to purchase live pets for their children, as well as access to parks with real lawns, plants, ponds, and to the most fashionable shops, surgical procedures, and other benefits. The recursivity among body, home and community is very apparent in the Y-S dictated universe. Here, coded bodies facilitate surveillance and control. Social and spatial production and reproduction remain firmly in the hands of the power brokers at the top. High-level and mid-level workers, for example, wear backless suits and sport hair styles that conform to the corporation's latest fashion dictates. Even movement is controlled from the top, as Shira reveals when she realizes that 'she never saw an adult run on these streets. Everyone was conscious of being observed, of being judged' (Piercy 1991: 5). In sharp contrast, day workers wear uniforms that are colour-coded according to their jobs. The coding makes subversion and resistance difficult: when Yod and Shira re-enter the enclave to retrieve her son, they decide to dress as landscape workers whose attire codes them for access to the particular area and the freedom of movement they need to accomplish their mission.

Day workers, like the landscape workers that Yod and Shira use for their disguise, are not even allowed to live in the enclave. They must commute from the outside, from the Glop, which provides an apparently limitless reservoir of proletarian bodies. In the Glop, elections are still held every two years, but have degenerated to highly bet-upon sporting events. Every quadrant in the Glop is managed by the remnants of the former United Nations and the eco-police, but little actual control is possible. A dismal dystopia, the Glop is a 'crowded violent festering warren of the half starved', a place where nine-tenths of the people on the continent live (Piercy 1991: 6). It is a place where hundreds camp and sleep 'in the filthy decaying passages' that mumble 'day and night of distant voices, muffled screams, drumming, zak music, running sewage, the hiss of leaking coolant' (Piercy 1991: 31–2). It is 'crowded, fetid with human smells and the overwhelming stench of pollution and decay' (Piercy 1991: 294). And it is a place of creolized Spanish, African and other languages, where most of the residents are of mixed race.

The Glop lacks the sophistication, and even the basic resources, available in Tikva and Y-S. However, it does have its own spatialized power structures and relations. Here, gangs control their turf against all outsiders, and elaborate, often arcane rules determine who may go where, when, and under what circumstances. Maintaining a hyper-elevated state of alertness is essential, for thieves steal not only belongings but also body parts, and murder goes unremarked. Here, what small measure of community – indeed of safety – may be had is found in belonging to a gang or in adjusting one's behaviour so as to render oneself as invisible as possible. Ignorance reigns. Unlike the technocratic world of Y-S, or even of Tikva where access to vast databases is universal from childhood onward, very few inhabitants of the Glop have computer connections. The very barriers posed by the squalor and violence of the Glop, however, provide an opportunity for organized resistance to the larger structural forces that surround them. By expressly valuing education and by opening up to contact with outsiders – notably the cohort from Tikva led by Riva – to acquire necessary knowledge and technology, Glop gang leader Lazarus is emerging as a potential, if masculinist, force for social change. An alliance between Tikva and Lazarus's group, approached very tentatively by both sides, suggests that a new and more liberatory inter-community geopolitics may be emerging.

The tensions among these three contrasting social constructions of material urban space allow Piercy to locate the existential lives of her characters in a larger context, one that facilitates exploration of how external structures and events alternately influence their freedom to produce and reproduce lives and geographies of their own choosing. Yet while the material is essential to the unfolding of their lives, interactions and conditions in cyberspace introduce an important element that must be considered.

## CYBERSPACE

Animated by developments and futuristic visions in the field of virtual reality and artificial intelligence, Piercy creates a parallel cyberworld into which her characters can mentally project themselves. As also occurs in cyberpunk fiction such as Gibson's *Mona Lisa Overdrive* and *Neuromancer*, the inhabitants of *He, She and It* can mentally project themselves into and through virtual space, wage virtual battles, and gain access to information from the files of their own and other large databases. The artificial intelligences that lie at the foundation of cyberspace include protective programming that can damage or kill cyber-travellers, or simply create diversions that lead travellers down spurious paths. Malkah's specialty is creating such diversions, called chimeras. Indeed, the marketing of sophisticated chimeras to the corporations is crucial to Tikva's efforts to remain independent. These artificial intelligences and the massive databases they support are essential to survival in the post-apocalyptic world that Piercy has created, and cannot be destroyed without imperilling life as it has evolved under the domes and wraps of the 'chosen'. However, they also constitute dangerous 'territory' where attack can come without warning, where knowledge can be used for nefarious or beneficial purposes, and where relations of power hinge on advanced knowledge of their structure and behaviour.

In *He, She and It*, cyberspace provides a level playing-field where gender, strength and bodily attributes do not pose barriers to entry. Thus, the cyborg Yod, the young female Shira and the old female Malkah are all able to navigate cyberspace, enter virtual worlds of data, change shape to avoid destruction by cyberweapons, and move at speeds impossible in the material world. In thus immersing her characters in this alternative world, Piercy poses provocative suggestions about the ways in which our understanding of the interactions between material and cyberspace – and between both types of space and social process – is changing as we gain ever-greater capacity to overcome distance, gender and body image, as well as intellectual and physical constraints. Our understanding of both material and metaphorical space is already being influenced by the possibilities and dangers of cyberspace, even in the rather rudimentary forms in which it exists today. If we follow Piercy's lead, we can envision even more radical changes in social, political and spatial relations as we come to be ever more transformed into cyborgs, with full capability to mentally project into and travel through cyberspace.

## GEOGRAPHIES OF POWER IN PIERCY'S
## POST-APOCALYPTIC WORLD

The concurrent blurring of boundaries between human and machine, male and female, material space and cyberspace provides Piercy with a rich context for exploring alternative geographies of power and social relations. Social relations in cyberspace prove crucial to the unfolding of the novel's plot, and at key moments provide the means to overcome the friction of both material space and embodiment. Yet it is material space in which the characters must live, and back to which they must return. Indeed, it is dangerous to remain plugged into cyberspace for long periods of time. Thus the built and natural environments provide equally essential contexts for the unfolding of the drama. It is not unimportant, in fact, that the residents of Tikva seek escape from their daily routine and the stresses of life not in Gibsonian cyberspace, but in the ocean beach outside the wrap that protects their town. The beach, with its dunes and clear view of the sky, provides a much-valued respite, particularly at night when ultraviolet rays are not a threat and organ scavengers have retreated until daylight. It is itself an in-between place that provides a buffer between the town and the wasteland beyond.

At its most powerful, *He, She and It* raises provocative questions about the nature of difference (see Young 1990) and the role of the body, the very 'stuff' of subjectivity (Grosz 1994). In spinning a tale of a male cyborg, Piercy is able to explore questions of gender and what it means to be 'human'. The social and spatial implications of how these issues are addressed are enormous. Should Yod be confined to the lab as an object, or should he, as a subject, have a home? Should he be allowed to wander about town freely, and be paid so that he can shop and engage in other distinctively human transactions? How does he need to behave in space in terms of body movements, posture, communication, in order to be accepted as human? Can he be prevented from causing great harm by his superhuman strength combined with his incomplete and ultimately unpredictable social persona? Should he be allowed to love and be loved, and engage in sexual relations? Does travel in cyberspace ever really level the differences between him and his human companions?

The collision between patriarchal and feminist world-views depicted in the novel provides equally provocative food for thought. The revelation of a very complex web of spatialities of social relations and geographies of power reflects Piercy's interest in inside–outside dipoles, and the possibilities that might emerge from a revival of the old 'free city' model of socio-spatial relations. Metaphors of centre, borderland, and outside versus inside recur repeatedly in her novel, with feminist interpretations of inside in terms of body, home and community providing attractive alternatives to the masculine realms of corporate enclaves and surrounding wastelands. Further, in fabulating a cyberspace where people are not always as they seem and where mind, not body, matters, Piercy produces abstract geographies of power that emerge from the interplay of minds, apart from the mediating influences of the material world. The universe of artificial intelligence creates the preconditions for imagining an almost limitless array of options and possibilities, but horrifying dangers as well. Ultimately, cyberspace constitutes a world where the potentialities and dangers of idealized non-gendered structures and interactions can be more fully explored than is possible in the material geographies of the real world.

Ironically, for all that *He, She and It* presents a compelling vision of alternative social and spatial relations, Piercy's construct contains several problematical elements. First, her geographies of inside, outside and borderland privilege the borderland position in ways that celebrate feminist knowledge gained from centuries of experience as marginalized beings. As Pratt (1998) argues, however, the use of such metaphors can close off avenues of thought, ones that might recognize the dynamic nature of society's geographies. According to hooks (1990), the margins offer a place to insist upon and indeed celebrate difference, and constitute locations of strength by virtue of their distance from dominant hegemonic cultures. But by valorizing outsider status, proponents of the benefits of margins as the sites of resistance (see also Anzaldúa 1987) fail to clearly articulate the serious issues involved. Pratt notes that 'even if boundaries are conceived as socially constructed, metaphors of inside/outside, centers/margins at least temporarily homogenize experience on either side of the boundary' (Pratt 1998: 16). Such metaphors constitute a 'representational strategy that rigidifies differences among women. The metaphors of exile and margin help us to see difference, but they encourage us to lose sight of commonalities' (Pratt 1998: 16). Such is the case with regard to the social relations constructed in *He, She and It*.

Second, for all that the narrative engages in an intriguing invention of a very specific feminist utopia, the nature of this utopia is fundamentally troubling. The narrative locates all good things in Tikva, a free town that is a homogeneous ethnic Jewish enclave and a prototypical geography of exclusion (see Sibley 1995). At the same time, the narrative portrays the antagonists as Asians or whites who are powerful, patriarchally oriented, corporately defined 'others'. The residents of the Glop, by comparison, are a racially mixed and ethnically impure collection of marginalized others. In constructing these dystopian geographies of power, Piercy comes perilously close to reproducing invidious racial and ethnic stereotypes. Likewise, by depicting Tikva as a sort of post-apocalypse 'gated community' where residential privileges are in the hands of the community itself, Piercy reproduces, in inversion, historical relations between Jews and their oppressors. At the same time, Piercy also reconstructs some of the elements of socio-spatial control that the Jews experienced both as ghetto residents in cities such as Prague and, until relatively recently, as American citizens explicitly excluded from elite country clubs and residential neighbourhoods in the United States. The question of whether such inversion is any more equitable than the original remains unasked.

On the surface, dystopias such as the Glop provide an effective trope for highlighting the values of feminist social formations. Such dystopias not only provide dramatic tension, but also allow a stronger light to play over how feminist values might provide a viable alternative way of structuring society. Such devices should provide a means for creatively thinking about how feminist alternatives might effectively redress profound wrongs through more egalitarian ethnic, gender and racial integration. However, Piercy's depiction provides little guidance for imagining how the residents of the Glop could be raised out of their abject poverty and degraded environmental and social conditions. The contradiction is troubling for its window into some of the limitations that continue to plague feminist politics. By focusing the novel's utopian ideals on the ethnically pure town of Tikva, the author reinforces political and social geographies of power that derive from some of the very same types of politicized differentiation that post-colonialist feminists continue to resist.

Piercy herself begins to recognize the dilemma towards the end of the book, when she portrays the following comment by Nili and Shira's reaction:

> 'You hear the weirdest hybrid languages in the Glop, not just Spanglish, but Chino-English, Mung-Japanese, Turko-Spanish. I don't know what'll happen to language in the end, but it sure is cooking in there.' Nili saw the Glop differently than Shira always had. Shira realized she had been trained automatically by her culture, especially by corporate culture, to treat the Glop as an unimportant place where nothing consequential happened. Nothing that mattered to the real, the significant, people could originate there. But Nili turned to the New Gangs for answers. In people living off the garbage of the preceding century, Nili found much to study and admire. Shira would have to mull it over.
>
> (1991: 361)

Shira is maturing, and becoming more socialized into a world of feminist alternatives. It is unfortunate that Nili returns home before the process has been completed.

In the end, Piercy's failure to fully delineate multiple subject positions for those outside Tikva reinforces a rather myopic construction of an otherwise attractive feminist alternative to contemporary socio-spatial relations. As Holly Youngbear-Tibbetts observed in a different context, 'when women writers couch their positioning – voluntary or involuntary – within a political analysis of perceived repression, the literature they produce resonates with metaphors of the political landscape, especially in respect to frontiers and boundaries, borderlands and exclaves', positions that are 'alternatively exalted or reviled' (1998: 39). We are left to imagine how the Glop might evolve in a narrative more fully informed by an inclusionary perspective.

### WHAT DOES IT ALL MEAN?

The above criticisms notwithstanding, Marge Piercy has created a rich, complex world in which to imagine alternative geographies arising from feminist social relations. The question then arises: what can be learned from her exploration, and how can the lessons be applied now? What sorts of alternative geographies of power and social relations might emerge as a result? Certainly the novel encourages readers to value relatively small communities where the scale is small enough to support a completely open, democratic form of governance, and where equality among residents can be assured through communal consent and cooperation. In posing the question of whether Yod could be accepted as 'human', for example, Piercy places the question directly in the hands of the community for consensual resolution. In the end, the town decides that Yod will be treated as a human with regard to his rights as well as to his obligations. In essence, he becomes a citizen of the town, a very important step in his humanization. Even though Yod is destroyed in the end, it is easy to imagine that the issue would be revisited in the future as the question arises about how far down the path towards full cyborgian enhancement of humans – like Nili – the town is willing to go.

Piercy's insistence on equal standing among individuals, regardless of their gendered identity, cyborgian status or sexual preferences, poses questions about what sorts of public and private spaces might come to be produced and reproduced as a result of such social processes. One alternative is, of course, Tikva. Yet it is doubtful that, should their relationship grow, Nili and Riva would ever produce the same kind of world. In this case, the reader is left to imagine what kinds of cities, and related geographies, might arise from alternative feminist world-views. This then poses the question: are there any existing urban models that might aid in envisioning alternative urban constructs?

Dear and Flusty (1998) examine explanations of urban dynamics developed by various writers for Los Angeles, California, and suggest a new model of some relevance to this discussion. Drawing on the work of Mike Davis (e.g. 1990), Edward Soja (1989, 1996) and others, the authors discuss a series of alternative views of urbanism. The first characterization, *edge city*, they borrow from Joel Garreau (1991). Such urban areas rise by virtue of their geographical location at key beltway–lateral road junctures and related proximity to abundant female labour, automobile accessibility, and access to advanced communications systems. In Piercy's post-apocalyptic world, the corporate enclaves constitute a close analogy to the edge cities of the late twentieth and early twenty-first centuries. A related residential form, the *privatopia*, is characterized by Dear and Flusty as 'perhaps the quintessential edge-city residential form' (1998: 55). It is more difficult, however, to envision this variant, based as it is on private housing developments administered by home-owner associations and arising from a particular spatialized form of patriarchal social relations, as fitting into the kind of radical feminist alternative envisioned by Piercy.

By contrast, the *heteropolis* might present a real possibility for a socially responsive, feminist urban form, for the heteropolis is characterized by an emphasis on cultural and racial diversity. Here, a hetero-architecture exists, demonstrating the virtue and pleasure to be derived from 'mixing categories, inverting customs and adopting the marginal usage' (Jencks 1993: 123, cited in Dear and Flusty 1998: 55). Heteropolises are vigorous, imaginative and reflective of cultural diversity and trend towards hybridized complexities reflecting dense concentration of cultural producers. It is entirely possible to imagine Nili, for example, living in a futuristic heteropolis. Further, Dear and Flusty go on to describe the built environment of the heteropolis as being 'characterized by transience, energy, and unplanned vulgarity . . .' (1998: 56), a description that might fit a new city form emerging from Piercy's Glop.

An even greater contrast is posed by the idea of city as *theme park*, wherein 'architectural landscapes are readily convertible into marketable commodities . . . prepackaged landscapes engineered to satisfy the fantasies of suburban living' (Dear and Flusty 1998: 56). This description accords closely with Piercy's description of the Y-S enclave, especially those areas that are reserved for the upper echelons. Like privatopia, it is difficult to imagine radical feminism adopting the spatial form in a theme park city, although creation of subversive theme park elements to underscore feminist values would not at all be outside the realm of possibility.

The *fortified city* and *interdictory space* present still other alternative urbanisms, ones that are organized around surveillance and social control. The fortified city, according to Dear and Flusty, represents Southern California's obsession with security, which in turn has resulted in the rise of a fortress urban form and mentality. Here, the city is 'divided into fortified cells of affluence and places of terror where police battle the criminalized poor' (1998: 57). The consequence is a *carceral city* where, through security by design, the poor are spatially sequestered, separate from affluent forbidden cities. In its most extreme form, the interdictory city space, a 'canopy of suppression and surveillance' extends across the entire city (1998: 57). In Piercy's novel, Y-S exemplifies the carceral city taken to its ultimate extreme as an interdictory space, complete exclusion of the poor and undesirable from the domed enclave. Interestingly, in this construct, Tikva emerges as an interdictory space, though in this case the community has apparently been driven to such extremes by the combined dangers posed by a poisoned atmosphere and poisonous geopolitical relations associated with the dominance of the multinational corporations and the anarchy of the Glop.

Contrary to these existing, and according to Dear and Flusty, outdated constructs of urbanism, the authors propose a new postmodernist explanation of urban dynamics, though one that anticipates a less apocalyptic future than that envisioned by Piercy. According to the authors, concentrated centres of production called '*global latifundia* are arising from contemporary globalization processes' (1998: 61). These latifundia, which have much in common with Piercy's corporate enclaves, are home to a newly emergent cybergeoisie (Dear and Flusty 1998: 62). At the same time, they see another, parallel urban form emerging: the *protosurp*, which encompasses the 'sharecroppers of the latifundia', the 'increasingly marginalized "surplus" labor' (1998: 62). This is the Glop in 'different clothes'.

In envisioning how the two realms co-exist, Dear and Flusty propose an overarching construct they describe as a 'dispersed net of megalopoles' which 'may be viewed as a single integrated urban system' (1998: 63). These megalopoles encompass the geographies of both the cybergeoisie and the protosurp. In many ways, the cities of the future envisioned by Dear and Flusty suggest what things must have looked like in Piercy's universe prior to the devastations of global warming, war, pestilence and disease. However, where Dear and Flusty's postmodern urban geography derives from an attempt to synthesize the work of a cadre of male urbanists, Piercy's science fiction virtually demands that the dialogue be opened to include feminist and post-colonial perspectives, including the radical, speculative voices of non-mainstream science fiction. As her narrative demonstrates, imagining alternative geographies is as much a matter of art as of science.

# 6

# THE SUBJECTIVITY OF THE NEAR FUTURE

## GEOGRAPHICAL IMAGININGS IN THE WORK OF J. G. BALLARD

*Jonathan S. Taylor*

The surrealist landscapes described in the fiction of J. G. Ballard portray the world transformed by flood, drought, and fire; a world where objects turn into crystals, and psychopaths fuse their sexual obsessions with car crashes. When not altered by catastrophe, Ballard's landscapes include a terrain of empty car parks, glowing neon advertising images, abandoned suburban swimming pools full of broken sunglasses, and crashed small aircraft. Resorts of endless sand replete with decaying movie actresses, cloud-sculptors, jewelled insects and singing orchids stretch into the future horizon. Primal violence breaks out in a high-rise apartment, vandalism and drug abuse enliven a deadened Spanish coastal resort. Are these landscapes *Myths of the Near Future*? Or perhaps glimpses of a disguised but true subjectivity hiding beneath the surface of the present?

The iconography described above comes from the distinct voice of James Graham Ballard, one of the world's most acclaimed science fiction authors, widely celebrated in literary circles,[1] and the one whose work is most closely associated with the avant-garde, and with postmodernism (see for instance Baudrillard's (1991b) article on Ballard's novel *Crash* (1973)). Ballard's work has drawn attention outside of SF; in fact, much of his work of the last two decades, from the semi-autobiographical *Empire of the Sun* (1984) and *Kindness of Women* (1993) to the dystopic 'adventure' novel of *Rushing to Paradise* (1994) cannot be classified as SF at all. Still, Ballard's vision, if not always his topical matter, and his repeated iconography are all concerned at heart with an overall SF topic: the subjectivity of the near future. And unlike many of the mainstream SF and fantasy writers of his generation, Ballard seems to always begin with the present and the possible, and then combine them in unsettling ways with an imaginary landscape of his own creation. Beholden more to the visions of the Surrealist painters than to any previous science fiction authors, Ballard creates stories set in settings which evoke, at times directly, the paintings of Dali, Tanguy, Ernst,

Magritte, De Chirico and Delvaux rather than the fantasy paintings of mythical beings or glossy illustrations of spaceships and aliens which tend to cover most SF pulp paperbacks. Ballard's prose style shows allegiances to the Surrealist writers as well, with its mixture of hard and soft description, and heavy use of metaphor and idioms (Pringle 1979). Ballard's world of fascinating and strange landscapes inhabited by obsessive characters has been inspirational to a younger generation of artists. Film-makers such as David Cronenberg; the editors of the Re/Search series of books; the mechanical destruction performance art group Survival Research Labs; and the so-called 'industrial musicians' of the early 1980s, the forerunners of the musical genres now known as techno or electronica (including SPK and Cabaret Voltaire) all refer to Ballard as a major influence (Bukatman 1993; Vale and Juno 1983). Yet it is difficult to characterize Ballard's work overall: it is a large body of work, written over a long period of time, with stories and novels disparate enough to be unrecognizable as the work of one author, save for the similarity of their iconography, the unique style in which they are written, and a number of recurrent themes.

Geography is central to Ballard's work, which is frequently based upon land-scape and landscape description, much in the manner of the Surrealist painters who inspired him. But these are no ordinary space-fiction landscapes. For the Surrealists, painting landscapes was one method of depicting the reality of the Freudian or Jungian unconscious. The moonlight and eroticized nightscapes of Paul Delvaux, darkly lush jungles of Max Ernst, empty cityscapes of De Chirico and strangely-filled lunar deserts of Tanguy and Dali were attempts to portray psychological truths of the unconscious mind through the representation of imaginary or impossible landscapes. Ballard, who confesses he would have liked to have been a painter but lacked the talent (Goddard and Pringle 1976: 9), does the same through prose. For as Ballard says, 'Landscape is a formalization of space and time. And the external landscapes directly reflect interior states of mind . . .' (Juno and Vale 1984: 159). Thus rather than stressing a sociological, political or psychological imagination, Ballard's vision is centred upon geography as both the expression and main agent of change in human subjectivity. Already often cited as a unique and important figure in modern fiction, this now makes him perhaps the unwanted focus of attention even to human geographers. Unwanted, because Ballard seems rather less than enamoured of theoretical literary critiques, especially postmodernist ones.

## BALLARD AND POSTMODERNISM

In 1991, the journal *Science-Fiction Studies* published a special issue on post-modernism in science fiction, including one article by Jean Baudrillard focused specifically upon Ballard's *Crash* (Baudrillard 1991b). It also included a number of responses, including a very short paragraph by Ballard (1991). Ballard's response demonstrated a singular hostility towards postmodernism in general, and science fiction studies in particular. This hostility is complex, distilled from notions of what is important in writing and criticism, what objects are worthy of critique, the value of fiction versus academic studies, and the debates about modernism versus postmodernism. Ballard sees his own work not as merely speculative, but as a dissection and recombination of the data of reality to form something new. This new creation may contain a higher truth or at least a more accurate description of reality than could be found in the standard modern novel, which Ballard insists is a highly dishonest model (Juno and Vale 1984). But when others initiate the same processes of dissection against his own writing, he has protested. One can read this not as a protest of method, for the post-modern method has been in many ways his own since before the popularization of the term – for instance in the non-linear medico-scientific narratives which form the book *The Atrocity Exhibition* (1979) – but of object. While Ballard is interested in dissecting and re-imagining significant objects of the twentieth century, he views dissecting and analysing science fiction, in his notable phrase, as 'the apotheosis of the hamburger' (1991: 329). As a result, perhaps few other contemporary figures more closely exhibit the disjunction between those who create works of art and those who then claim these works to be postmodern.

A major reason for Ballard's dismissal of postmodern criticism of science fiction is because the elements from which Ballard constructs his works are generally everyday objects; objects of significance to many people in the con-temporary world, for example car crashes; or in other cases objects of the media landscape – Ronald Reagan, Ralph Nader, Jacqueline Kennedy and Charles Manson. As an imaginative enterprise, science fiction does not fall within any of these categories. In other words, those elements of reality that call for critical investigation and rearrangement do not include science fiction. This is because not only is science fiction not a vital component of our commonplace reality, but as an imaginative enterprise it poses a challenge to this reality itself. Thus for Ballard, it should not be subjected to the same analytical processes as ordinary objects. He admonishes postmodern critics to 'Turn your "intelligence" to the iconography of filling stations, cash machines, or whatever nonsense your enter-tainment culture deems to be the flavor of the day' (1991: 329). Because the imaginative process has already been completed in Ballard's works, further ana-lysis and reconfiguration is unnecessary, hence his comments to the effect that the people engaged in postmodern science fiction critique have little imagin-ation. This is perhaps the ultimate insult, since for Ballard the imagination is perhaps the main quality of importance in writing.

Beyond these issues is the fact that contrary to those like Baudrillard or Bukatman (1993) who claim him as a postmodernist, Ballard views himself as a modernist writer. There are reasons to be sceptical of this characterization. Ballard's work from the late 1960s and early 1970s on the mediascape, his use of 'cut-up' methods and his repudiation of literary modernism make him appear to in fact prefigure postmodernism in many important ways (Bukatman 1993). As early as the brilliant 1963 story 'The Subliminal Man' Ballard saw that advertising and the media played a huge, transformative role in our experiential reality.

Moreover, like many postmodern thinkers, Ballard feels that history, and more than history, contemporary society and perhaps the average sum of modern-day contemporary lived experience, is contingent: much of what we take for granted easily could have been or could be vastly different. Some of his novels, such as *Crash*, attempt to illustrate this by describing what the present could very well be like if, as Baudrillard writes, 'all of the models which surround us, all mixed together and hyper-operationalized in the void' (1991a: 312) had been accelerated. In this way Ballard's view of social reality does not differ markedly from realists, phenomenologists and other schools of critical social theory (Warf, this volume). But beyond this point, the similarities grow less and the differences greater. Ballard's goals are not the same as those of social theorists. While in some way bourgeois society does figure as a common enemy for both, for Ballard, the more insidious enemy is *normalcy*. Thus Ballard may fit more neatly into the modernist tradition of the transgressive amoral moralist, like De Sade, Bataille or Burroughs, than he does in the company of Baudrillard or Lyotard. Ballard should be considered a modernist mainly because his predominantly geographical imagination focuses on the interrelationships between landscapes and the psyche in order to sketch the possibilities of transcendence which lie within these relationships (Wagar 1991). Although this transcendence can be repeated by many individuals and perhaps even eventually the society at large, it is largely a mystical, not social, transcendence, and is largely achieved at the level of the individual. Furthermore, Ballard believes in 'truth' and 'reality', those concepts most distasteful to postmodern philosophers, and insists that his literature and the characters within it are engaged in searching for truths (Juno and Vale 1984). Unlike postmodernism's goal of exploding truth and demonstrating reality to be fictive, Ballard seeks to find 'true' reality through his fiction. Contrary to postmodernism's dead end – where do we go when all has been deconstructed, all myths have been exploded? – Ballard's goal is to create new myths of human transformation and, ultimately, transcendence, made possible by the transformation of the external world underway. The tools which make this possible are imaginative writing, the imagery of landscape, and the method of Surrealism – pure psychic automatism.

From what I presume to be Ballard's vantage point, literary critiques such as this run into two possible problems. By analysing texts of imaginative fiction through rigid predetermined categories we may reduce a text which previously worked by acting upon the imagination to a sterile prose whose effect upon the imagination is largely deadening, closing possibilities rather than opening new ones as it decides what the author is *really* up to. Alternatively, critiques might become largely parasitic, piggybacking off one writer's imagination to create a new work distinctly lacking in the originality of the texts it discusses. Ballard's own book, movie and art reviews, as published in the non-fiction collection of essays *A User's Guide to the New Millennium* (1996b), avoid these traps by writing articles only peripherally connected at times to the subjects they are ostensibly discussing. Yet since Ballard's work may not be familiar to some readers of this volume, this technique would probably prove disappointing if used here. Frankly, I think it impossible to completely avoid the pitfalls I have just set out in analysing Ballard's writings, but my overall intention is not to cast Ballard's work within a body of postmodern theory that he largely reviles, but instead to explicate some ideas found within Ballard's writing by reorganizing them thematically and making their conclusions clear. The starting point for this exploration is that rather than being a postmodernist, Ballard is best described as a surrealist writer.

## BALLARD AND SURREALISM

Ballard's impatience with postmodern literary criticism is related to both its jargon and the importance which it places upon text and textual analysis, presumably since Ballard's self-proclaimed influences are far less literary then visual. In numerous interviews he has stated that his primary influences are the painters of the Surrealist movement. Surrealism is both a style as well as a broad artistic, literary and philosophical movement. The art of one of the movement's chief progenitors, the painter Giorgio de Chirico, has been described as 'a naturalism of the inner mind' which 'represented the psyche as architectural space' (Short 1980: 77). De Chirico later inspired members of the Surrealist movement, such as Yves Tanguy. Tanguy painted mental and emotional states as landscapes, using the technique of automatism and creating new worlds of organic and inorganic ambiguity where nature fused with technology. Going beyond what was still considered Tanguy's passive recording of the inner mind, Salvador Dali used the 'paranoic-critical method' to create new landscapes representative of psychic desires (Short 1980). Similarly, Ballard's intention also is to represent the psyche through the use of landscape imagery, and then to reconfigure it according to the template of his desires. However, Ballard is a novelist, not a painter, and his textual canvases are backdrops for characters whose own unconscious desires are also bleeding out in strange obsessions and behaviours.

For Ballard as a surrealist, the nature of our reality is that we do not really know our reality until it begins to manifest itself through our obsessions and desires. This reality is both the reality of the unconscious as well as a true knowledge of the external world. Surrealism sets the imagination in motion against the seldom-seen but omnipresent nature of social reality: 'this huge network of ciphers, and encoded instructions ... which surround us' (Juno and Vale 1984: 43). Frequently, however, our obsessions and dreams will only begin to manifest themselves when we are exposed to notable stimuli: major changes in the external landscape, an atmosphere of deviance, or the presence of strange and incongruent objects – much as the Surrealist painter Max Ernst's initial revelation of automatism came while he was examining the strange juxtaposition of objects in a catalogue of scientific items designed for demonstrations. Thus Ballard's books are doubly surrealist: his novels sketch surrealist landscapes from his own mind, which themselves are the inspirations for his characters to then follow their own blossoming obsessions and desires. For the Surrealists there was little difference 'between a changed perception of the world and the actual, objective changing of the world' (Short 1980: 84). And so in Ballard's fiction, as actual transformations in our physical and social worlds occur they are mirrored by purposeful transformations in individuals' subjectivities and behaviour. And these changes in subjectivity, while at times frightening, are ultimately in some way desirable since they militate against 'that smothering set of conventions that we call everyday reality' (Juno and Vale 1984: 47).

My primary focus is thus on the role of the geographical imagination in this process and the way in which through surrealism this imagination envisions the new subjectivities which may accompany the changing multiple geographies of the present and near future. For the purposes of this explication, Ballard's novels and short stories can be loosely classified into three types, which correspond only slightly to three periods in his work. First are the natural disaster novels. These works, *The Drowned World* (1962a), *The Wind from Nowhere* (1962b), *The Drought* (1965) and *The Crystal World* (1966), are set in the near future, in a world where radical shifts in nature have led to the collapse of civilization, or at least to drastic changes in human society. As the landscape changes in accordance with new environmental conditions, human subjectivities also begin to mutate. Two tendencies generally reveal themselves, one a fascinated and enraptured drawing towards the newly altered landscape, the other a descent into human selfishness and a regressive desire for the satisfaction of childish, often cruel, desires. The theme of fascination and obsession first revealed in these works is later explored further in the second of Ballard's main themes: changing human subjectivity towards the built environment.

This second body of work is found especially in Ballard's mid-1970s trilogy of *Crash* (1973), later made into a major motion picture by David Cronenberg, *Concrete Island* (1974) and *High-Rise* (1975), but also in a number of earlier short stories. In these works, the protagonists find themselves in situations where their subjectivity is altered by changes in the built environment. In the case of *High-Rise* this is a return to primitivism and tribal warfare inside the new urban enclosure of the high-rise apartment building. In *Concrete Island*, the protagonist finds himself trapped and forced to survive and create a new life in a large grassy median between highways. In *Crash*, we follow the activities of a group obsessed with the erotic nature of violent car accidents. All of these works implicitly critique a modern urban society that has produced types of environments containing the freedom to explore new psychopathologies. But at the same time there is little sense of condemnation. Instead, Ballard explicates the nature of the unconscious desires that underlie our technological world.

The third body of work continues to focus on the built environment as the locus of changing subjectivities, but replaces the urban desolation of the trilogy discussed above with a leisure environment: tourist resorts and suburbia. In works such as *Vermilion Sands* (1971) and *Cocaine Nights* (1996a), new forms of expression, lifestyle, social breakdown and accompanying subjectivities emerge out of the leisure landscape. In these works we see less of a social critique of the leisure class than a glimpse of what Ballard seems to hope the future will actually look like.

## THE INNER LANDSCAPE TRANSFORMED BY NATURAL CHANGE

In the first of the categories of Ballard's work, the 'disaster novels', changes in the natural environment of the earth give rise to changes in the inner landscape of the novels' characters. As these physical changes are near-apocalyptic in scale, so are the changes in human subjectivity. Unlike 'normal' disaster novels, however, Ballard's works 'operated by "inverting" the logic of the genre; no longer narratives of heroic survival in the midst of global disaster, the protagonists of *The Drowned World* and *The Crystal World* "accept" catastrophe and willingly seek ecstatic dissolution in death' (Luckhurst 1994: 688). As Ballard explains, 'These are stories of huge psychic transformations, and I use this external transformation of the landscape to reflect, and marry with, the internal transformation, the psychological transformation, of the characters' (Pringle 1984: xxii–xxiii).

The most notable of Ballard's early 'disaster novel' works is the first, *The Drowned World*. Prefiguring the current likelihood of global warming, in the near future solar radiation has increased and a change in the earth's gravity has led to the diminution of the outermost layer of the ionosphere, leading to a dramatic warming and subsequent 'drowning' of all but the Arctic and Antarctic extremes of the Earth. Polar ice caps and glaciers have dissolved, and massive soil erosion has created silt dams in rivers, flooding large sections of the continents. Major European cities have become drowned lagoons, hemmed in by tropical forests and swamps of strange species of Carboniferous-era-like vegetation, as increased radiation has led to increases in plant mutations, and iguanas gaze down on the few humans still left outside of the Arctic circle colony. Much of the power of this work is in the imagery of the reclaiming of cities by a hungry tropical nature:

> An immense profusion of animal life filled the creeks and canals: water-snakes coiled themselves among the crushed palisades of the water-logged bamboo groves, colonies of bats erupted out of the green tunnels like clouds of exploding soot, iguanas sat motionlessly on the shaded cornices like stone sphinxes.
>
> (Ballard 1962a: 53)

As the main characters of the book, scientists preparing maps of the changing continents, come to realize, internal changes in subjectivity mirror the changes in the landscape. Thus the main character, Kerans, 'wondered what zone of transit he himself was entering, sure that his own withdrawal was symptomatic not of a dormant schizophrenia, but of a careful preparation for a radically new environment, with its own internal landscape and logic, where old categories of thought would merely be an encumbrance' (1962a: 14). The protagonists of *The*

*Drowned World* realize that 'A more important task than mapping the harbours and lagoons of the external landscape was to chart the ghostly deltas and luminous beaches of the submerged neuronic condition' (1962a: 45). As the book continues, the protagonists begin to have dreams harking back to prehistoric memories of the Triassic lodged deep within their cells. Dreams and reality, prehistoric past and future, real and super-real become mixed.

In the last and perhaps most haunting of the disaster novels, *The Crystal World*, a section of forest in Africa is beginning to enter a strange process of crystallization. Orchids, plants, fungi become jewelled objects emanating an uncanny powerful light from within. Here is an 'enchanted world, where by day fantastic birds fly through the petrified forest and jeweled crocodiles glitter like heraldic salamanders on the banks of the crystalline rivers' (Ballard 1966: 203). People as well are caught up in the spread of the crystallizing phenomenon. As in *The Drowned World*, some characters end up welcoming this transformation of the environment. The magnificence and brilliance of the transformed forest, where man himself can be transformed and immortalized in crystalline form, is too much for some to resist: 'There is an immense reward to be found in that frozen forest . . . the transfiguration of all living and inanimate forms occurs before our eyes, the gift of immortality a direct consequence of the surrender by each of us of our own physical and temporal identities', the main character Sanders writes (Ballard 1966: 202).

As in many of Ballard's works, these changes in the external landscape produce changes in inner landscapes, but not in a uniform manner. In *The Drowned World*, many of the characters experience a similar pattern: dreams of heat and water, a huge red sun, the sound of their amplified heartbeat like a drum, visions of giant reptiles. Drawn by their dreams they long to stay in the lagoons and move towards the equator – representing primeval nature – instead of moving to the less altered world of civilization in the Arctic camps. But other characters are inspired to move towards ever-greater criminality and sociopathology. In *The Drowned World*, the character Strangman, a latter-day pirate indiscriminately plundering the underwater cities for works of art, only reverts to his most bestial state when he pumps the water out of the city and returns to its streets. This backward movement to claim the landscape back from nature is the spark which sets alight his sociopathology. Thus for Ballard, in contrast to Golding's *Lord of the Flies* (1959), it is neither nature nor human society itself which brings out the worst in man. For that we must wait until Ballard turns his eye to modern urbanism and technology.

## PSYCHOPATHOLOGICAL SUBJECTIVITIES AND THE BUILT ENVIRONMENT

In three novels from the mid-1970s, *Crash*, *Concrete Island* and *High-Rise*, Ballard demonstrates some of the new subjectivities that emerge as alienated individuals react to the technological surroundings in which they live. This theme had been contemplated much earlier in the short story 'The terminal beach' (1964), as Ballard bibliographer David Pringle describes: 'Set in the present, the story involves an ex-bomber pilot who feels compelled to visit the nuclear-testing island of Eniwetok in the Pacific. Haunted by visions of war, flight, and apocalypse, he finds psychological solace in the "synthetic landscape" of concrete blocks, plastic mannequins, and junked aircraft . . . In this piece, Ballard is, almost literally, delineating an inner landscape, a terrain of the soul which has been brought into existence by modern technology' (Pringle 1979: 11). This landscape is filled out, quite unpleasantly, in the controversial novel *Crash*. Here Ballard depicts the subjectivities of a small group of individuals obsessed with the interrelationships between death, car crashes and sexuality. They are led by the imagination of a man named Vaughan, who like the Surrealists reacts to the contemporary world by following his own perverse erotic imagination:

> He dreamed of ambassadorial limousines crashing into jack-knifing butane tankers, of taxis filled with celebrating children colliding head-on below the bright display windows of deserted supermarkets. He dreamed of alienated brothers and sisters, by chance meeting each other on collision courses on the access roads of petrochemical plants, their unconscious incest made explicit in this colliding metal, in the haemorrhages of their brain tissue flowering beneath the aluminized compression chambers and reaction vessels.
>
> (1973: 13)

In writing *Crash* as well as the later *Concrete Island*, Ballard did research on highways and automobile landscapes as well as copying medical texts for some passages (Goddard and Pringle 1976: 34). The landscape of *Crash* is unrelenting, a landscape wholly created by the prevalence and importance of the automobile, but liberally shaded with blood and semen. 'In this overlit realm ruled by violence and technology he was now driving for ever at a hundred miles an hour along an empty motorway, past deserted filling stations on the edges of wide fields' (Ballard 1973: 16). The landscape is utterly technological, but strangely barren, like the downtown of a deserted city at night. Significant human contact is achieved only through the car accident.

The impact of this external world on the subjectivities of the protagonists is clear, the main effect is on their sexuality, which is 'liberated' from its reflections upon nature and the body and directed instead towards the union of the body and technology.

> This obsession with the sexual possibilities of everything around me had been jerked loose from my mind by the crash. I imagined the ward filled with convalescing air-disaster victims, each of their minds a brothel of images. The crash between our two cars was a model of some ultimate and

yet undreamt sexual union. The injuries of still-to-be admitted patients beckoned to me, an immense encyclopedia of accessible dreams.

(Ballard 1973: 29)

*Crash* has been variously read as an amoral work of fiction and thus a truly postmodern novel (Baudrillard) or as a moral cautionary tale about the alienation of technology (most sympathetic critics). Yet neither morality nor amorality appears to be the main goal of Ballard's writing. *Crash* is best read as a work of speculation about the possible subjectivities produced by a technological society oriented around the automobile. Yet of course it is also not value-neutral – there is a social critique implicit in the way in which technological change and changes in our built environments create the preconditions for individual transformations of a particularly disturbing type.

In contrast, the protagonists of *High-Rise* are drawn less by sex and more by violence as over the course of the novel social order breaks down and the residents of a high-rise apartment building resort to vandalism, tribal warfare and mayhem. The violence, however, seems to emanate not from some deep flaw of human nature, but from a reaction to the architecture and enforced community of the high-rise building itself:

By its very efficiency, the high-rise took over the task of maintaining the social structure that supported them all. For the first time it removed the need to repress every kind of anti-social behavior, and left them free to explore any deviant or wayward impulses . . . the high-rise was a model of all that technology had done to make possible the expression of a truly 'free' psychopathology.

(Ballard 1975: 43)

A self-contained universe, with its own natural logics, the high-rise enables the residents to choose to react in a particular manner.

Ballard himself best sums up the message of these two works:

In *High-Rise* the whole point of the book, as in *Crash*, is that the characters eagerly embrace these revelations about themselves and the new life that technology has made possible. The whole logic of the book and their behavior only makes sense if you assume that they *want* this apparent descent into barbarism. It is willed by them all, either consciously or unconsciously . . . The environment makes possible the whole set of unfolding logics, like those that unfold on the highway in *Crash*. That technology as a whole has a sort of alienating effect . . .

(Juno and Vale 1984: 162)

Yet it is not a determining effect, but merely suggestive of new possibilities.

The built environment also has a similar effect in the short story 'The overloaded man' (1961). The main character, Faulkner, is slowly going mad. This is largely the result, we learn, of his surroundings, a planned community known as the 'Bin'. Designed to 'avoid producing a collection of identical hutches, as in most housing estates, and secondly, to provide a showpiece for a major psychiatric foundation which would serve as a model for the corporate living units of the future', the Bin was constructed using 'the so-called psycho-modular system . . . a sprawl of interlocking frosted glass, white rectangles and curves, at first glance exciting and abstract (*Life* magazine had done several glossy photographic treatments of the new "living trends" suggested by the Village) but to the people within formless and visually exhausting' (Ballard 1961: 81). Faulkner's reaction to his environment is to learn to mentally disassociate the houses as visual objects from their meanings as his symbolic prison. Relaxing on his veranda, he stares at the buildings until they are transformed into abstract geometric shapes of a cubist landscape. He has found that this mental exercise was easiest on consumer goods: 'Stripped of their accretions of sales slogans and status imperatives, their real claim to reality was so tenuous that it needed little mental effort to obliterate them altogether' (1961: 83). The effect is similar to a hallucinogenic drug experience. Quitting his job and all activities except his meditations and peeping at his attractive female neighbour, eventually Faulkner is able to employ this method so successfully that he kills his hectoring wife, now a collection of abstract forms – 'moulding her angular form into a softer and rounder one' (1961: 91) – and then himself.

While some have referred to the Ballard of the disaster novels as a utopian (Wagar 1991), are these actually works of dystopian fiction, in which the near-future offers us few choices beyond obsession, violence, or escaping through efforts of altered consciousness? Perhaps it is more true to state that Ballard is attempting to objectively inform us of the new possibilities that technological and modern urban environments are opening up. In resorting to these methods of dealing with their environment, the characters of these works are not necessarily taking the only course of action, the correct course of action, or certainly the most moral one, but simply a new course suggested by their lived environments. Ballard is telling us that insanity, sexual obsessions and violence are one way of embracing the new technological landscapes that we have created. But Ballard's future is not unrelentingly bleak and pessimistic. In the more peaceful lived environments of his stories of the leisure future, alternative courses of action are suggested.

## OUR FUTURE: THE LEISURE SOCIETY

The Vermilion Sands stories, written over a period of more than ten years, represent Ballard's hope for the future, a timeless resort of endless sand, where a leisure class has the time and money to explore infinite possibilities of aesthetic experimentation and contemplation, to play elaborate games, and to contemplate their strangely haunted environment, which fuses natural and technological elements. Here people may live in 'living' psychotropic homes designed from bio-plastic, work on making metallic sound-emitting sculptures, grow singing plants, cruise on sand-sailships, make avant-garde films, or fly in hang-gliders, sculpting the clouds. Ballard explains his purposes:

> I suppose I was just interested in inventing an imaginary Palm Springs, a kind of world I imagined all suburbs of North American and Northern Europe might be like in about 200 years time. Everyone will be permanently on vacation, or doing about one day's work a year. People will give in to any whim that occurs to them – like taking up cloud-sculpture – leisure and work will mesh in. I think everybody will be very relaxed, almost too relaxed. It will be a landscape of not so much suburbia but exurbia, a kind of country-club belt, which will be largely the produce of advanced technologies of various kinds, for leisure and so forth. So you will get things like computers meshed into one's ordinary everyday life in a way that can be seen already. I'm just writing about one direction that the future is taking us. I think the future will be like Vermilion Sands, if I have to make a guess. It isn't going to be like Brave New World or 1984: it's going to be like a country-club paradise.
>
> (Goddard and Pringle 1976: 23)

The near-future will thus offer a leisure landscape, perhaps one also similar to the present-day landscape of the imaginary community of Estrella de Mar described in Ballard's novel *Cocaine Nights*. On the Spanish Costa del Sol, the narrator is investigating his brother's arrest and guilty plea for an arson mass-murder in a wealthy coastal resort community. All around, the resort towns function as a terminal resting place for retirees, 'a world beyond boredom, with no past, no future and a diminishing present' (1996a: 35). For Ballard, this is the reality of 'a leisure-dominated future . . . [where] Nothing could ever happen . . . where entropic drift calmed the surfaces of a thousand swimming pools' (1996a: 35). In contrast, Estrella de Mar is different from its surroundings, enlivened by artists, theatre, tennis and a host of other activities. Yet as the narrator finds in his investigation, the key to Estrella de Mar's liveliness is vice: drugs, adulterous sex, and especially crime. These activities create community, excitement and passion, much as the strange obsessions and habits of the residents of Vermilion Sands enliven their sun-filled lazy lives. In the near future, as technology enables a leisure-filled existence, vice, crime and obsession will fuel the daydreams of a population in an otherwise permanent stupor. But rather than being a negative, we should look at this as a positive. Play, despite its hazards, will awaken us.

## CONCLUSION

To understand J. G. Ballard's writings as a unified body we must see him not as a postmodernist or a futurist, but as a surrealist. For the goal of the surrealist is clear: the artist is 'leading the struggle to raise reality to the level of man's dreams' (Short 1980: 87). Ballard's mission is to offer us alternative views of what our world truly looks like underneath the veneer of our conventional understandings of it; what it could look like should the future direct us along particular trajectories; and at times what he hopes it will look like. These works are written in opposition to normalcy and the lack of imagination which prevents us from refiguring our realities; the antidote is the bringing forth of hidden desires and obsessions; and the method is literary surrealism. The results are not always pleasant, but this, like whether the characters in the novels act morally, is not the point. As individuals living in a strange and changing time, we accept too much for granted. But if we allow our imaginations, no matter how perverse, to break free of the conventional logics, codes and ciphers, we may begin to see what a very strange world we actually inhabit.

Baudrillard is quite probably correct in his claim that *Crash* is an amoral novel, but its amorality is not the quality that makes it unique, postmodern or even particularly interesting. Amorality is a side effect of the protagonists' surrealist transformation of the conditions of their existence. Having escaped from the web of conventional social reality, their obsessions and desires have led them to shed all common-sense understanding of the nature of their existence – including morality – and enter into a new relationship between their bodies and their obsessions with technology. In the same way the protagonists of the early 'disaster period' come to welcome and willingly are transformed by the changes in their environments; while those of the suburban works similarly embrace the new possibilities created by the built environments they inhabit. Ballard is less interested in making a moral statement than in exploring the ways in which we relate to our built environments.

Ballard is of course offering a social critique in *Crash* as well as in many of his other novels and stories, for not to do so would be difficult, given his subject matter. The mediascape, the technoscape and suburbia are disturbing landscapes in which individuals can act out disturbing obsessions. In the urban settings of *Crash* or *High-Rise* the characters gain inspiration from socially pathological environments to pursue their own individual pathologies, indicating that for Ballard both our outer environments and our inner lives can be polluted. While it is tempting when reading *Crash* or *High-Rise* to view Ballard as a romantic crying out against the perils of a modern technological society, one cannot make the mistake of assuming he romanticizes nature as set against civilization or technology. In the novel *Rushing to Paradise* about an abortive attempt to save a Pacific island from nuclear testing and create a nature-based utopia, the characters follow their own ecofeminist obsessions to a dementia fully the equal of the technophiles of *Crash*. In fact, many of Ballard's works actually romanticize the built environment, for no matter how we may see them, the protagonists of *Crash* or *High-Rise* or even 'The overloaded man' do reach a type of spiritual fulfilment in their own way, while the mixed natural/technological landscapes of *Vermilion Sands* enchant with their surreal beauty.

It is difficult to sum up Ballard's overall attitude because of the great differences in content between many of his novels and short stories. A large number of the latter are overtly political in nature, revealing deeply held scepticism about government, the world of commerce, the consumer society, the media and advertising. Thus those who see Ballard as a social critic of a condition some term postmodernism are undoubtedly correct. But in the works I have discussed, Ballard's theme can be seen as more simple in nature, telling us that the key element in transforming the relationship between humans and their changing socio-spatial environments is simply *obsessiveness* and showing us that the obsessive individual, who embraces the possibilities inherent in their specific time and place, is in some ways more *real* than the rest of us. Rather than telling us what we should or should not do, as individuals or as a society, Ballard attempts to demonstrate to us what is possible, that we can in some way liberate ourselves by taking the surrealist path. Our own obsessions and desires can be pursued, if we wish, to the logical conclusions that our changing environments suggest.

### NOTE

1 Ballard's work has drawn praise from Susan Sontag, William S. Burroughs, Anthony Burgess, Kingsley Amis, and other literary luminaries.

# 7

## TUNING THE SELF

## CITY SPACE AND SF HORROR MOVIES

*Stuart C. Aitken*

It is midnight and the skyscrapers erupt, erect and twist into new forms as the city is remade and its characters are reworked to fit new narratives. The movie is Australian director Alex Proyas's *Dark City* (1998), the process is called 'tuning' and it is masterminded by 'the Strangers', a band of sinister aliens who inhabit the bodies of the city's dead[1] (see Figure 7.1). These gothic-clad zombies work their machinations on the buildings from below the city through a series of weird telepathically controlled gears, cogs and mechanisms. They work their plot twists

*Figure 7.1* Publicity material for *Dark City*.
(*Source:* Ronald Grant Archive)

on the people who inhabit the city with the help of Dr Daniel P. Schreber (Kiefer Sutherland), a human scientist who is coerced to alter memories and contrive the stories that form the basis of the Strangers' experiments. John Murdock (Rufus Sewell), the protagonist of the movie, awakens during tuning as the doctor attempts to inject him with the narrative of a serial killer. Because Murdock possesses nascent abilities to tune he is a threat to the Strangers, but they also believe he may have what they are seeking: the key to individuality and, apparently, the human soul. Telepathically and cognitively connected with each other, the aliens seek individuality as a way to save their dying race. Murdock is chased through the city picking up clues about his identity from family members and repressed childhood memories (which are not really his) of a seaside resort called Shell Beach. Schreber characterizes Murdock's subject position to his wife (Jennifer Connelly) as follows: 'Wherever your husband is, he is searching for himself.' The search is contrived through alleyways and across rooftops that strongly resemble the city setting of Fritz Lang's *Metropolis* (1926).

There is no day, but at the stroke of midnight the humans in Dark City fall asleep and the city contorts and twists. During one tuning, Murdock escapes the Strangers by jumping to safety on the tip of an extending chimney. Sometimes a chimney is just a chimney but in *Dark City* such symbolism is clearly meant to evoke. There is something obvious and unacceptable about phallic iconography such as this, but it insinuates image after image in the urban spaces of SF films. In *Dark City*, Proyas brings all the Freudian artefacts that hallmark SF horror movies into stark relief: slashed women/prostitutes; repressed memories; womb-like spaceships; psychotic scientists/doctors; medusa-headed zombie aliens. If we assume that movie genres endure because they have something to say about how we negotiate our day-to-day lives, then, as Linda Williams (1991) argues, to overlook the horror genre as bad sexual or violent excess or as bad racial perversion is to miss its function in cultural problem-solving. The violence and horror of contemporary SF horror movies cannot be dismissed as evidence of a monolithic racism and unchanging misogyny. Their very existence and popularity hinges upon changes that take place in social relations and by changing notions of gender, sexuality and 'race'/ethnicity. Movies like *Dark City* are the dark side of the *Star Wars* epic mythology-making. The astonishing acceptance of these movies' iconography as an important part of our societal character raises questions regarding not only the content of myth but also its power.

Understanding the power of myth as it relates to fantastic urban spaces requires that we hold on to the possibility of formulating some kind of articulation between the sphere of the social and that of the psyche. Steve Pile (1996: 174) argues that if bodies are constituted by 'seeing and recognizing' and cities are conceptualized 'visually and spatially', then their alignment enables a particular kind of power. The way political power is mobilized has something to do with the resonance between the space of the body and spaces of the city and Pile believes that this resonance can be understood psychoanalytically. It is perhaps inappropriate to heed the counsel of some feminists (e.g. Kuhn 1984; Gledhill 1988) and jettison cine-psychoanalytic perspectives but, at the very least, I want them unshackled from *fixed* notions of identity. I am particularly interested in the ways spaces are portrayed in the SF horror genre and how these relate to changing political identities and the stability of narrative solutions. With this chapter I want to think broadly about the ways city spaces are portrayed in popular SF horror by touching lightly on a swathe of movies from *Metropolis* to *Dark City* and a smattering of ideas from feminist and psychoanalytic perspectives. Ultimately, this is an attempt to tap into the grammar of man-made spaces from the window opened onto them by popular SF horror movies. My aim is not to uncover underlying principles (as stable grammar) by which cities work, but to understand at least in part the forms of social practice that SF movies articulate. To do so, I assume that cities develop a morphology set by specific conceptions of space (in the Lefebvrian sense) which are embedded in political power (in the Foucauldian sense) and that this power is not only reproduced and maintained through social space but it does so by excluding other concepts of space. I want to relate these exclusionary tactics to fantasies, fears and phobias. My enduring argument is that city architecture is used to reorder fear and anxiety and that fear finds representative form through the fantastic dystopian and utopian aesthetics of popular science fiction movies.

I begin by considering the power of film genre and relate this to ways that SF movies have changed over the last few years. I argue that what seems to endure are identities and spaces suffused with Freudian iconography. Fantasy theory provides a lens through which this iconography can be broadened away from the suggestion of fixed identities. I then relate fantasies to fears and phobias and demonstrate how these are articulated in the enduring spaces of SF cities. That these fantastic cities are mythic brings me back to a consideration of how power is effected by the alignment of body space and city spaces, and what is excluded in popular SF city configurations.

### GENRE AND REPETITION IN SF MOVIES

The genre of the SF movie has evolved significantly over the last thirty years. Dominated by sentimentality and positive meetings between humans and aliens in the 1970s and 1980s with films like *2001: A Space Odyssey* (1968), *The Man Who Fell to Earth* (1976), *Close Encounters of the Third Kind* (1977), *E.T.: The Extraterrestrial* (1982) and *Starman* (1984), the SF movie is for the most part now dominated by terror, dystopia and destructive inhuman associations (two notable exceptions are *Contact* (1998) and *Mission to Mars* (2000)). 'SF horror' is perhaps more than a genre, given its status as a consumer category in many video-stores along with 'family' and 'adult' movies. The immense box-office popularity of the Terminator and Alien series helped propel a cultural movement that includes *Species* (1995), *Independence Day* (1996), *Mars Attacks* (1996) and *Starship Troopers* (1997) among many others. Central motifs in these movies include monstrous, dripping, insect-like aliens and (sometimes equally monstrous) cyborg systems that embrace human and machine components.

That the SF horror genre is immensely successful suggests that, in Mikhail Bakhtin's (1994: 5) terms, it engages in a 'truly historical struggle' moulded by intertextual relations and interdependence with social experiences. For example, whereas *Metropolis* questioned the moral soundness of making robots 'in the likeness of man', it also spoke to 1930s American fears of working-class revolt (the mass uprising of the workers in the movie was patterned after the communist attempt to take over Bavaria). Over half a century later, Ridley Scott's *Blade Runner* (1982) broached similar themes (the revolt comes from androids, but their 'race'/humanness is a central narrative question), but its critical acclaim derived from postmodern sensibilities that marked the 1980s (Bruno 1987; Harvey 1989). The process by which texts are shaped by their interaction with social and historical forces is the driving force of the Bakhtinian project, of which I'll have more to say at the end of the chapter. The form and content of communication depends on anticipated responses or 'dialogics', which ultimately create a chain of meaning whereby each word (and image) carries the inflections of all its previous usages in any number of social situations. As Williams (1991) points out, genres thrive first on the persistence of the social problems that they address and, second, on their ability to recast the nature of those problems.

The persistence of genres lies in their adaptability and the ways they cater for and create cultural capital, but their survival is also dependent on the provision of a coherent framework and a recognizable iconography from which varied narrative material engages social audiences. In a social and cultural sense, film genres deny 'closure' to any particular film when the curtain falls and the house-lights come up. But also, like the aliens in the Alien series, genres are slippery and constantly evolving or dissolving their borders with other genres. For example, Martin Flannigan (1999) notes that whereas *Alien* (1979) capitalized on the slashing-teeth horror genre inspired by *Jaws* (1975), this genre was waning by the 1980s to be replaced by the action/war genre that *Aliens* (1986) embodied. Enduring amongst these changes is the merging of classic gothic horror and film noir genres with SF, perhaps represented best in *Alien*, *Blade Runner* and *Dark City*. The *mise en scène* and urban iconography that plays the narratives of these movies was first conceptualized by Lang in *Metropolis* (see Figure 7.2)

City space as part of the SF horror film genre turns on how to think about what it is that frightens when someone's experience of his or her milieu is felt as overwhelmingly threatening. While *Metropolis* may pass as ironic parody rather than horror today, many of Lang's innovative techniques and methods of inciting horror endure. For example, Lang's use of shadow and facial close-ups persists as a fundamental part of film noir in the 1940s and SF horror today. The shadow of the evil Rotwang stalks Maria through the catacombs of Metropolis in precisely the same way that Murdock is stalked by the Strangers in Dark City, that Roy Batty stalks Deckard in the Bradley Building, and that the alien stalks Ripley and her crew in the spaceship *Nostromo*. These scenes repeat, *en abyme*, to the extent that some feminists would argue that they are aspects of patriarchal duplicity in the fixing of gender. This is a contentious point that I want to

*Figure 7.2* Cityscape from *Metropolis*.
(*Source*: Ronald Grant Archive)

elaborate upon with three examples of cine-psychoanalytic repetition: the Medusa's head, the monstrous womb, and the stalker/slasher.

When Rotwang successfully creates a robot in Maria's image, she/it transfixes the men in the ballroom with an 'evilly seductive' look (later she/it leads the workers' revolt that destroys the city). Is it a coincidence that the head-dress of the robot appears snake-like (see Figure 7.3)? When Murdock slices the top of the head from one of the Strangers (using the mechanical arm of a bikini-clad woman in a billboard advertising Shell Beach), the tentacles of an alien form squirm from the cranial cavity. Freud (1955), in his famous essay entitled 'Medusa's head', reinforced his theory that the terror of castration is linked to the sight of female genitalia and, similarly, 'the sight of the Medusa's head makes the spectator stiff with terror, turns him to stone'. At the same time, he argues, consolation is offered because 'the stiffening reassures him'. Teresa de Lauretis (1984), in her equally famous essay 'Oedipus Interruptus', asks the question: how did Medusa feel? Following some anti-Lacanian thinking, she points out that when Medusa is looked at straight on she is not deadly, but beautiful and laughing:

> The problem is that to look at the Medusa 'straight on' is not a simple matter, for women or for men; the whole question of representation is

precisely there. A politics of the unconscious cannot ignore the real, historical, and material complicities, even it must dare theoretical utopias.

(1984: 136)

Portrayed otherwise, de Lauretis suggests, the Medusa is 'death at work' not only for the male but also for the female because it contrives the conditions

Figure 7.3 'Medusa's head' from *Metropolis*.

of vision and meaning-production. To echo Pile's (1996) concerns, mapping politics onto body space is effected by how the body is seen and recognized.

Another SF repetition that is worth looking at from the perspective of sexual politics is the portrayal of the impure womb. The dark, cavernous interior of the alien 'mother ship' in *Independence Day* is penetrated by two of the movie's protagonists, who then leave a deadly virus that ultimately destroys the alien threat.[2] In *Aliens* and *Alien Resurrection* (1997) Ripley is pitted in the penultimate scenes against the most terrifying alien of all: a pregnant mother. That the lair of the mother looks and feels like the inside of a womb raises the spectacle of the monstrous feminine. And elsewhere, the Strangers' sub-city control room features an androgynous face that opens vulva-like at tuning time. Less obvious, but still dark and dripping, are *Metropolis*'s catacombs and *Blade Runner*'s Bradbury Building. Barbara Creed (1986) draws on Julia Kristeva (1982) to suggest that the notion of the monstrous feminine represents a 'primal fantasy' in terms of 'the abject'. Abjection, defined by Kristeva, is derived from something we do not like but from which we cannot divorce ourselves. The abject does not respect borders and definitions such as self and other. Kristeva (1982) argues that aversion to bodily excretions is a social construct which is metaphorically and linguistically linked to symbolic aversions to the other embodied in racism and sexism. It is the dissolution of social constructed borders between the internal and the external (self and other) that the SF horror film repeatedly enacts. From Borg-like cybernetic implants to the draping of human flesh over Terminators to images of spewing innards and gushing blood, there is preoccupation with the transgression of the corporeal. In all of this, and graphically in the Alien series, 'the alien is more than a phallus; it is also coded as toothed vagina, the monstrous feminine as the cannibalistic mother' (Creed 1986: 69). But it is important to get beyond Freudian symbolism of the all-devouring womb to understand more fully *the desire that is linked with transgressing boundaries*. For Creed, the reasons we are fascinated by transgressions that include both cyborg portrayals and gushing entrails relate specifically to problematic social constructions of the abject. But what of the violence that often accompanies these transgressions?

Cine-psychoanalytic theory would position as gender-linked to male fears of castration the disembowelling that concludes the alien's stalking (and its birth) in the Alien series and the seeming joy of the Strangers in *Dark City* when slashing prostitutes with multi-pronged knives. In her classic discussion of the slasher film, Carol Clover (1989) notes that spectator identification along gender lines (authorizing impulses towards sexual violence amongst males and passive victimization amongst females) is much too simple an explanation. She wonders how to explain the appeal to a large male audience of a film genre that invariably features a female victim-hero. She characterizes these women – such as Ripley – as Final Girl and notes that men's ease at engaging with them is an indication of cross-gender identification. But this also is too simple an explanation because the gender of Final Girl is compromised by her masculine interests, her sexual reluctance (Ripley's only sexual encounter is in *Alien*[3] (1989) and her lover is quickly dispatched by the monster) and her apartness from other girls. Perhaps most important, her unfemininity is marked by her abilities with 'the active investigating gaze normally reserved for males' (Clover 1989: 93). Tentatively at first and then with considerable aggression, Final Girl looks for the monster, tracks it down to its womb-like lair and finally looks at it and thereby brings it fully (and often for the first time) into our vision. Clover points out that this encounter puts Final Girl and the monster on terms that are about something more than sexual repression and fears of castration, they are also about shared identity. In the mother alien's nest in *Aliens*, Ripley's protection of the little girl Newt parallels the mother alien's protection of her eggs. For a brief moment they look at each other and understand this desire before Ripley discharges her flame-thrower on the eggs and blows apart the alien workers with her high-powered automatic weapon. According to Clover (1989: 94), the association between Final Girl and the monster is a 'shared masculinity, materialized in all those phallic symbols – and it is also a shared feminity, materialized in what comes next: the castration, literal or symbolic, of the killer in her hands'.

At one level, cinematic conventions of genre and repetition provide means through which the private structuring of desire can be represented in public form. I am persuaded that the fantasies, fears and desires embodied in SF spaces reflect and refract what Kaja Silverman (1992) notes as a series of male masochistic fantasies, and what Kristeva (1982) designates as abject, that is, the fantasized 'impure' maternal body. But if we are to believe Clover, we need to accept multiple spectator positions to reconcile the appeal of a female victim-hero to a largely male audience. The cine-psychoanalytic tradition demarcates the essence of male in Freudian opposition to the 'dark continent' of a monolithic mother figure. But the spectator's identification is shifting, unshackled from ethnicity, biological sex, cultural gender or sexual preference. The use of fantasy theory by feminist film critics suggests a valuable lens on a more mobile form of subjectivity. It is also useful for what I am interested in here because it suggests multiple connections between subjectivity and space.

## FANTASIES, PHOBIAS AND THE SF CITY

In their now classic essay 'Fantasy and the origins of sexuality', Laplanche and Pontalis (1986) argue that fantasy is the staging of desire, its *mise en scène* rather than its object. Some feminists use this essay to suggest a move away from film theorists' preoccupation with cinema's power to gender-fix its spectators. The reverse is also possible: cinema offers its fantasizing spectators shifting and multiple positions (Thornham 1999: 229). Williams (1991: 11) points out that fantasies 'are not ... wish-fulfilling linear narratives of mastery and control leading to closure and the attainment of desire. They are marked, rather, by the prolongation of desire, and by the lack of fixed position with respect to the objects and events fantasized.' Fantasy is a place where conscious and unconscious, part and whole, may meet. It is a place that enables what Gillian

Rose (1993) calls an oscillation between self and other. In this sense, it reflects some common feminist thinking that coalesces around object relations theory and, in particular, Donald Winnicott's (1971) notion of transitional spaces. Transitional spaces enable play and exploration of the interdependencies of an expanding self without repercussions of outside (paternal or maternal) judgement. We are always present in transitional spaces but our position is not fixed. In their book on psychoanalysis, Laplanche and Pontalis (1973: 277) note that people live their lives through their object relationships, through a spatial relationship to the world that is 'the entire complex outcome of a particular organization of personality, of an apprehension of objects that is to some extent or other phantasized'. What needs further articulation is the way fantasies relate to phobias, and how this relation turns on an understanding of social space.

It is appropriate to think not only about structures of fear and perversion in SF horror genres, but also about structures of fantasy. There is a link, argues Williams (1991), between the appeal of horror genres and their ability to address but never really 'solve' basic social problems related to sexual (and racial) identity. She goes on to note that Laplanche and Pontalis's (1986) understanding of fantasies is structurally linked to 'myths of origins' which try to cover the discrepancy between two moments in time: an irrecoverable original experience and the uncertainty of its imaginary revival. The SF horror genre provides the signs that evoke both this existence and its absence. The important point that Williams raises is that the juncture of this irrecoverable real event and the totally imaginary event has no fixed temporal or spatial existence. Her argument melds well with how contemporary object-relations theorists, pulling from Melanie Klein and Julia Kristeva, understand 'the origin of the subject' as unfixed, unstable and transitional. Laplanche and Pontalis's tripartite division designates (a) fantasies of the primal scene that image the origin of the individual; (b) fantasies of seduction that image the origin and upsurge of sexuality; and (c) fantasies of castration that image the origin of difference (Thornham 1999). These fantasies are about mythic origins, and their power derives from social reality as well as the unconscious. For what I am trying to do here it is necessary to consider more fully the relation between the realm of the unconscious and social space as it relates to fantasies, fears and phobias.

Felicity Callard (2000) notes that the phenomena of fear and anxiety require that we take seriously the difficulty of formulating the articulation between the sphere of the social and that of the psyche. She highlights how fear (and desire) infects social relations through 'pathological' experiences of anxiety and how fear can emerge in particular social and spatial settings to beset those who otherwise appear 'sane'. An articulation of the social and the psyche around fantasy and horror assumes that a discrete individual and a discrete 'object' (or condition of desire or threat) are put into question. If horror ties into phobias, then both are about disruption of an individual's connection to a symbolic/spatial hegemonic norm. In the case of agoraphobia taken by Callard, it may be possible for an individual to reorder space with 'props'. For example, skirting an open plaza enables the agoraphobe to remain close to buildings, or perhaps the crossing is possible when accompanied by a child in a buggy. Callard notes that in the late nineteenth century, commentators circled around two problematics: the difficulty of adjudicating what it was that the agoraphobe, in his/her fear of the agora, actually feared; and the dilemma posed by the fact that 'the will' seemed utterly inadequate for overcoming the disorder. The question that Callard raises relates to what models of the social and the spatial underlie these two problematics. She notes that they are still in evidence in geography today and rely on a presumption that fear is precipitated by causes external to the individual.

The point I want to make here is that 'social pathologies' such as agoraphobia, vertigo, hysteria and schizophrenia are embedded in the landscapes of science fiction films to the extent that the space marks our collective responses to what is not hegemonic (and, thus, to what is pathological). In *Dark City*, schizophrenia is raised for Murdock when he yells at his wife 'I'm living someone else's nightmare'.[3] That the people in Dark City live out other people's lives under the direction of the Strangers is a motif of 'schizophrenic vertigo' with which Giuliana Bruno (1987: 69) typifies the replicants in *Blade Runner*. Indeed, schizophrenia and vertigo are conflated with castration fears in *Dark City*. Detective Bumstead (William Hurt) is tipped off that Murdock's story may ring true when an insane hysterical colleague ('nothing like a little healthy paranoia') draws spiral images on the walls after he awakes during tuning. These spiral images evoke Hitchcock's portrayal of male hysteria in *Vertigo*. They are repeated in Dr Schreber's rat maze experiment, but also on the bodies of the slashed prostitutes. Near the end of the movie, Bumstead is engaged in a fight with one of the Strangers as the exterior wall of the city is broken down. Empty space is exposed in the rift and the detective is hurtled into the void and, as he expires, he (and the audience) views the Dark City spaceship in its entirety for the first time.

For some people labelled as schizophrenics, time is discontinuous. This is clearly the case in Dark City, a place of perpetual night-time. Indeed, time-pieces are a central icon of the movie, featuring with not only clocks in shops and watches on arms, but a huge clock face that hides behind the androgynous face in the Strangers' lair. Doel and Clarke (1997) posit further that for the schizophrenic/replicant, not only is time discontinuous but the 'perpetual present' is lived with more intensity. In addition, for the inhabitants of Dark City and the replicants in *Blade Runner*, the present is always part of a larger experiment controlled by the 'law of the father' (the Strangers, Tyrell).[4] Doel and Clarke outline in detail how *Blade Runner* positions the replicants on Oedipal journeys that are their attempt to accede into the symbolic order, and how Roy Batty fails spectacularly to bend to the 'law of the father'. But his patricidal actions are also the beginnings of his 'subsequent acceptance of terminal breakdown' (Doel and Clarke 1997: 149). Doel and Clarke point out that other commentators on the film fail to appreciate the film's obsession with the differences between replicant and human and go on to argue its 'diegesis and its cybernetic mimicry of subjectification remain conventional, banal, and predictable inasmuch as they are essentially combinatorial and kaleidoscopic . . . the margins of difference may have been diminished, but everything remains frozen in the categories of the Same' (Doel and Clarke 1997: 151).

Schizophrenia is about the erasure of difference. Caroline Knowles (2000) points out that the condition is really about an interpretation of particular forms of social divergence from norms (and their political regimes) which are assumed to hold in place the behaviour of the 'no-mad', as well as being a description of the behaviour manifestations of particular forms of private terror and anxiety. In many of his novels, Philip K. Dick (whose *Do Androids Dream of Electric Sheep?* (1968) is the basis of *Blade Runner*) thematized the peculiarity of the schizophrenic nightmare that strands the protagonist in a phantasmagoric world and dramatized the disintegration of that world through the fear that perceived processes of decay are internal rather than external. The relationship between schizophrenia and identity comes into sharper focus in Dick's novel than it does in the movie. At one point, Rick Deckard is concerned that schizo-phrenics will be unable to pass the Voigt-Kampff Empathy Test designed to catch androids. Deckard's boss declares (Dick 1968: 33):

'They want the latest and most accurate personality profile of analytic tools used in determining the presence of an android – in other words the Voigt-Kampff scale – applied to a carefully selected group of schizoid and schizo-phrenic human patients. Those, specifically, which reveal what's called a "flattening of affect." You've heard of that.'

Rick said, 'That's specifically what the scale measures.'

'Then you understand what they're worried about.'

Deckard originally designates Roden's (Tyrell's in the film) niece Rachel as schizophrenic (p. 48), but what I want to emphasize here is the importance of this particular narrative's conflation of schizophrenics with non-people. This is precisely the point that Knowles makes when she describes how schizophrenic people are typecast and politically hidden in the streets of cities. Non-people are designated as such because they deviate from standards set by society. As Doel and Clarke (1997: 157) point out, the Voigt-Kampff test is an imposition of a statistical norm around which deviations may be distributed.

What the work on fantasies and phobias in film calls into question is the assumption of, first, a discrete individual and an external threatening object or condition, and, second, a majoritarian standard around which normality and humanness are judged. And so we can understand fear of open space, heights or snakes in the same way as we understand fear of blood, guts and other bodily transgressions because each is constructed through a fixed symbolic/spatial hegemonic norm. A central concern, then, revolves around ways that certain 'social pathologies' – hysteria, vertigo, agoraphobia, paranoia and schizophrenia – are *embodied* in future urban spaces because these speak to changing social/spatial hegemonic norms.

## FUTURE URBAN SPACES

By and large . . . horizontal space symbolizes submission, vertical space power and subterranean space death. These associations offer unequivocal responses to demands for meaning. But they need be tempered by some notion of ambiguity . . .

Lefebvre (1991: 236)

Science fiction cities are constructed out of a very clear three-dimensional space. Mary Anne Doane (1982) notes that this is an illusory depth inhabited and controlled by (white, affluent) men. Scott Bukatman (1993: 128) argues further that although the oppressive scale of SF cities is emphasized, it is also presented as 'a weightless space, an area of suspension and vertical boundlessness'. This contrived depth and weightlessness transcends the seventy years between *Metropolis* and *Dark City*: elevators transport the workers of Metropolis to the subterranean 'workers' city' while the secret stairways are known only to Rotwang and John Fredersen, the father of Metropolis; hover cars in *Blade Runner* are seen to be used only by city officials; only those who can tune are able to fly through Dark City.

The vertical exaggeration of some SF cities is not only a symbolic but also a literal construction. From their lair, the Strangers (curiously, there is a rather nasty white child but no women or minorities amongst these Zombies) scrupulously replace buildings to reconceptualize and relocate the contexts of the lives of the humans who live in the city above. As one of the Strangers explains to Murdock: 'We fashioned the city on stolen memories: different eras, different pasts.' Installed memories enables them to 'localize' and 'punctuate' people's activities in space and time in a classic Lefebvrian sense. During the final battle between Murdock and the leader of the Strangers, the duellists levitate from the subcity lair to high above the city. With Murdock's win (his opponent explodes into a startlingly good representation of a toothed vagina before dissipating), there is no doubt on whose side the greatest power resides. The vertical space of power also bears meaning for the Tyrell Corporation's Aztec-like pyramid and in *Metropolis*'s elite garden of the bourgeoisie ('where there is the sun and life').

For Lefebvre (1991: 227), buildings (vertical space) are a 'homogeneous matrix of capitalist space' and, as such, they narrate stories of the intersection of particular forms of power with a specific form of political economy. Buildings contain activities in socially controlled spaces and sites equipped for particular kinds of production and reproduction. The power of capital to assert its requirements dominates this cityscape but, as Pile (1996: 213) points out, Lefebvre is also unequivocal in his assessment that buildings and monuments conceal both a 'phallic realm of (supposed) virility' and a repressed space of panoptic surveillance and voyeurism. From this perspective monuments and monumental buildings present and re-present the phallus. Pile continues:

They both make visible and 'mirror' back to the 'walker on the street' their place in the world, geographically, historically and socially; they reproduce repressive spaces which, while ostensibly acting as celebrations of events and people, have both feet in terror and violence; and they repeat not just people's experiences of themselves and their relations to others but also modalities of power. Symbols on the royal road to the 'unconscious' of urban life may not be that hard to find; indeed, it is possible to analyze urban spaces as if they had been dreamt.

(Pile 1996: 213)

The future space of *Metropolis*, with its *mise en scène* of monumental buildings linked by concourses, alleyways, and transportation hierarchies, is repeated *en abyme* in SF movies. It finds new utopian heights in the City of Coruscant as represented in *Star Wars Episode I: The Phantom Menace* (1999). Coruscant hosts the powerful Jedi Council in a slender tower that overlooks the city. Even the dream-like Theeb City perched on a waterfall in Naboo is monumental in the sense created by George Gurney in his Dinotopia book series (indeed, Theeb is a direct copy of his Dinotopia City). It is worth noting further that Otoh Gunga, the city of Jar Jar Binks, is comprised of separate underwater bubble spaces. That the character of Jar Jar drew significant and appropriate criticism for racist stereo-typing resonates with the way his city is portrayed as segmented. A darker side of this same coinage is represented in *Blade Runner* and *Dark City* by cities that are equally monumental and segmented, but where the space of the city is used to amplify rather than hide the horror and terror. The monumental spaces of utopian cities like Coruscant and Theeb both displace and condense meaning or substitute one set of meanings for another while the power of the phallus is highlighted in dystopian cities like Metropolis and Dark City. This urban aes-thetic (inspired by Le Corbusier's 'Contemporary City for Three Million' (1922)) is effectively conjoined by Lang with images of huge cogs, gears and pistons to represent the oppressive system that enables the city to function. These metaphors evolve into stark psychotic realism in both *Dark City* and *Blade Runner*.

The cities portrayed in these movies embody the power and authority of 'the law of the father'. *Metropolis*'s John Fredersen is an intellectual entrepreneur whose only concern is the well-being of his creations. In a motif that is repeated by Tyrell in the form of replicant slaves on off-world colonies, Fredersen helps his inventor Rotwang create 'a machine in the image of man that never makes mistakes' in order to replace those who work the machines and live far below the city. The SF city is constructed as a space of patriarchal corporate/institutionalized power that not only constrains the subject but replaces her/him. The prospect of toppling this power mobilizes desire (to know oneself): Roy Batty against Tyrell; Murdock against the Strangers; Ripley against the Hyper-dine Corporation (embodied by Ash and the *Nostromo*'s computer 'Mother' in *Alien*); Sarah Connor against Skynet in *Terminator II*. In Doel and Clarke's

(1997: 149) formulation (following Bruno 1987), the protagonists desire to accede into the symbolic order of the Oedipal journey, but at another level the institution conspires a hidden agenda of domination through 'the law of the father'. Patriarchal power is not only reproduced and maintained through a social space that thwarts resistance, it does so by excluding other concepts of space. Question arises about what these spaces may look like and about the staying power of a genre that combines immense towers with corporate power and the law of the father in a grotesque phallic display. As Mike Davis (1992: 1) points out, Ridley Scott's caricature of 2019 Los Angeles 'fails to imaginatively engage the real Los Angeles landscape – especially the unbroken plains of aging bungalows, dingbats and ranch-style houses – as it socially erodes into the 21st Century' (quoted in Doel and Clarke 1997: 145). That Los Angeles of 2019 will perhaps be more like Frank Lloyd Wright's Broadacre City than Le Corbusier's Contemporary City for Three Million begs the question of why dystopian cities in film are rarely portrayed as sprawl. A decaying two-dimensional (submissive) sprawling landscape is a central feature in Dick's novel, but *Blade Runner* focuses only on the deterioration. Doel and Clarke (1997: 146) pull from Bruno's original essay on *Blade Runner* to suggest that an aesthetic of decay is a submission to, a flattening out of, the patriarchal logic of binary opposition:

> The archetypical hollow Tyrell Corporation implies monopoly capitalism disseminated to the n[th] degree through subcontracting and outworking; whilst the explosion of a Fourth World underclass in the interstices of the city speaks of the hyper-deskilling of labour.

If the grotesque and the phallic are but hollow symbolism, then Doel and Clarke point to possibilities of the 'law of the father' changing its face.

### THE PHALLIC POWER OF AUTHORITY

Steve Pile uses the work of Kevin Lynch (1960) and Meagan Morris (1992) to suggest that there is some doubt about the phallic power of buildings and monuments. He does so by not necessarily denying that cityscapes such as the Manhattan skyline have phallic power – Lynch, after all, noted that New York's vitality, mystery and greatness was erected upon Manhattan's towers. It is well known that the look of *Metropolis* was inspired by a trip Lang and his wife made to Manhattan. Like *Blade Runner*'s Los Angeles of 2019, the power of Manhattan is spoken by its skyline. To use Lynch's terms, these cities provide 'imageability' – a sharp picture that reinforces meaning. The point that Pile (and Morris) makes is that the virility of this phallic arrogance is too easily caricatured. For Morris, the tower must be something other than phallic space simply because it can be exposed as an unseemly, laughable penile display. She argues, rather, that these phallic jokes serve to mask the brutal, vicious, complex and contradictory power of corporate capital by reducing the urban landscape to a singular, monolithic psychosexual edifice. Pile shows through the work of Lynch and Morris that the power and the face of capital is not in the edifice which is hidden by the phallic joke, but in the image, the spectacle, the façade and the facial. And so, too, it seems that SF movies mimic this imagery. That these movies focus on the detrimental consequences of these urban spaces to the film's protagonists (Ripley, Murdock, Connor, Deckard, Batty) denies the contexts of the various marginalized and excluded who actually live in these cities. That the forces making the urban landscape are multiple and not necessarily focused in the hands of one almighty father figure (Tyrell or the unitary minds of Strangers) denies arbitrary and contradictory urban spaces. That one or two wo/men, or in the case of Metropolis a single-minded proletarian mob, can overcome the law of this father denies the reality of various, multiple, continuous and repeated contestations.

For Pile (1996: 223), the shift from the phallus/penis to the face/faciality is significant, for it marks the shift from one masculine space to another. Allegoric-ally, the substitution of the body of the White Man by a disturbingly andro-gynous Face (e.g. *Dark City* and *Mission to Mars*) may be read as the substitution of the brutal, penetrating body politic of urbanized capital by 'the cityscape as a collection of postcard scenes'. From this perspective, Pile argues, the skylines of Manhattan and Los Angeles become the perpetually acceptable face of capital-ism. In *Dark City*, Poyas uses a postcard of Shell Beach to beckon John Murdock and to spur his memory for the authenticity of something that does not actually exist (except as a vague memory for all the city's inhabitants) until Murdock tunes it for himself and his wife at the edge of the city. In *Blade Runner*, elec-tronic postcards of colonial life on Mars continually beckon the engloomed and rained-upon inhabitants of Los Angeles. The face of patriarchal capitalism resolves in these movies with postcard-perfect narrative solutions.

### DISTURBINGLY HAPPY ENDINGS

The reason Broadacre City is an inappropriate symbol for SF horror cities is that it is too close to *home*. This symbolism is magnificently turned around in Tim Burton's *Edward Scissorhands* (1990), where the gothic castle is an aesthetically pleasing refuge and the suburb is a nightmare. But *Scissorhands* is a fairy-tale rather than the kind of SF horror where the phallic towers invariably are toppled. In *Independence Day*, the world's major cities erupt in a series of spectacular conflagrations and, at the movie's conclusion, the womb-like alien spaceships share a similar fate. The *Nostromo* (a mining ship with gothic towers) self-destructs at the end of *Alien* while Ripley escapes with the ship's cat in a seed-like pod. In *Terminator II*, the Skynet Corporation headquarters are destroyed. In the 1982 version of *Blade Runner* and in *Dark City* the city is not destroyed but the protagonists escape beyond the 'law of the father' by crossing the border of the city. Deckard and Rachel drive away from Los Angeles to find an idyllic natural beauty 'to the north'. Murdock and his wife find their way to Shell Beach which, through Murdock's ability to tune, exists beyond the law of the fathers/ Strangers.[5]

The convention of the happy ending establishes a loving heterosexual couple (*Blade Runner, Dark City, Metropolis*), a family (*Independence Day*) and/or a community (*Metropolis, Independence Day*). Indeed in the latest Alien movie, the ending encompasses the global community as Ripley and Call (her android buddy recalls another movie genre) stare dreamily at the Earth from space in the knowledge that it is safe from threat. These endings involve narcissism when two characters constitute a couple and this motif turns upon a further component of fantasy: that love, family and community are good and will last, defying time and even death. This narrative ending contrasts with the graphic mortality and symbolic castration portrayed throughout these movies. Once control is eliminated with the death of the father (the Strangers, Tyrell), loving heterosexual relations can be formed and community can be built. Hence, escape to Shell Beach or to nature completes a chain of equivalencies that reflect larger values represented by the couple, the family and the community that exist in defiant opposition to the law of the father/Corporation. Steven Neale (1990a) notes these equivalencies in *Blade Runner* and *Alien* and suggests that the common theme at its denouement is almost overtly a process of wish-fulfilment, progressively displacing the Law, the Father and the impure Mother in favour of values and qualities associated in fantasy with the 'good' Mother.

I share Susan Jeffords's (1993) concern that these endings do not displace the 'law of the father' but replace it with a new picture-postcard-perfect face. In a detailed discussion of *Terminator II*, she points out that with the changes in behaviour of the Terminator from the first movie a new masculinity emerges. Learning, for the new Terminator, is a non-discriminatory attitude of this new masculinity. Not only the Terminator but scientists such as Miles Dyson, the African-American scientist who constructs Skynet, are able to learn new modes of behaviour:

> The message here is clear: in this narrative, masculinity transcends racial difference, suggesting that forces of change – killing to non-killing, silence to speech, indifference to love, external display to internal exploration, absent to active paternalism – not only cross racial boundaries but draw men together.
>
> (Jeffords 1993: 254)

The vehicle to the transformation, Jeffords continues, is a particular kind of fathering that transcends the spectacle of violence, technology and castration with the even greater spectacle of male individualism in the act of self-sacrificing fathers. The narrative here is particularly insidious because it also involves a serious reversal from the first movie: the police are no longer good or well-intentioned but conspiratorial and deadly, protecting corporate property rather than people. Jeffords argues that these oppositional representations of police power distinguish individual actions from organized institution. In *Dark City*, the fastidiously professional detective Bumstead finally abdicates his institutional affiliation to side with Murdock. Individual men – Murdock, the Terminator, Deckard – are made to seem not only effective but necessary. Jeffords's arguments about fathering are compelling. The Terminator series offers a reassuring framework – the world as the family – for many white male viewers in an era when the public realm is no longer a stable source of authority and power. Rather, men can achieve this authority through individualism and a force of will.

Towards the end of *Dark City*, Dr Schreber confronts Murdock with 'There is no Shell Beach, only City. The only place home exists is in your head.' And in the penultimate scene of the movie they meet again and Murdock, realizing his abilities to tune, declares: 'I can make this world anything I want it to be . . . Just as long as I concentrate hard enough.' Murdock creates a Shell Beach that hangs fibroid-like to the periphery of the Strangers' spaceship/womb. And through the sheer force of his will, in a final act of god-like omnipotence, Murdock causes the sun to rise over his ocean. The law of the father has a new face and it is shining benevolently down upon its children.

### CLOSURE?

SF movies are nothing if they do not embody fantastic special effects and improbable subjects, places and events. At the level of fantasy, form and *mise en scène*, little has changed in representations of SF cities in the seventy years between *Metropolis* and *Dark City* and this should be of some concern. I want to argue with Linda Williams (1991) that criticisms of these films as unrealistic, as lacking psychological complexity and narrative closure, and as repetitious become moot if such features are intrinsic to their engagement with fantasy and desire. As Lucie Armitt (1996: 1) points out, fantasy is the intangible source of unconscious fears and desires 'that fuels our dreams, our phobias and therefore our narrative fictions'. The notion of fantasy embracing both the positive and the negative returns me to Bakhtin's project and, in particular, his work on desire and the grotesque (cf. Bakhtin 1984). As Rosemary Jackson (1981: 15) puts it, Bakhtin 'points towards fantasy's hostility to static, discrete units, to its juxta-position of incompatible elements and its resistance to fixity. Spatial, temporal, and philosophical ordering systems all dissolve; unified notions of character are broken; language and syntax become incoherent.' For Bakhtin, the horror of the grotesque and the monstrous is simply the flip-side of carnival laughter, the point at which something ominous and sinister emerges out of something careless, fanciful and free. Desire for the grotesque emanates from desire for the other, in a Kristevian sense, but it is also linked to purely fantastic caricatures where the creator (and our collective selves) gives rein to an unchecked fancy. Science fiction's horror, its grotesque and monstrous, takes us into a fictive space that is not of our world, it is a world of anxiety and terror inspired by bodily transgressions (the monster oozes, people are ripped apart).

Armitt (1996) and Williams (1991) point out that this is an important world that should not be dismissed as formulaic or escapist. Among other things, there is a link between the appeal of fantastic science fiction forms and their ability to address basic problems that relate to sexual and racial identity. This link, according to Laplanche and Pontalis, is the irrecoverable 'origin of the subject'. This irrecoverability, this lack of wholeness, is vicariously and momentarily restored in fantastic filmic places. The horror and the symbolic womb in some of the films I discuss above represent respectively a genre that seems to endlessly repeat the trauma of castration as if to 'explain', through endless repetition, the original problem of sexual difference, and a related, and again endlessly repeated, sense of the loss of origins. The latter, then, is the embodiment of an impossible hoping to return to but remain apart from an earlier state which is most fundamentally represented by the body of the mother (Williams 1991). In noting this, Lucie Armitt (1996: 185) argues that the positive aspect of this is that 'we are left with a state of ongoing desire, perpetuating our endless, but always hopeful returns'. In this sense, the horror of SF and the monstrous gothic city point to something with liberatory potential. Fantasy as a source of both fears and desires beckons on endlessly the furtive and playful imagination. This is a good thing. I agree with Armitt that fantasy and the fantastic are potentially liberating if we focus on their abilities to highlight the uncertainty and the ambiguity that is woven into the accepted conventions of 'normal reality'. But to get to that place, we need to resist the restrictions of genre. What I am arguing here is that the genre of SF horror and its attendant monolithic city perpetuates narrative solutions and closure around patriarchal norms. This is not a good thing. This is not liberatory.

Pulling from Judith Butler (1993), it can be argued that the mythic proportions of these forms of fantasy suggest the 'naturalness' of the ideal of fixed binary opposition despite the spectator's unfixed position in the fantasy. Unfixing is good; fixing is bad. The appearance of naturalness that accompanies heterosexual white political identity is simply the effect of a repeated imitative performance that ultimately presupposes fixivity. What is being imitated is only a fantasized ideal, it is not Armitt's playful and liberatory desire. With this motif, heterosexuality and the couple and, by extension, the family, the home and the community are circumscribed by the man, the father, the hero, the saviour. The possibility that there is no closure on this patriarchal form of representation, and that it continues *en abyme* as a spiral of infinite regression, is of considerable concern. It is a concern that I raise in the face of the optimistic suggestion by a number of science fiction fans, including some of the authors in this book, that science fiction opens up the taken-for-granted. Some individual films may do so but, alternatively, I argue that the restrictions of genre close down and problematically fix a heterosexual norm.

If we agree with Pile (1996: 215) that when Lefebvre (1991: 121) notes that 'the relationship between Home and Ego . . . borders on identity' he is placing himself in a position to mix and match seemingly separate scales of analysis, then the point I want to make in closing is that the narrative resolutions of *Metropolis*,

*Blade Runner* and *Dark City* are imagined in terms of a white couple/family that continues (forever) and reproduces. It is a solution that leaves behind the repressed eroticism of the city and finds resolution in the country, the seaside and nature. We are left with a disturbingly normalized and naturalized white hetero-sexual geography that leaves behind but does not wholly dislocate not only the terror and horror, but also the law of the father. But in gaining the country/seaside/nature, space is once more produced under the tyranny of three intersecting lines of power that begin with masculinity and align with the bourgeois family and capitalism.

### NOTES

1 I am aware that what I am writing about here smacks of auteurism. This analytic framework is used extensively on prominent directors like Fritz Lang and Ridley Scott and the argument from feminists is that male critics celebrate auteurs like these for their complexity and irony or for rising above their material (Thornham 1999: 9). Sharon Smith (1972: 21) called auteur theory 'the most incredible of all male fantasies'. I am more convinced by feminist film critic Claire Johnston's (1973: 26) admonition that the test of any theory should be the degree to which it produces new knowledge, and auteur theory has certainly achieved this to the extent that it is able to delineate the unconscious structure of film. What we learn from auteurism – and what I try to articulate in my work on Peter Weir, Gus van Sant, Terry Gilliam and Bill Forsyth – is not about creativity, art and the intentionality of the director. Rather it is through the force of his preoccupations that an unconscious, unintended meaning can be decoded in films.

2 Parallels with contemporaneous speculations about the 'unnaturalness' of the AIDS virus and its decimation of African populations suggest a thinly veiled racist story-line. See Nast (2000) for a fascinating discussion of the Oedipal racist family, primal fantasies and their spatial manifestations.

3 In the director's cut of *Blade Runner* (1992), Deckard dreams of a unicorn that later in the movie is revealed to be an implanted fantasy dream, thus precipitating his feelings of living someone else's memories and his insecurities at not being himself.

4 Time-travel is also implicated in the SF phobias because it provides 'schizophrenic loops' whereby, in the words of Fredric Jameson (1992: 35), 'the protagonist became his own son and father simultaneously, and in which this particular alternate world gradually grew away from the real historical one, sealed in an icy solitude that, excluding all difference by virtue of its power to rewrite the past (or future), thereby leaves the protagonist stranded forever as a private monad'. In her discussion of the Terminator series, Susan Jeffords (1993) adds that time-travel in these movies is about repeating the fantasy of the primal scene and the male child (John Connor) exerting control of his own conception. Constance Penley (1990: 128), in her classic essay on the topic, calls the primal-scene fantasy of time-travel 'imaginary reminiscence'.

5 Terry Gilliam's *Brazil* (1986) ends with the protagonist escaping to nature with his girl-friend, but the final shot shows him still strapped to an interrogation chair. The escape was nothing more than a final flight of fantasy.

# 8

## SCIENCE FICTION AND CINEMA

## THE HYSTERICAL MATERIALISM OF PATAPHYSICAL SPACE

*Paul Kingsbury*

Science fiction has always been attracted by speeds greater than that of light. Far stranger, however, would be the register of lower speeds to which light itself could descend.

Jean Baudrillard (1999: 18)

So, too, slow motion not only presents familiar qualities of movement but reveals in them entirely unknown ones . . . Evidently a different nature opens itself to the camera than opens to the naked eye – if only because an unconsciously penetrated space is substituted for a space consciously explored by man.

Walter Benjamin (1968: 237)

Pataphysics . . . is the science of that which is superinduced upon meta-physics, whether within or beyond the latter's limitations, extending as far beyond metaphysics as the latter extends beyond physics . . . Pataphysics will be, above all, the science of the particular, despite the common opin-ion that the only science is that of the general. Pataphysics will examine the laws governing exceptions, and will explain the universe supplementary to this one; or, less ambitiously, will describe a universe which can be – and perhaps should be – envisaged in the place of the traditional one . . . *Pataphysics is the science of imaginary solutions.*[1]

Alfred Jarry (1996: 21)

One of science fiction's most disturbing scenes occurs in the film *Alien* (Ridley Scott, 1979) when, amidst a relaxing meal, a crewmember suddenly falls ill on the table and an alien violently bursts into view from his stomach and disappears into the shadows of the spacecraft. The intensity of this scene involves not merely the sight of an abdomen ruptured by the head of a menacing alien, but also the familiarity, or even banality, of people eating around a table. This event is exemplary of how cinematic worlds of science fiction vibrate between the alien and the familiar. Such movements, I argue, entwine, on the one hand, stable and determinant variations of space maintained by assumptions in what Jacques Derrida calls the 'metaphysics of presence' and, on the other hand, surreal spaces of entropy that destabilize and haunt the former, which I call (following Alfred Jarry) the 'pataphysics of absence'. Science fiction's panoply of aliens, flying saucers, invisible men, giant women, human flies, overgrown animals and faulty cyborgs are pataphysical entities *par excellence* that invade and evade what are presumed to be unshakable regimes of space underpinned by presence. Pataphysically unhinging space can be as monstrous as the monsters themselves. Likewise, Georges Bataille (1985: 55) notes that '[m]onsters thus would be the dialectic opposites of geometric regularity'. The shock of the pataphysical may induce outbursts of what could be termed hysterical materialism, a reaction to extreme ruptures of presence. Geometric regularity or any other certitude in the presence of material constancy or the quotidian securities, such as eating around a table, is liable to pataphysical transgressions. Pataphysical spaces without measure are often hysterically disavowed in the screams of earthlings running away from gigantic blobs and simultaneously facing a suspension of belief in the certainties of presence and space. Hysterical materialism also occurs in the pataphysical convulsions of materiality itself. In the film *Close Encounters of the Third Kind* (Steven Spielberg, 1977), the domesticated presence of kitchen appliances, toys, mailboxes, cartons of milk and car radios twitches and then stutters hysterically when brought under the sway of the pataphysical electromagnetism of flying saucers. Thus, like the scene in *Alien*, by ratcheting the staging of presence in a *mise en scène* through the usually secure geographic imaginaries, science fiction films can sacrificially plunge their lulled characters and viewers towards a *mise en abîme* of absurd geographical nightmares.

However, as I hope to show in this chapter, science fiction films often demonstrate that differences between the metaphysics of presence and the pataphysics of absence are neither distinctly oppositional, nor do they involve a linear procession whereby one element is coherently superseded or eclipsed by another. Rather, many science fiction films affirm, on the one hand, that spaces of presence are momentary arrests, out of joint in the first instance, and, on the other hand, how the pataphysical is swayed by the requirements of presence. Together, the qualities of science (fixing presence) and fiction (realizing absence) may involve ludic double-movements whereby the familiar becomes strange and the strange becomes familiar. For example, in the film *Invasion of the Body Snatchers* (Philip Kaufman, 1978), with its skilful camera techniques that expose the uncanny in everyday objects, flowers from outer space land in San Francisco and discreetly abduct humans by possessing the inner spaces of their minds. The wife of an abducted husband becomes aware that her husband is 'weird but not the way he normally is'. And alternatively, when the strange becomes familiar, children make friends with aliens despite huge differences in neck lengths, and, in order to remain invisible, invisible men have to be careful about eating.

Nonetheless, the porosity of everyday and alien spaces may be sealed over in science fiction films in the violent binaristic struggles between good and evil, as earthlings battle aliens for epistemological *lebensraum* at intergalactic and urban scales. This chapter, then, is not only an attempt to show how the geographies of science fiction films may be mapped in terms of the metaphysics of presence and the pataphysics of absence. It is also, more broadly, an attempt to show how the spacing of these differential forces in science fiction films can prompt new possibilities for geography and understandings of space elsewhere. It is to these differential forces that I now wish to turn.

## THE METAPHYSICS OF PRESENCE

Metaphysics concerns the highly disputed branch of philosophy that questions the ontological composition of the universe as well as realities that lie beyond the empirically knowable. With developments in modern science, the expansion of metaphysics to include scientific knowledge and methods became one of the major objectives of metaphysicians. Metaphysical issues are intimately linked with recurrent philosophical questions of truth, illusion, form, substance, presence, time, space, causality and free will.

According to Derrida, the history of Western philosophical inquiry, in spite of all its variations and contrary to anti-metaphysical claims within phenomenology, positivism and pragmatism, consistently assumes, requires and necessitates validity in terms of presence. For Derrida (1988: 93), metaphysics has been Western thought being mobilized through the assumption and imposition of hierarchical dualistic language.

All metaphysicians, from Plato to Rousseau, from Descartes to Husserl, have proceeded in this way, conceiving good to be before evil, the positive before the negative, the pure before the impure, the simple before the complex . . . And this is not just *one* metaphysical gesture among others, it is *the* metaphysical exigency, that which has been the most constant, most profound, and most potent.

Here, Derrida points out that one half of binaries are privileged with the quality of full presence while the supplementary half of binaries are subordinate and ascribed within terms of absence. He links this metaphysical enterprise to the search for an undivided, ultimate point of origin whereby metaphysics ascribes truth to the *logos* (e.g. logic, reason and God). Derrida calls this pursuit of *logos* the 'metaphysics of presence'. Derrida suggests that any claim, philosophical or not, is founded on notions of presence. Derrida's examples include the presence of the object to sight, the immediate presence to sensation and the co-presence of self and other. Thus, presence is (already) spatialized in terms of nearness, immediacy and adjacency. Presence is also configured temporally through assumptions of the present as the now, that occurs without delay, lapse and deferral. Derrida's project is not one of resolution, but is rather a (pataphysical) strategy that works *differently* to unsettle and overturn traditional metaphysical binarism. This strategy involves the displacement of either/or logic and the reversal of the hierarchies through what he calls 'undecidables' such as '*différance*', 'trace', '*supplément*' and 'spacing'. Derrida has also aligned his deconstructive process to a shaking, a movement of *sollicitation* (see Derrida 1987). A comparable shaking of presence occurs in science fiction films when presence configured in objects such as buildings is rattled by monsters and destroyed by laser beams. Pataphysical erasing of presence shakes our assumptions that people will not be invisible, will not turn into animals, and will not shrink or grow bigger. Thus, science fiction films can be considered as a deconstructive genre that invites characters and viewers to identify with Gayatri Spivak's urge to 'render delirious that interior voice that is the voice of the other in us' (Spivak 1988: 294) and confront the pataphysical other by loving the alien.

## THE PATAPHYSICS OF ABSENCE

The late nineteenth-century French writer Alfred Jarry (1873–1907) 'formally' initiated the pataphysical project and his work is regarded as an important precursor to French avant-garde literature, Surrealism and Dada, which in turn would have influenced twentieth-century science fiction. Like these artistic and literary projects, Jarry's work seeks to portray worlds governed by anarchic surprises and nihilistic blasphemy. In the book *Exploits & Opinions of Doctor Faustroll Pataphysician: A Neo-Scientific Novel* (published posthumously in 1911) Jarry promotes the pataphysical as a science of imaginary solutions. Pataphysics, as a mode of scientific inquiry, was more influenced by the work of the eccentric British scientists Sir William Thompson (Lord Kelvin), Sir William Crookes, Arthur Cayley and C. V. Boys, than by Jarry's French contemporaries, Louis Pasteur, Jules Henri Poincaré and Marie Curie (see Jarry 1996: xiv).

Pataphysics speculates about the realm beyond metaphysics and investigates the laws that govern exceptions. Jarry's characters are radical spatial scientists who explore and are informed by surreal idiographical imaginations. The pataphysician Dr Faustroll becomes the size of a mite and voyages across the 'Squitty Sea' and 'Paris to Paris via the sea', to explore the pataphysical morphologies of the subterranean canals in cabbage leaves. Dr Faustroll reports in a telepathic letter to Lord Kelvin that:

> The sun is a cool, solid, and homogeneous globe. Its surface is divided into squares of one meter, which are the bases of long, inverted pyramids, thread-cut, 696,999 kilometres long, their points one kilometer from the center. Each is mounted on a screw and its movement, *if I had the time*, the rotation of a paddle at the top end of each screw shaft, in a few meters of viscous fluid, with which the whole surface is thinly veiled . . .
>
> (Jarry 1996: 105)

Jarry's world parodies the Cartesian will to measure, by pushing it to its logically absurd limits (see also Jarry 1969). The pataphysical 'sensibility' seeks to render delirious precarious metaphysical assumptions about presence and is comparable to the exasperating logic of invisibility, dissolution and reversibility in science fiction films. As I argued earlier, in science fiction, the pataphysical and the metaphysical, however, do not negate one another, but rather oscillate under perpetual erasure, mixing what is thought to be the strange and the familiar. That this double-movement of science fiction echoes the dialectic of Enlightenment (Horkheimer and Adorno 1998) means that the pataphysical wrath of aliens and earthling hysteria proceed *not* from a lapse in reason but from a faith in reason's presence. As Georges Bataille (1985: 17) notes, '[i]t is known that civilized man is characterized by an often inexplicable acuity of horror. The fear of insects is no doubt one of the most singular and most developed of these horrors.' I would now like to attend to the important role cinema has on visually casting and screening the spaces of science fiction as film.

## SCIENCE FICTION AND CINEMA

As a story-telling medium and transformer of presence, cinema functions like a time and space machine that shuffles the temporality of narrative and condenses the effects of proximity (see Natter 1994). Cinema is a magical flickering, a spacing between presence and absence, whereby for every second of projected image there is a second of darkness.[2] We may consider cinema as a science fiction, or perhaps a sci-finema, focused to reproduce the allure of the visible as 'reality effects' whereby the strange becomes stranger the more real it looks. Film, like Baudrillard's description (see epigraph) of science fiction, can assimilate light to slower speeds through slow motion and replay to produce what Walter Benjamin (1968: 237) calls 'unconscious optics'. Science fiction and cinema may reside very much on the same planet, but they still require careful consideration. Cinema is not merely a mirror that faithfully re-presents societal opinions or authorial intent, but rather acts as a screen of immanence. Marcus Doel and David Clarke offer this premise in their Deleuzian critique of cinema and *Blade Runner*. They argue that:

> Cinema does not re-present, re-produce, re-play, or re-flect . . . [C]on-ceptualization should work 'alongside' rather than 'on' the cinema: resonance, rather than reflection; encounter rather than capture; invention rather than re-presentation . . . [T]he screen is always already immanent to itself.
>
> (Doel and Clarke 1997: 141)

The epistemic *dis*order immanent to science fiction's things is never wholly destructive but, as I argue, is continually re-registered and re-mapped through the *presumably* secure presence of everyday familiarity. Presumably secure, and this is crucial, because everyday space is not a lucid presentation that is cinematically re-presented, but is rather a tremulous representation that is represented (Jones 1995: 87). Science fiction films seek to radically trip up the contrived maintenance, through metaphysical assumptions grounded in presence, of everyday spaces that already presuppose the possibility of pata-physical incursions. Thus, the supposed alien that allegedly came from outer space, or from outside of space, already resides and permeates so-called everyday inner space. How else could one explain the bizarre frequency of humanoid aliens?

The *grands récits* of presence (Lyotard 1984) are spectacularly dismantled by science fiction's bellicose aesthetic of hysterical vaporization of metal, buildings and people. These epistemic suicidal yearnings produce what Susan Sontag (1965) has described as a fundamental trope in science fiction as the (geographical) 'imagination of disaster'.

> Science fiction films are not about science. They are about disaster, which is one of the oldest subjects of art. In science fiction films disaster is rarely viewed intensively; yet it is always extensive. It is a matter of quantity and ingenuity. If you will, it is a *question of scale*.
>
> (Sontag 1965: 454, my emphasis)

At once subtle and devastating, the undoing of presence may occur when just one metaphysical strand as a basic unit of everyday presence is pataphysically tweaked to become the film's or a scene's primary motif. I seek to unravel these various strands and show that they are thoroughly spatial. In making these spaces at once more recognizable *and* more monstrous, I would like to disentangle the geographies of science fiction films in terms of scale, the invisible, the bestial, and the cyborg.

## OBSCENE SPATIAL ODDITIES

The geographies of science fiction films are perhaps most immediate in terms of the surreal juxtapositions and the warping of scale ranging from giant 450-metre-long desert worms in *Dune* (David Lynch, 1984) to microscopic alien lifeforms in *The Andromeda Strain* (Robert Wise, 1971). The usual friction caused by the tyranny of distance (Latour 1997), where the far is beyond, is tamed by intergalactic space travel; scale also dissolves when moons are mistaken for space stations as in *Star Wars* (George Lucas, 1977). The pataphysical not only disrupts conventional morphologies but, through disruption, places space into question and, therefore, meaning itself. For example, when characters and viewers are confronted with the sexuality of a giant woman in *Attack of the 50 Ft. Woman* (Nathan Juran, 1958) or giant creatures amidst urban landmarks in *King Kong* (Merian Cooper and Ernest Schoedsack, 1933), space visibly incorporates the pataphysical. Alongside Baudrillard, we may consider these

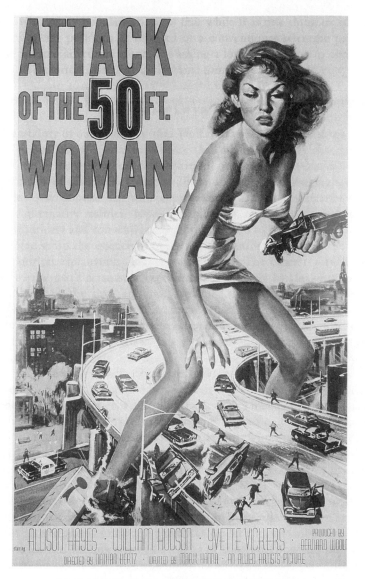

*Figure 8.1* Poster for *Attack of the 50 Ft. Woman*.
(*Source:* Ronald Grant Archive)

pataphysical objects as a form of obscenity, 'because they have too much meaning, because they take up too much space' (1999: 57).

The effects of these reconfigurations of space are often registered in science fiction films as volatile geopolitical or, rather, cosmopolitical conflicts in the will to pataphysical power. For example, in *Dune* the substance spice (mined on the planet Dune) is valuable because it enhances life force required for space travel by 'folding space' and 'travelling without moving'. By ingesting spice, one is endowed with limitless power. Nevertheless, *Dune*'s way of linking power and space as geopolitics is highly reminiscent of Halford Mackinder's Heartland thesis ('he who controls the heartland, controls the world'), when we learn in *Dune* that 'he who controls the spice controls the universe'. Victory is assured for the protagonist Paul, who, having overcome the metaphysics of presence conferred in frightening illusions ('I must not fear: Fear is the mind killer'), successfully harnesses the pataphysical power of the spice. Paul proclaims:

> Some thoughts have a certain sound, that being the equivalent to a form. Through sound and motion you will be able to paralyze nerves, shatter bones, set fires, suffocate an enemy or burst his organs.

Pataphysical power, then, operates by forcibly disrupting the containment of presence, but this empowering manoeuvre is partial and subject to slippage into presence. Missiles and bullets are often portrayed as ineffective weapons against the alien threats to extinction of humanity. Catastrophe is averted, however, when towards the end of many science fiction films the aliens' metaphysical weak spot is discovered. For example, mere salt water is deadly for the alien plants in *Day of the Triffids* (Sekely, 1962), and bacteria kills the alien creatures in *War of the Worlds* (Haskin, 1953).

*The Matrix* (Andy and Larry Wachowski, 1999), which significantly opens with the line 'is everything in place?', portrays ensuing struggles to utilize the pataphysical power of the cyberspatial matrix. Early in the film, the character Neo avoids capture by being guided by an unknown voice on a mobile telephone through the labyrinthine office space. Thus, the hitherto maze-like presence of the office is made legible, and the threat of Neo's pursuers is subdued for Neo with the guidance of the pataphysically empowered voice from nowhere. In a later scene, Neo meets a Matrix controller called Morpheus and is given the choice whether to swallow a blue pill and return to his everyday context, or a red pill to enter the Matrix. Neo chooses to take the red pill and embraces the pataphysical. Like Alice's descent into her pataphysical wonderland that defies conventional understandings of space and presence, the Matrix is a world where spoons bend like rubber, helicopter flight instructions are downloaded, bullets travel in slow motion and bodies split into pieces, collapsing time and the illusion of real geographies. Science fiction's spectacles of obscenity and spatial oddities promote pataphysical bravado and *jouissance*. In *The Matrix*, the limitations of presence as the logic of iterability are breached when Neo is faced with the logical challenge: 'no one has ever done that before.' He revolts with pataphysical defiance, 'and that's why it's going to work'.

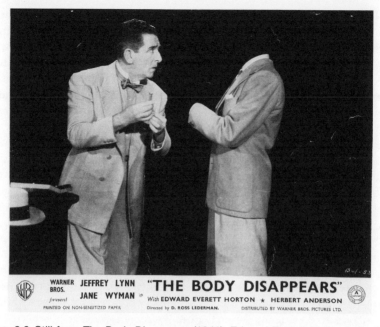

*Figure 8.2* Still from *The Body Disappears* (1941). Edward Everett Horton talks to an invisible friend.
(*Source:* Ronald Grant Archive)

### THE INVISIBLE AND UNMAPPABLE

In addition to scale, vision is a crucial register of presence (Jay 1994). The ocularity of presence is severely problematized in *The Invisible Man* (James Whale, 1933), a film advertised as containing 'acts of unspeakable terror'. These acts that are caused by the Invisible Man, which include threatening voices in thin air, people falling into village ponds, and ink being suddenly thrown into a policeman's face, occur amidst the familiar backdrop of rural England. The 'unspeakable terror' of these hardly terrible acts is a result of the invisibility (pataphysics of absence) of cause (metaphysics of presence), paradoxically making these effects more present. For example, the absurdity of the ocular centricity of presence is manifest in a '100,000 people strong' manhunt for the Invisible Man that involves prodding hedges with sticks. The seeing and visible hunters become the haunted as they enigmatically scream, in the Invisible Man's pataphysical absence, 'Help! Help! He's here! He's here!' The Invisible Man performs the role of an epistemological Antichrist, who threatens to 'sweep the world with invisible armies' and conquer a global order founded on its metaphysics of presence ('the whole world is my hiding place'). As the civilized and discontented villagers' pataphysical other, the Invisible Man is pathologized because he is 'invisible and that's what's the matter with him . . . But he's human and we shall get him . . . But at all costs we must avoid a panic.' The villagers believe they can find him because despite his alienating invisibility, the Invisible Man is, after all, just a human. Despite the villagers' humanist faith, the Invisible Man maintains his elusiveness and confronts an old scientist friend, who is duly shocked by his invisibility. The Invisible Man puts his friend at ease in his absence by wearing a smoking jacket and saying 'now then, we can talk as man to man ... You'd prefer to see me, wouldn't you.' The Invisible Man asks his friend to become his partner in pataphysical crimes. He revels in the pataphysical power of invisibility but warns of its fallibility in the presence of soot, mist, dirty fingernails and eating food. Later in the film, the Invisible Man is heard snoring in a barn and the police are notified. Having set fire to the barn, the police and villagers form a giant human chain to finally locate the Invisible Man's material presence. Footprints in the snow signify his presence and this allows the police to take aim and shoot. In the final scene, the Invisible Man's pataphysical death is coupled with a metaphysical re-birth. He becomes visible.

The threats of the unmappable and miasmic are central to *The Andromeda Strain*. In this film, a state of global hysteria is threatened when a two-microns-wide alien lifeform lands in a remote hamlet in Nevada, North America. Suspicions arise when the bodies lack empirical evidence to discern the cause of death. The plot becomes pataphysical upon the discovery of powdered blood within the victims' bodies. Eventually, the remains of a strange capsule are discovered and transported, along with the two survivors, an unconscious drunkard and a baby, to a secret alien germ research centre composed of five underground floors, each with an increasing level of purity. The scientists, suddenly and mysteriously plucked by the police from their homes, undergo thorough decontamination and immunization procedures. The presence of everyday germs and other impurities are washed, burnt and radiated off the scientists' bodies.

Having calculated the approximate size of the alien using filtration methods to distinguish it from spatters of orange paint, consternation ensues when it is observed that the microscopic alien is growing in size. Fortunately, immunity to the alien is discovered using the quarantined survivors. An alcoholic and a baby share abnormal pH levels in their blood, the former because of alcohol and the latter because of high respiratory rates from crying. *The Andromeda Strain* revels in the methods and methodology of modern science's disease control. The film pedagogically delimits the metaphysics of presence in the scientific procedures of 'detection, characterization, and control' that can outwit the tiny pataphysical disease. Science fiction's struggles over life and death can also be understood in terms of the struggles in bounding the human body with the bestial and the technological.

## THE BODY DE-FORMED: CREATURE DISCOMFORTS AND CYBORG MALFUNCTIONS

The much-written-about Foucauldian 'death of the subject' is in many ways a death of a metaphysic of presence configured in the human body and mind as a materially contained, distinct and generative site for self-identical knowledge and psychic experience. Some science fiction films seek to edify and celebrate this death by diminishing the autonomous space of the human body's being through the pataphysical collapse of the bestial and mechanical. Bataille (1985: 59) once noted that 'man does not have a simple architecture like beasts, and it is not even possible to say where he begins'. Science fiction graphically reinforces Bataille's proposition that these metamorphoses are truly threatening to everyday cartographies in depicting a human subject turning into chitin and being disseminated into a constellation of madness, ruthlessness and excessive libidinal energy. In the film *The Fly* (David Cronenberg, 1986), the genetic codes of a fly and the eccentric scientist-cum-pataphysician Seth Brundle accidentally get combined during a teleportation experiment. This precipitates the gradual rancid disintegration of Brundle's human body, which begins with the protrusion of thick hairs that break his electric shaver, and finally the presence of human subjectivity and ethical concerns disintegrates into a fly's 'insect politics'. Seth Brundle's teleportation-computer username becomes 'Brundle-Fly', which signifies the erasure of a metaphysically present human body and identity. Even the *conventions* of cannibalism (human eats human) are pataphysically breached when he warns his girlfriend that she has not only become edible but also liable to dissolution by his salivary acids.

Like the bestial, the mechanical is another motif that disturbs the presence of human(ist) sensibilities. Donna Haraway (1989: 180) draws upon science fiction to claim that the cyborg (cybernetic organism) subject avoids a binary logic conferred in the metaphysics of presence that constrains possibilities for multiple (feminist) subjectivities:

> A cyborg body is not innocent; it was not born in a garden; it does not seek unitary identity and so generate antagonistic dualisms without end (or until the world ends); it takes irony for granted . . . The machine is us, our process, an aspect of our embodiment.

While Haraway acknowledges that the cyborg is far from innocent, and already part of our subjectivity, cyborgs in science fiction films such as the computer HAL in *2001: A Space Odyssey* (Stanley Kubrick, 1968) are guilty of pataphysical malfunctions. HAL, a computer that speaks and responds to humans, is lauded as being incapable of error. However, during a space mission we witness HAL's gradual and perhaps wilful descent into malfunction, made all the more poignant through his human-like and indeed neurotic responses to his human colleagues' doubts of his computational abilities. The pathos of HAL's demise exceeds that of his human colleagues when, close to his death, he utters the words 'take a stress pill and think things over . . . I'm afraid Dave . . . I'm losing my mind, I can feel it.' Interestingly, HAL, like many other cyborgs in science fiction films (for instance R2-D2 and C-3PO in *Star Wars*), derives a cyborg identity from a mechanical rather than human end of the spectrum (C-3PO takes showers), in contrast to Haraway's somewhat more down-to-earth cyborg subject (a human takes a shower). The cyborg, then, pataphysically blurs the distinction between the machine and the human and, in so doing, re-enacts certain presences that are human, all too human.

## CONCLUSIONS

I began this chapter with the premise that the 'science' of good science fiction films largely depends on their ability to subtly fix the normality of a given situation so that its staged presence can be radically unfastened by something fictive enough to be recognized as alien. This movement, I have argued, involves directing spaces under the aegis of the metaphysics of presence and the pataphysics of absence. Science–Fiction is an unstable binary that shakes hysterically in its unfixing of the metaphysics of presence conferred in scale, visibility and the human body. Any fixings of presence, however, as Derrida reminds us and science fiction shows us, cannot hold indefinitely. Thus, the pataphysics of absence is like a catalytic spectre. It provides a cosmic counter-mapping of conventional earthbound *geo*graphical imaginations that brushes against the grain of presence to the extent that it reveals the contingency of any neat fix of spatial certitude.

It follows, then, that an understanding of the metaphysics of presence and the pataphysics of absence and, therefore, their subsequent geographies need not be confined to the analysis of science fiction films. Close encounters with science fiction films should resonate with geographical inquiry when one considers how the geographic tradition has straddled (lauded by Alexander von Humboldt and derided by Richard Hartshorne) the factual imperative of science and the fictive qualities of aesthetics (see for example Livingstone 1992). In more recent times, geographers have sought to emphasize the 'uncertainty' of space (Natter and Jones 1997) and the plasticity of space and geography itself as a disciplinary Frankensteinian 'freak show' (Doel 1999b). Geographers can further their understandings of pataphysics by visiting the Collège de 'Pataphysique in Paris, founded in 1948, an institution composed of artists and writers that once included Marcel Duchamp, Max Ernst and Man Ray. Similarly in Japan, one encounters the pataphysical art of *Chindohgu* that seeks to invent 'unuseless' machines that echo the cartoons of North American Rube Goldberg who specialized in drawing whimsical, complicated machines to perform very simple tasks.

Perhaps the fatal observation of Baudrillard (1999: 7), a self-confessed pataphysician, that 'the world is not dialectical – it is sworn to extremes, not to equilibrium, sworn to radical antagonism, not to recognition or synthesis' may help to guide pata-physical-geography's sensitivity to the possibilities of space. If so, we may add to Jarry's (1996: 24) fatal observation:

[L]et us reflect, in this connection, upon the irreverence of the common herd whose instinct sums up the adepts of the science of pataphysics in the following phrase:

**ACKNOWLEDGEMENTS**

Heartfelt thanks to Dr Francis Harvey and Dr John Pickles for providing the Digital Places/Spaces seminar that allowed for my pataphysical musings, and their insightful comments on an earlier draft of this chapter. I would also like to acknowledge the support of my fellow graduate students, particularly Matt McCourt and Josh Lepawsky, during and after these seminar discussions.

**NOTES**

1  The word 'pataphysics' first appeared in print in an article entitled 'Guignol' in the April issue of *L'Echo de Paris Littéraire Illustré* (1893). Accordingly, the word's precise meaning is unclear, perhaps created from an alteration of the Greek *ta epi ta metaphusika* (things after the metaphysics). Jarry (1996: 21) writes that the 'actual orthography *'pataphysics*, [is] preceded by an apostrophe so as to avoid a simple pun' such as *patte* (paw) or *pâté*.
2  Thank you to Josh Lepawsky for directing me to the article 'E-cinema' in *The New York Times Magazine*, 5 December 1999, p. 59.

# 9

## AN INVENTION WITHOUT A FUTURE, A SOLUTION WITHOUT A PROBLEM

## MOTOR PIRATES, TIME MACHINES AND DRUNKENNESS ON THE SCREEN

*Marcus A. Doel and David B. Clarke*

In this chapter we consider film as a science fiction. However, rather than restrict ourselves to the genre of science fiction, we take the very medium of film itself to be an exemplary form of science fiction. Film engineers space and time. It renders space-time malleable and therefore amenable to the most extraordinary forms of human intervention: real, symbolic, and imaginary. However, while today we take such renderings of space and time for granted, in the first few years of film-making no one really knew what to do with film. It was anything but a space and time *machine*. In this chapter, then, we have chosen to explore the emergence and shaping of the practices which support film production, exhibition, and reception as a literal science fiction. This brought us to consider the period 1895 through to 1913, 'an all but lost continent of invention and discovery', as Christie (1994: 8) put it. 1895 witnessed the public début of 'animated photography': a technology without an application; a solution without a problem; a medium without a message; an address without an addressee; an invention without a future. Nothing was set: not even the rate of hand cranking . . . By 1913, however, the global film industry had become dominated by so-called 'feature' films, which were explicitly arrayed in terms of distinct genres and increasingly centred on stars. Meanwhile, film-making and exhibition had more or less ossified into a certain kind of narrative cinema centred on the interpolation of the audience, diegetic realism, and the adoption of continuity editing to give a coherent sense of space and time.

Treating early films as science fiction also brought us to England. For in addition to its manufacturing and technical supremacy, England had the advantage of a highly sophisticated visual culture, which was already very well acquainted with 'moving pictures', not least because of the massive industry built up around magic lantern slides and lectures. Furthermore, all of this was served by a plethora of trade journals devoted to the conjugation of technical innovation, animated photography, and imperial citizenship. To that extent, this chapter takes the English film trade and discourse between 1895 and 1913 as its focus. The empirical claims in the chapter are supported by our study of almost all of the 500-or-so surviving British-made 'fiction' films held by the National Film and Television Archive (NFTVA) at the British Film Institute (BFI). Nevertheless, the chapter deals in most detail with one idea that never came to fruition: a preliminary patent application made by the film-pioneer Robert W. Paul in 1895. His patent was for a cinematic 'Time Machine', an idea which came to him after witnessing the fortuitous success of his kinetoscope and H. G. Wells's *The Time Machine*. Along the way, we will also encounter motor pirates, drunkards, and the shocking case of a little old lady exposed on the screen.

## WE HAVE EXPLOSIVES ...

Looking back on the histories of science fiction and film, it seems unremarkable that they should have emerged together. First and foremost, film is an exemplary medium for presenting science fiction. One thinks of such films as *Metropolis* (1926, directed by Fritz Lang), *Alphaville* (1965, Jean-Luc Godard), *2001: A Space Odyssey* (1968, Stanley Kubrick), *Star Wars* (1977, George Lucas), *Blade Runner* (1982, Ridley Scott) and *The Matrix* (1999, The Wachowski Brothers). In addition, film is literally a *science fiction*: a fabrication lent plausibility by scientific technique. And just as science fiction derives its energy from drawing out and accentuating facets of the present that are disturbing or fantastic, film is able to project space and time beyond the pre-existing co-ordinates of the real. Although the interpolation of the viewer into the diegesis of a film is not an established part of early film-making and exhibition, the attempt to connect real space and filmic space (real-to-reel) is already there in the Lumière brothers' seminal *Arrivée d'un train en gare à La Ciotat*[1] (*c.* 1895), which darted out of the screen like an arrow. While this film marked the eruption of filmic space into real space, the 1900 Cecil Hepworth film *How It Feels to Be Run Over* re-marked the boundary between them. A car races towards the camera until it 'hits' the audience. More ambitiously, James Williamson's 1900 film *The Big Swallow* strives to take the space occupied by the audience into itself. Upon realizing that he is being filmed by a 'camera fiend', a man advances menacingly towards the camera until his open mouth fills the frame. Through stop-motion trickery we see the camera fiend fall into the now-cavernous mouth, whereupon the man draws back, munching in triumph. Whether or not contemporary audiences were taken in by such duplicity is a moot point. Indeed, one of the founding myths of the cinema is that filmgoers were terrified by suddenly encountering 'the absolute novelty' of animated photographs and stationary trips (a myth parodied in R. W. Paul's 1901 film *The Countryman and the Cinematograph*, in which the countryman flies in terror from the train coming out of the screen). This neglects the fact that in the wake of the camera obscura, phantasmagoria, spirit photography, automata, the waxwork Chamber of Horrors and so on, most audiences were well versed in how to 'suspend their disbelief' in readiness for such dark attractions. It also neglects the fact that there was considerable pre-cedent in terms of moving images: thanks in no small part to the ingenious devices dreamed up by the lanternists. An 1892 issue of the *PRR*,[2] for example, reports a demonstration in Bath of Rudge's Bio-phantascope, 'an adjunct to the ordinary magic lantern by means of which [whatever is] depicted on the screen can be made to move with life-like accuracy'. In the example reported,

> there are a number of photographs on glass of a man's face, taken under different conditions. In one the face is at rest, in another it is smiling, in a third frowning; in others the tongue protruding, or the eyes alone that move, so throughout the whole series. It is by throwing the light of the lantern alternately through first one then another of these various photo-graphs, making each image fall upon the same portion of the screen as the preceding one, and without any intermediate loss of light, that the life-like movement of the portrait is obtained.
>
> (*PRR* 1(4), 15 April 1892: 138)

Such life-like facial expressions evidently exerted considerable fascination in their time, insofar as they also featured in some of the earliest films, including the 1898 films *Comic Faces – Old Man Drinking a Glass of Beer* directed by George Albert Smith and *Grimaces – The Fateful Letter* (probably also directed by Smith), and the 1901 films *Masques and Grimaces* and *Mister Moon* (directors unknown). Likewise, other early films directly borrowed techniques from the lanternists: in the 1896 film *Footpads* (director unknown), for example, to depict the sequential, letter-by-letter illumination of advertising signs for 'Bovril' and 'Vinolia' in a painted night-time city backdrop to a scene of violent crime.

Rather than cast science fiction as little more than a technologized version of utopianism or dystopianism, Baudrillard treats it as symptomatic of the altered status of space, time, motion, rhythm, duration and reality under conditions of mechanical reproduction and simulation (Benjamin 1969).

> To the limited universe of the pre-industrial era, utopia *opposed* an ideal, alternative universe. To the potentially infinite universe of production, science fiction *adds* the multiplication of its own possibilities.
>
> (Baudrillard 1994: 122)

One thinks of editing, montage, multiple exposure, double printing, parallel action, flashback, close-up, slow motion, split screen and time lapse. Through the operations that it performs on space and time, film came to express a 'ver-nacular relativity' (Christie 1994: 33). It did this in two ways, both of which

posed specific problems for early film-makers, exhibitors and audiences. The first
concerns motion; the second involution.

With regard to motion, films 'reproduced the mechanization, jerkiness, and
rush of modern times'. Moreover, 'of all the technology that affected the pace of
life, the early cinema most heightened public consciousness of differential speed'
(Kern 1983: 117 and 130, respectively). For example, the *OLCJ* repeatedly fretted
about the 'well-known circumstance of Anima-photography', such 'that unless
the projecting of the subject upon the lantern screen is conducted precisely at a
speed corresponding to that at which the negative picture was taken, false representations of nature will result'. Worse still: 'Our beloved art becomes a cause for
laughter when men march at a running speed; when artillery guns skate over the
ground on carriages with stationary wheels; and when the wheels on the Royal
carriage revolve backwards' (*OLCJ* I, November 1904: 11). The inconsistency of
both exhibition and audience reaction was a recurrent theme in the *OMLJPE*.

> Two young men recently began a tour with a few very indifferent cine-
> matographic films. When they were exhibited in a large town the report in
> a certain paper described them as 'blurred, streaky, and uninteresting,'
> whereas, when the same pictures were exhibited at the village of ———,
> the local paper said they were 'highly artistic, clearly defined, and of such
> great interest that they fairly brought down the house.'
>
> (*OMLJPE* 8(96), May 1897: 78)

To help rectify this situation, journals such as the *OMLJPE* and the *OLCJ*
advocated a standard rate of 24 frames per second to replace the convention of
sixteen frames per second, along with the professionalization of camera and
projector operators to ensure a consistently good quality of hand cranking: 'We
should then rid the art of illusional freaks, which, though curious and interesting, are undesirable' (*OLCJ* I, November 1904: 11). When the *OLCJ* became the
*OLKJ*, the editor, Theodore Brown, struggled in vain to convince film-makers
that the extra expense of shifting to 24 frames per second was worthwhile (*OLKJ*
II, June 1906: 156–8). And when the journal became the *KLW*, the campaign
against flicker, unnatural motion and the jerkiness of fast-moving foreground
objects across the screen was still being waged. Films have rendered a 'continuity
of impression' but not 'true motion' (*KLW* 2(37), 23 January 1908: 179). This
accords with the widespread suspicion of film trickery. 'Several of our contemporaries have lately taken to heart the increasing success of the trick film, and
deplore their position in popularity over what they are pleased to term the
"straightforward cinematograph picture"' (*OLCJ* I, May 1905: 145). The *KLW*
(2(38), 30 January 1908: no pagination) was especially scathing of that 'class of
trickery' in which 'the laws of nature are assumed to be set at variance'. The
journal even went so far as to deplore the use of lenses which gave 'false perspective' and therefore 'false motion' (*KLW* 2(35), 9 January 1908: 141–3). So, given
'the various illusions to which the art is subject, it becomes a problem taxing the

greatest genius, how best to avoid giving false effect upon the screen' (*OLCJ* I, November 1904: 11). Whilst one may sympathize with this reservation, it is clear that the journal fails to consider the possibility that so-called 'true motion' may itself have become variable, discontinuous and jerky: that modernity itself may have set the 'laws of nature at variance'. Such a possibility is precisely the theme of Robert W. Paul's 1906 film *How to Make Time Fly*, in which the action accelerates and decelerates depending upon the movement of an erratic clock whose pendulum has been stolen (cf. *Onésime Horloger*, a 1912 Gaumont comedy in which Onésime invents a special clock that accelerates him through twenty years of Parisian life in order to claim his inheritance, only then to reverse the clock to twenty years before so that he can enjoy his new-found wealth, and the 1924 film *Paris Qui Dort*, directed by René Clair, in which a mad scientist, Dr Craise, freezes all human motion across Paris using an invisible ray).

The second problem posed by film-making concerned the possibilities opened up by editing. This allowed time to be abstracted from its regular flow, so becoming a material that could be engineered: stopped, expanded, diminished, reversed, accelerated, decelerated, cut, spliced, quoted, iterated, reconcatenated, transformed, et cetera. 'The compacting of events in time was best suited for the new art form of the period – the cinema.' 'Film expanded the sense of the present' by allowing one 'to splice open a moment and insert a number of simultaneous activities' (Kern 1983: 279, 70 and 71, respectively). Film lets one 'interpolate endlessly into what has been' (Benjamin; quoted in McCole 1993: 7). It has the potential to make events stutter and to force reality to turn against itself. Hence Benjamin's intuition of the revolutionary and explosive potential of film: not just in terms of content, but especially in terms of form. It has the power to defamiliarize and counter-actualize what would ordinarily be experienced as self-evident by 'penetrating the formerly inviolable surface of the visible world' and replacing it with a discontinuous surface rendered through the disjunctive synthesis of montage (McCole 1993: 6). Accordingly, Benjamin characterized this 'progressive mode of reception as a critical, testing attitude', and the mass of filmgoers were 'entitled to be considered experts' in it (McCole 1993: 201). It is not surprising, then, that bourgeois cultural intermediaries should have so vocally championed the cause of realism, of eradicating 'illusional freaks' and 'false motion', and of muffling film's explosive potential by the imposition of a smooth and anaesthetizing form of space-time continuity.

## AN UNTIMELY TIME MACHINE ...

It is often said that science fiction and film were unleashed on the world in the same year, 1895, with the public début of the Lumière brothers' cinématographe, and the publication of Herbert George Wells's *The Time Machine*, whose title came to provide an apt characterization of the cinematic experience. As if to shatter the fortuitous origin of science fiction and film, however, we should note that *The Time Machine* was in fact based on *The Chronic Argonauts*, published by

Wells in 1888. But as if by magic, 1888 also turns out to be a seminal year in the pre-history of film, for it was in that year – during the boom in chrono-photography inspired by Muybridge, Anschutz and Marey – that Louis Le Prince reputedly took the first ever sequence of moving photographs in his home town of Leeds, before mysteriously disappearing in France (Rawlence 1990). It is perhaps no mere coincidence, then, that the original serialization of *The Time Machine* in the *New Review* of 1895 should open with the line: 'The man who made the Time Machine . . . was well known in scientific circles a few years since, and the fact of his disappearance is also well known' (cited in Moorcock 1993: xxix).

From the off, then, film and science fiction have been imbricated. Yet in his Introduction to the 1931 edition of *The Time Machine*, Wells noted that the story had 'lasted as long as the diamond-framed safety bicycle, which came in at about the date of its first publication'. That the safety bicycle loomed larger in Wells's memory than film is telling: though not unreasonable, especially since Wells himself became an avid cyclist during the 1890s (Austin 2000). Despite the apparent affinity of science fiction and film, Wells had little to do with cinema until his collaboration with Alexander Korda on the 1936 science fiction epic *Things to Come*, which was based on Wells's 1935 novel *The Shape of Things to Come* (Richards 1999). Indeed, to illustrate the initial estrangement of the emergent science fiction literature and the nascent medium of animated pictures, it is instructive to note that R. W. Paul – 'noted for his technical and mechanical excellence, film quality and originality, and "up-to-dateness"', according to the 'Who's Who' of the English film industry that appeared in the first issue of the *KLW* (no. 1, 16 May 1907) – courted Wells's collaboration on a filmic project as early as 1895: but to no avail. According to the showbusiness newspaper *The Era* on 25 April 1896, Wells's 'weird romance' *The Time Machine* 'had suggested an entertainment to [Paul], of which animated photographs formed an essential part'. When one recalls that the staple of English film production and exhibition in the period 1896 to the early 1900s was actuality shots and 'screamingly funny' comics, with the occasional pathetic subject and trick film (the latter of which, exemplified by Georges Méliès, a Parisian magician-turned-film-maker, owed as much to still photography as it did to animated photography), one is struck by Paul's prescience. To conceive of film as a time machine was almost unthinkable. More obviously, film appeared to operate on space: allowing audiences to see as if they were elsewhere, such as in London, the provinces, the colonies or 'Wild Wales'. Nevertheless, one should not overlook the popularity of so-called 'local' subjects. 'The showman who has not tried a "local" does not really know what success means' insisted the *KLW* (2(44), 12 March 1908: 315). Likewise, *The Bioscope* reported on the success of 'see yourselves' films in Sebright and Islington (*B* no. 130, 8 April 1909: 23). Indeed, their popularity led the *KLW* to ask whether 'any exhibitor has tried the drawing effects of a continuous series of local subjects?' (*KLW* no. 4, 6 June 1907: 59). Film was not yet a time *machine*: it did not manufacture time, nor did it manufacture space. At most, film seemed to offer the possibility of making time endure, although many were at best ambivalent towards, and at worst appalled by, the reduction of time to a succession of stills (Bergson 1984; Douglass 1999). Suffice to say that the vast majority of made-up subjects before 1900 consisted of one unedited shot of a rigidly framed frontal presentation set against a plain painted backdrop that lasted barely one or two minutes. They were literally animated pictures, not portals onto other worlds. To that extent, it was not self-evident that someone like Paul should make the leap of imagination from science fiction to film, a leap that Wells would or could not make.

With the idea of time travel planted firmly in the public imagination in the wake of Wells's novel, and having witnessed the success of his kinetoscope during the Empire of India Exhibition at Earls Court (which ran from May to October 1895), Paul applied for a preliminary patent to mount a 'novel form of exhibition whereby the spectators have presented to their view scenes which are supposed to occur in the future or past, while they are given the sensation of voyaging upon a machine through time' (Patent No. 19984, lodged 24 October 1895; cited in Barnes 1976: 37). Paul's plan involved the projection of moving photographic images onto a screen, a technical achievement yet to be accomplished, that would serve as the 'window' of the Time Machine. In the event, however, Paul's idea was never to materialize. News of the success of the cinématographe-Lumière in Paris, and of its imminent exhibition in London, caused Paul to abandon his plans in order to produce a projector of his own: the Theatrograph, which was reputedly designed and produced within two months. And although Paul later revealed that he had regarded the Lumières' projector as 'superior in steadiness and cleanliness' to his own (*Proceedings of the British Kinematograph Society* no. 38, 3 February 1936: 4), the principle he devised was ultimately to serve as the prototype for the modern film projector.

### A SOLUTION WITHOUT A PROBLEM ...

Apart from attesting to the possibility of a connection between the filmic imagination and the emerging genre of science fiction, Paul's Time Machine demonstrates something of far greater significance: that the new technology of animated photography did not have an obvious use beyond its tautological role of taking animated photographs. Films were neither evidential nor destined to tell stories: they were attractions 'in and of themselves', and English trade journals struggled in vain to promote them as an edifying, educational and scientific medium. At best, films were illustrative. Hence the interest shown by lanternists and lecturers, as well as music hall managers and showmen. As an attraction, however, films were in a precarious position. For in the latter part of the nineteenth century the entertainment industry raced through an enormous number of attractions, all of which were sold as 'novel' and most of which disappeared very rapidly. For example, in 1889, the *OMLJPE* (I(6): 44) characterized 'a peculiar kind of camera' invented by Friese-Greene as 'a startling optical novelty', while in 1894 the *WB* (IV(91): 754) all but dismissed the small and indistinct images made by Thomas Edison's kinetoscope, claiming that it should 'only be regarded as an amusing toy'. And recalling how in 1896 'people flocked in crowds' to see the Lumière films shown at the Empire Theatre, London, which represented 'the latest triumph of modern science', the *KLW* (no. 8, 4 July 1907: 125) noted that this success was not assured: the Alhambra Theatre, London, was also offered the Lumière show but 'threw a cold blanket on the proposed enterprise'. Indeed, Louis Lumière famously declared films to be 'an invention without a future' (cited in Christie 1994: 95), and both the Lumières and Paul abandoned film-making to return to their real passion for the manufacture of equipment.

As a one-time 'novel' attraction in a world hooked on the cult of the new, it should come as no surprise to learn that film's future was not assured. In fact, the history of film provides an excellent example of Ellul's (1964: 19) insistence that a technology 'is nothing more than *means* and an *ensemble of means*'. It 'makes possible a very large number of "solutions" for which there are no problems' (Ellul, miscited in Bauman 1993: 187). When it came to film-making, no one really knew what one should do with either the equipment or the films: how they should be made, exhibited and received were all problematic, despite the fact that they appeared within highly sophisticated visual and technical cultures (Christ and Jordon 1995; Schwartz 1998). The earliest films were typically made by engineers, chemists, travelling showmen, photographers, lanternists and lecturers. Little wonder, then, that film-makers, exhibitors and audiences were seeking problems for which moving photographs would become the solution. Such was the contingency of film's future. Consequently, the English trade journals were full of appropriately 'novel' suggestions: everything from political propaganda and caricature to medical training and labour relations. Nevertheless, the problems first posed for animated photography were problems that had already been 'solved' by other devices such as the flick book, thaumatrope, magic lantern, diorama and still camera (e.g. animated pictures, animated photographs, transformation views, multiple exposures, and ghosting). It took a long time for specifically filmic problems to be formulated.

For now, suffice to say that in the 1890s and early 1900s, it was a struggle to maintain interest in animated pictures, especially among the middle class. Even in 1907, the *KLW* (no. 4, 6 June 1907: 59) still lamented the fact that '[i]n the music hall programme the kinematograph is merely regarded as a turn instead of a separate entertainment ... "American Bioscope" ranks on the equal to "So and so, the comedian"', while the *OLKJ* (III(5), March 1907: 115) once again laboured the virtues of those few music hall managers who were 'awakening to the fact that the kinematograph should be regarded as something more than a stop gap' between other entertainments. 'No one went to see a *particular* film until around 1907 at the very earliest', observes Christie (1994: 8). 'They went to the biograph, the cinematograph, the moving pictures, the nickelodeon: it was a *place* and an *experience* long before identifiable works and their makers emerged to claim their niche in history.'

Despite their novelty and trickery, early films appear to have been no more attractive than, say, X-rays – whose eerie form of nakedness had both a macabre and an erotic quality. Thus, Bottomore (1996: 146) notes evidence that in the first few years of the twentieth century films slipped down the order of attractions and disappeared entirely in some places:

> The lanternists maintained that the cinema was a sensation of the moment, comparing it unfavourably to the quality and solid tradition of the lantern; many in the variety professions suggested that the movies were but another sensational act, which could only last for a brief time on their bills; early actuality producers wondered whether, once all the world's sights had been recorded on film, there would be anything left for the cameras to do; finally, representatives of the legitimate stage maintained that spectators would never prefer mere celluloid entertainment to the presence of live performers.

So, while novel in 1895, the projection of animated photographs and living pictures was not actually *that* novel. The Lumières' cinématographe brought together and refined a whole series of previous inventions. Likewise, as attractions, films were not necessarily *that* attractive. According to Schivelbusch (1988) they were arguably less attractive than the panorama, the diorama and the peep show, since these devices had taken the frame from around the picture and put it in front of the picture: so becoming an aperture to look through. This resulted in the interpolation of the spectator. The picture lying behind the aperture appeared to be unlimited, while its realism was consequently heightened. Through their frontal presentation, depthlessness, fondness for painted backdrops, histrionic acting and obtrusive framing, the earliest films thereby undid the work of interpolation, effectively expelling the viewer from the scene. So, films were *not* groping towards narration, nor were they *fated* to express a smooth and coherent diegesis. They were attractions: less representational than presentational; less optical than haptical. The haptical cinema of attractions:

> invokes an exhibitionist rather than a voyeuristic regime . . . Rather than a desire for an (almost) endless delayed fulfilment and a cognitive involvement in pursuing an enigma, early cinema . . . *attracts* in a different manner. It arouses a curiosity that is satisfied by surprise rather than narrative suspense.
>
> (Gunning 1996: 75)

In this regard it is salutary to read the account of 'Our first kinematograph show' by Sylvanus, which appeared in a 1907 issue of the *KLW*. Sylvanus tells us of an English village 'out of the beaten track': 'it seldom saw a motor or any of the latest marvels of science.' What would the villagers make of film?

Suddenly a picture appears – but what is this? The figures are moving, trees are waving in the wind, and everywhere is to be seen life and motion. It was a comic film that was being presented to our eyes, and intensely amusing, but there was no roar of irresistible laughter to be heard; all was utter silence for a few minutes, then awe found relief in a long-drawn exclamation of wonderment. Presently a sound of laughter was heard, but it was of a very subdued nature, for to the ignorant country mind there was a touch of the uncanny about it all. But as the evening wore on . . . enjoyment began to take the place of wonderment.

(*KLW* no. 8, 4 July 1907: 128)

However, what was most notable for Sylvanus was neither awe, nor uncanniness, nor wonderment, nor enjoyment. Rather, the principal legacy of the evening was disillusionment. 'Presently there came upon the screen a picture of their own Queen Victoria, but this, I must confess, was a big disappointment to many of them . . . It took them some time to recover from the knowledge that their Queen was apparently like any other old lady' (*KLW* no. 8, 4 July 1907: 128).

Not that novel. Not that attractive. And mostly involving running about, falling down, and being beaten. Little wonder, then, that while preaching edification, instruction and enlightenment – in short, embourgeoisment and imperial citizenship – when it came to reviewing 'the latest film releases' the English trade journals simply adored 'screamingly funny' and 'thrilling' subjects. For example, while the first issue of the *CBM*, published in April 1906 by the St Albans-based Warwick Trading Company, gave pride of place to an article on 'The educational value of the cinematograph', subsequent issues made the most of the firm's exclusive access to films of the aftermath of the San Francisco earthquake. In May 1906, the journal ran an advertisement for the films under the headline: 'The Appalling San Francisco Disaster!!' 'Awe-Inspiring! Thrilling!! Startling!!!' In June 1906, and without a trace of irony, the journal took the moral high ground against firms supplying 'faked' and 'dramatic' films of the disaster: 'a shock of three minutes duration which can lay the heart of a great city in ruins, is too awful to sport with. Such scenes [as that of a gloating devil rising above the ruins], we do not look upon as even "playing to the gallery"; they are inhuman, debasing and intolerable' (*CBM* June 1906: 40–1). This is immediately followed by a reannouncement of their 'San Francisco Disaster' films, this time under the less sensational heading 'Latest Films: topical'.

If the novelty and attraction of early films rested on their rendering of space and time, it is interesting to note that this science fiction of form was not complemented by a science fiction of content. To the contrary, the staple of British non-actuality films in the 1890s and 1900s was slapstick comedy, typically precipitated by the calamitous encounter of different social types: tramps and aristocrats, millers and sweeps, villains and policemen, cyclists and pedestrians, gypsies and stolen babies, would-be lovers and their chaperones, soldiers and natives, children and adults, curates and convicts; often entailing escalating chases and invariably involving beatings – especially of policemen. *The Adventures of a Role of Lino* (1907, Alf Collins), *His Only Pair of Trousers* (1907, A. E. Coleby), *Everybody Against the Policeman* (1908, director unknown) and *The Messenger Boy* (1911, director unknown) are exemplary. A common device for effecting disastrous encounters such as these was the park bench: attesting to the ambivalence of the new-found English pride in public space (e.g. *Weary Willie*, 1898, director unknown; *The Tramp and the Baby's Bottle*, 1899, director unknown; *The Postman and the Nursemaid*, 1899, Charles Goodwin Norton; and *The Bathers' Revenge*, 1904, William Haggar). Only gradually did modern technology begin to make an appearance – bicycles, telephones, motor cars, aeroplanes, airships, submarines, clocks, radio control, et cetera – and almost always to comic effect. And if such technologies appeared threatening, it was invariably because of their comic malfunctioning rather than their inhuman machinations (see for example Alf Collins's 1904 film *The Electric Shock*; W. R. Booth's 1907 film *A Juvenile Scientist*; Percy Stow's 1909 films *A Lesson in Chemistry, Juggins' Motor Skates* and *Put a . . .(Penny in the Slot)*; and the 1907 film *Accidents Will Happen*, director unknown). The one exception to this rule was the railways, which were widely used for both actuality and made-up subjects (not least because they provided a ready-made means for getting the camera moving). In general, however, scientific, industrial and technological content was the preserve of actuality films. Imagine our anticipation, then, as we came across a viewing copy of Arthur Melbourne-Cooper's 1906 film *Motor Pirates*, ostensibly the first British-made 'science fiction' film. The film opens with a bizarre twin-cannoned motor vehicle resembling a cross between a tank and a submarine speeding through country lanes. The vehicle arrives at a farm, opens up, and draws in a number of ducks and hens (using reverse-action cinematography), at which point a gun battle ensues between the motor pirates and farm workers. Leaving the latter for dead, the vehicle speeds off, only to draw alongside a motor car, robbing the occupants whilst in motion. Meanwhile, the police have been alerted and give chase. The viewing copy ends abruptly as the vehicle careers into a pond. Such was the occultation of science fiction by everything from animal rustling and highway robbery to comic capers and escalating chases.

In his first prospectus, dated 1897, Méliès sought to distinguish his work from the Lumières', saying that it lay 'mainly in fantastic or artistic scenes, etc. . . . thus creating a special genre which differs entirely from the customary views supplied by the cinematograph – street scenes or scenes of everyday life' (cited in Chanan 1996: 33). While Méliès' success may seem to suggest that he catered for demands left unsatisfied by the Lumières' realism, it would be more accurate to say that he 'created new appetites'. 'Realism à la Lumière and fantasy à la Méliès [were] only two among various orders of imagery which populated early cinema' (Chanan 1996: 33 and 35). Nonetheless, apart from the occasional foray into Vernean scenes of space travel – as in Méliès' 1902 film *Le Voyage dans la Lune* and Paul's 1906 film *The ? Motorist* – anything resembling science fiction was not amongst them. This absence is hardly surprising. Science fiction assumes a narrative form, soliciting the interest of the viewer through the posing of an enigma that lends itself to dialectical suspense and resolution. This in turn tends to evoke a stable and coherent, character-centred diegesis within which the enigma is to be played out. As we have seen, however, the earliest films did not do this.

So, when Telotte (1999: 21) tells us that the earliest science fiction films were 'narratives about great physical, cultural, or epistemological distances and the struggle to overcome them' – distances that technology, in the guise of 'rockets, submarines, radio-telescopes, tunnels, aircraft and various sorts of rays', promised to bridge – it is important to bear in mind that in the British context these were anything but *early* films (W. R. Booth was one of the first English film-makers to produce such films: *Airship Destroyer*, 1909 and *Aerial Submarine; A Startling Forecast – Piracy in Sea and Air*, 1910). That said, these films do demonstrate that technology embodies a central ambivalence: it provides the means for 'coping with a threatening distance' which technology itself has engendered. For the machine age fashioned 'a world that was fundamentally *defined by distance*' (Telotte 1999: 22), a world knowable only at a distance and accessible only via numerous technological intermediaries. Film was just such a technology: and as we have sought to demonstrate, that estrangement was most powerfully felt in the form, if not the content, of the very earliest films.

### TECHNOLOGICAL JERKS AND TECHNOLOGICAL SMOOTHIES ...

With its well-rehearsed screams of fear and delight, its adoption of the traits of the 'living tableau' and 'living waxwork' and its reliance on the histrionic code of stage acting, film, as a late nineteenth- and early twentieth-century 'attraction', does not accord with what has since come to be the dominant use of the medium: narration, which is founded precisely on articulated depth, space-time continuity, verisimilitude, dialectical progression and interpolation. (Although already in 1898 R. W. Paul was promoting the 'clever and natural acting' in his latest films, each of which 'tells a tale' that will 'appeal to the better class audiences'; 'It will probably pay you even to burn your films, and start afresh with a series of the new ones': *E* 8 October 1898: 27.) The move from a 'cinema of attractions' to a 'narrative cinema' was neither inevitable nor easily achieved (Bowser 1990; Burch 1990). 'The shift from a cinema of frontal presentation to a cinema of articulated depth' and 'the installation of perspective in the cinema – the fulfilment of its "three-dimensional vocation"' – was not immediate and obvious, despite the physics of the photographic lens, but was striven for and awkward, producing discontinuity in the spatial worlds early cinema offered spectators' (Lant 1995: 53 and 69, respectively). Hence Gunning's (1996: 71) description of how he 'began to envision early film as less a seed bed for later styles than a place of rupture, a period that showed more dissimilarity than continuity with later film style'. Likewise, Pearson (1996: 154) insists that 'so-called "primitive" cinema should be considered a fully realised mode of filmic communication, constructed around alternative, not inferior, conceptions of story-telling and spatio-temporal continuity' (cf. Brewster and Jacobs 1997; Elsaesser with Barker 1990; Pearson 1992).

It was not inevitable that films would come to express space-time continuity. Nor were they destined to tell stories (Doel 1999a). However, both required living pictures to break out of their rigid enframement. An early example of this appears in the 1899 film *Women's Rights* (possibly directed by James Bamforth), in which the camera position cuts from one side of a fence to another in order to reveal two men nailing the ladies' skirts to the fence with amusing consequences. While a change of camera position and occasional panning became increasingly common, the use of off-screen space, zooms and tilts remained most uncommon. Paul's 1903 *A Chess Dispute* uses off-screen space during a fight sequence, while Lewin Fitzhamon's 1907 *The Busy Man* makes the camera zoom in by mounting it on a trolley. However, it was especially within the chase genre that a number of early film-makers began to devise ways for linking shots to give a continuous sensation of the passing of space and time, and therefore a frame of reference for developing causal relations, reaction shots, parallel action and dialectical progression (e.g. *Fire*, directed by James Williamson 1902; *A Daring Daylight Burglary*, 1903, Frank Mottershaw; *Desperate Poaching Affray*, 1903, William Haggar; and *The Convict and the Curate*, 1904, Percy Stow. James Williamson's 1908 film *The Rival Cyclists* was one of the first English-made films to feature parallel action). Cecil Hepworth, the Sheffield-based film-maker, is widely credited with making a significant contribution to the creation of a coherent filmic space-time through continuity editing. In the 1905 film *Rescued by Rover*, Hepworth produced what Barr (1997: 15) describes as 'a precocious model of the cinematic system'. The film follows a dog as it pursues a kidnapper to her hideout, returns home to summon help and then goes back to the hideout to precipitate a rescue. The systematic sense of visual organization anticipates most of the later hallmarks of narrative cinema, although there is no parallel action and the camera remains almost totally immobile for the duration of each shot. Perhaps unsurprisingly, *Rescued by Rover* quickly became a classic film, giving rise to a number of other chase and rescue films centred on dogs and horses (e.g. Lewin Fitzhamon's 1907 films *Dumb Sagacity* and *Black Beauty*). Nevertheless, Hepworth turned his back on the continuity editing that he had done so much to engender.

> Smoothness in a film is important and should be preserved except when for some special effect a 'snap' is preferred. The 'unities' and 'verities' should always be observed, to which I should add the 'orienties'. Only the direst need will form an excuse for lifting an audience up by the scruff of the neck and carrying it round to the other side, just because you suddenly want to photograph something from the south when the previous scene has been taken from the north.
>
> (Hepworth 1951: 139)

It has been a constant source of disbelief amongst film historians that Hepworth should have produced a film so advanced so early, only to reject it in favour of what Barry (1972: 233) regarded as a singularly exasperating directorial failing: 'the one, common in England, of using the screen as though it were a stage with exits left and right, the actors free to move only across a circumscribed oblong area, with a low skyline and the movements all parallel to the plane of the screen, not, as they should be, for the sake of depth illusion, at angles to it'. However, Hepworth's retreat from continuity editing can be interpreted not as an affront to what 'should be', but as a restitution of the inviolability of the audience's point of view. This inviolability is precisely what is at stake in Paul's 1895 patent for a sedentary filmic Time Machine.

## AN AMBIVALENT TIME MACHINE ...

Since one should think of early films as very short, tightly-framed animated pictures, as wholly enclosed moving tableaux, which over time gradually began to be shown in sequence, more for effect than narration, and at the whim of exhibitors rather than film-makers, two things are striking about Paul's 1895 patent. We are struck, first, by Paul's equation of film with an operation on *time* rather than on space; and second, by his linking of film to science *fiction* rather than science fact, such as X-rays and the microscopic (see for example *The X-Rays*, 1897, G. A. Smith; *The Unclean World*, 1903, Percy Stow). Even for Méliès, perhaps the greatest exponent of 'transformation scenes' and 'fantastical scenes' in the first decade or so of film-making, a 'film's scenario never amounted to much . . . because it merely served as a "pretext" for *trucs* or tricks and striking tableaux' (Abel 1994: 62). On further inspection, however, Paul's *time* machine is distinctly odd. In fact, it is not a time machine at all.

According to the patent, the spectators are to be seated on an enclosed plat-form and 'given the sensation of voyaging upon a machine through time'. This is to be achieved through 'the forward propulsion of the platform' by cranks, cams or worms over a short distance, perhaps augmented by 'a gentle rocking motion', 'a current of air to be blown over it', and 'alternations of darkness and dim light' to feign the swift passage of night and day, the duration of which will signify the elapse of 'a certain number of centuries', whereupon 'the mechanism may be slowed and a pause made at a given epoch' so that the spectators can 'have presented to their view scenes which are supposed to occur in the future or past'. Clearly, the sensation of time *travel* is to be achieved through media other than film: moving platforms, gusts of air and flickering lights. The spectators will really travel: not through time, but through space. Moving pictures are to be shown only when their travel has come to a stop. And these will show *scenes* and *views*. There will be 'a number of powerful lanterns, throwing the respective portions of the picture, which may be composed of, (1) A hypothetical land-scape, containing also a representation of the inanimate objects in the scene. (2) A slide, or slides, . . . of objects such as a navigable balloon etc., which is required to traverse the scene. (3) Slides or films, representing in successive instantaneous photographs ... the living persons or creatures in their natural motions' (i.e. 'made up characters performing on a stage, with or without a suitable background blending with the main landscape'). Paul's vision is still one rooted in the tradition of the magic lantern and panorama, with its superimposition of multiple images and animated slides. Like a living tableau, movement is restricted to persons and creatures within an essentially immobile scene, enlargement, diminution and dissolving of the scene notwithstanding. As if to underscore this essential stasis, the patent states that Paul prefers 'to arrange the film to travel intermittently instead of continuously and to cut off the light only during the rapid displacement of the film as one picture succeeds another, as by this means less light is wasted than in the case when the light is cut off the greater portion of the time, as in the ordinary kinetoscope mechanism'. In effect, Paul treats the roll of film not as a complete sequence of real-time living pictures, and still less as a space-time unto itself, but as a succession of animated photographs and slides. This accords with the view that what attracted so much attention was the simple, but astounding, fact that the picture was animate: not in its totality, which was already a commonplace, but in its detail. This is why the *OLCJ* (I, February 1905: 73) could casually mention that '[s]ea pictures have always been the most popular of animated subjects', and why it is said that audiences were amazed not by the movement of people, but by the animation of leaves, grass and dust.

Just as Paul's time machine grinds to a halt, however, the patent proposes to heighten the effect of time travel by allowing the spectators to alight from the platform at certain locations and 'be conducted through grounds or buildings arranged to represent exactly one of the epochs through which the traveller is supposed to be travelling'. By implication, Paul considers the scenes and views to be both temporally and spatially retarded: one cannot go into them; one can only scan their surface. With regard to the slides that represent those vehicles required to traverse the scene (2 above), the patent notes that they may only be 'traversed horizontally or vertically'. So, although animated (a portion of the image moves) and dated ('the future', 'the past'), we infer that Paul's films will appear both depthless and timeless. They will not be 'static vehicles' like the Lumières' train darting out of the screen like an arrow.

In fact, setting aside its novel technological basis, Paul's proposed 'journey through time' was a variation on a well-established theme. Were it to have been operationalized, it would have found a ready audience in a public accustomed to being magically transported 'elsewhere' by panoramas, dioramas, peepshows and related attractions (Oettermann 1997; Robinson 1996), and taken on imaginary 'journeys' by the illustrated travel lectures that formed a popular part of the magic lanternists' repertoire (Barber 1993). Walter Tyler Ltd of London advertised over 800,000 items for the 1906–07 lantern season, with sets of slides and lectures that embraced the instructive, the comical and the political (*OLKJ* III (1), November 1906: 13). No small wonder, then, that many of the technological innovations of the day (including animated photographs) seemed to lend themselves to the staging of stationary voyages of one kind or another. Once film-makers began to make their cameras mobile by mounting them on moving trains they began to cover 'almost every exotic railway journey, from the Alps to the American West' (Christie 1994: 18). Here the 'parallel tracks' of the railroad and the cinema came together to launch what Virilio (1989: 110) has aptly dubbed 'the first static vehicle'. Indeed, so-called 'phantom rides' which were filmed from the front of a speeding train were common subjects, and Paul himself made an innovative contribution to the genre by filming from a roller-coaster in his 1898 film *A Switchback Railway*. One of the most ambitious examples of a 'motionless trip' of this kind was Raoul Grimoin-Sanson's cinéo-rama, a simulated balloon ride mounted at the Paris Universal Exposition of 1900 (an event which did much to rekindle public interest in film, especially amongst the bourgeoisie). It involved hand-coloured film footage, shot by no less than ten cameras during a real ascent, projected onto a wrap-around polygonal screen by an equal number of projectors, the results being viewed by an audience positioned in a mocked-up basket. Perhaps unsurprisingly, it was dogged by operational problems, although the myth persists that it was closed down by the authorities, who judged it a fire risk (Abel 1994). A less ambitious and far more commercially successful attempt to stage a simulated trip was devised by George C. Hale, an ex-fire chief from Kansas City in the USA. This involved actuality films taken from moving railway engines being projected to an audience seated in a mocked-up railway carriage (Fielding 1983). Needless to say, this contrivance bore a striking resemblance to Paul's patent. Hale's Tours were launched in America in 1904, coming to England in 1906.

> In 'Hale's Tours' we have one of the cleverest optical illusions of modern times, and the scheme of taking a company by apparent travel through all the countries of the world, has taken the public fancy and brought to the promoters a phenomenal success ... The sensation of the actual travel is made intensely realistic by the various means provided ... Indeed, as we step out of the car, with our auditory and visual faculties still vibrating, it seems a contradiction of nature to find ourselves still in Oxford Street, London.
>
> (*KLW* no. 3, 30 May 1907: 44)

### RENDERING TIME ...

Whether we consider Paul's Time Machine or Hale's Tours we are led to perhaps the greatest conceptual difficulty early film-makers experienced. By filming and projecting a complete sequence of 'instantaneous' photographs (which had hitherto been impossible because of the relative light-insensitivity of chemical emulsions and the inadequacy of the mechanisms for drawing the film stock through the various apparatuses) such devices as the kinetoscope, cinématographe, animatographe and bioscope seem ostensibly to function as *time* machines. They record the passage of time and enable it to be re-presented in another time and place. However, abstraction was a necessary but insufficient basis for engineering space and time. For film truly to become a time *machine*, film-makers and exhibitors needed to devise ways of working with time as if it were a raw material. They needed to render time malleable. But in the first few years of film-making, manufacturing time was almost inconceivable. Consider in this regard a letter sent to the editor of the *OMLJPE* in 1897 (8(93), February: 39), published under the title 'DRUNKENNESS – ON THE SCREEN', and the editor's ironic reply:

> DEAR SIR, – Might it not be of interest to the temperance cause, by means of quick exposures and the cinematograph, to publish a roll of pictures showing the effect of alcohol upon the system by starting with a person perfectly sober, and plying him with drink until he becomes incapable, meantime taking pictures all the time so as to show the results until the patient, in common parlance, 'falls under the table.' Such slides as this would, I think, do much good in showing people what beasts they may become by drink. If you know of any such set of slides, will you kindly let me know where I can obtain such, as I would then at once purchase one of the cinematographic apparatus, and include this subject in a series of lectures. Yours, etc., BARTOS.

> [Seeing that many exposures are made per second, and that the effects of which 'Bartos' speaks would take some considerable time, it is likely that a film to embrace this subject would have to be several miles long. As a film about 70 feet long costs a few pounds, we wonder if 'Bartos' would have sufficient ready cash to purchase one of the desired length, say twenty miles for £7,000 pounds. We do not know where such may be obtained commercially, but if 'Bartos' has money to spare, there will probably be little difficulty on his part in procuring a subject, if the requisite quantity of whisky is forthcoming. – ED.]

Two months later, the *OMLJPE* (8(95), April 1897: 62) published an interesting rejoinder by the *Alliance News*: 'The editor is too humorous in his reply, and Bartos too wholesale in his suggestion to be practical. Photographs of a tippler gradually "getting forrarder" taken at quarter hour intervals, would answer every purpose of instructive illustration.' Even now, however, it is unclear whether any of the writers can conceive of the possibility of recording anything other than real-time or a discrete series of still photographs and slides. Others, however, were beginning to sense that film could render time otherwise. Also in 1897, Birt Acres filmed clouds at about a frame per second, 'thus exaggerating the movement but retaining the form' (Birt Acres, 1897 lecture to the Camera Club, London, quoted in Barnes 1983: 21). A similar type of 'speed magnification' was employed in the 1902 Biograph film of the demolition of the Star Theatre in New York, where time-lapse photography enables the building to 'melt into the ground' in a matter of minutes. And in 1905, the *OLCJ* (I, April: 143) reported Mrs Dukinfield H. Scott's three-year experimentation with the time-lapse kammatography of germinating seeds (early efforts with a cinematograph failed because of the disastrous effect of dampness on the film).

Like Paul's Time Machine, then, early English film-making remained trapped within the problematics set by the magic lantern and the still camera. And just as the manufacture of time was virtually unimaginable, so too was the working of space. For example, Hepworth's *Fatal Sneeze*, made in 1907, follows the increasingly destructive effects of a man's sneezing in accordance with the conventions of the chase genre. Towards the end of the film, a massive sneeze makes the world rock. For the benefit of readers who did not realize that the camera, rather than the world, had been set in motion, the *KLW* speculates that the 'ground oscillation' was *probably* produced by rocking the camera on a see-saw (*KLW* no. 12, 1 August 1907: 181–2). Let us take up this inability to manufacture time and space by examining one final twist to Paul's patent. Having sensed the coming affinity between science fiction, malleable time, and film-making, Paul proposed to convey an astounding sensation of time travel. After the last scene of future ages has been presented, says Paul, 'the spectators should be given the sensation of voyaging backwards from the last epoch to the present', which may be 'accidentally passed', and upon 'coming to a standstill, after which the impression of travelling forward again to the present epoch may be given, and the re-arrival notified'. As we have already established, by moving, shaking, blowing and narrating, Paul hopes to give his customers the sensation of travelling *in* time. Assuming for the sake of argument that travelling in space can be made to feel like travelling 'in' time, we are at a loss to understand how this sensation could be given a *direction*: specifically, forwards or backwards. This indiscernability is the basis for one of the earliest operations that film-makers and exhibitors made on time: *reversal.*

As early as 1900, audiences were treated to filmic palindromes. Cecil Hepworth's 1900 film *The Bathers* and *The House That Jack Built*, also made in 1900 (director unknown), are good examples. In the latter, a boy knocks over a house of bricks. An intertitle reads: 'Reversed.' Then the boy magically 'rebuilds' the house as the original sequence is shown in reverse. Similarly, and despite the Lumières' fondness for actuality, their 1896 film *Démolition d'un Mur* was routinely run backwards as well as forwards. Stop-motion (*arrêt de caméra*) is employed in G. A. Smith's 1898 film *Santa Claus*, Cecil Hepworth's 1900 films *Explosion of a Motor Car* and *Clown and Police*, and Percy Stow's 1902 film *How to Stop a Motor Car*, in which one policeman is run over whilst another stops the car when it 'bounces' off him into a hedge. Indeed, stop-motion – which could be more accurately described as 'substitution splicing' – provided the means for the development of frame animation around 1900. W. R. Booth's 1907 film *The Sorcerer's Scissors*, Arthur Melbourne-Cooper's 1908 film *Dreams of Toyland* and Percy Stow's 1910 film *The Jealous Doll* are exemplary. Added complication appears in James Williamson's 1901 film *The Puzzled Bather and His Animated*

*Clothes*, which uses stop-motion to effect a looping of time so that a would-be bather tries in vain to undress, dives into the water fully clothed and reverses out in a swimsuit, whereupon his clothes leap out of the water and 'magic' themselves onto him. Stop-motion time loops also feature in the 1901 film *Man in Bedroom* (director unknown), in which a man repeatedly undresses only to find himself magically dressed again. A similar effect is employed in W. R. Booth's 1901 film *Undressing Extraordinary; or, the Troubles of a Tired Traveller*, although on each occasion the man is re-dressed in a different costume, which gives the impression of magical transformation rather than a looping of time. Double printing was used to ghostly effect in films such as W. R. Booth's 1901 *The Haunted Curiosity Shop, The Magic Sword; a Mediaeval Mystery* and *Scrooge; or, Marley's Ghost*, and Cecil Hepworth's 1904 film *The Johan Man; or, the Traveller Bewitched*. Meanwhile, in *The Frustrated Elopement* of 1902, directed by Percy Stow, protagonists slide up a ladder using reverse motion. This effect was perhaps most famously used in Frank Mottershaw's 1905 film *An Eccentric Burglary*. Other notable spatial and temporal operations include the cutting from one scene to another, such as in G. A. Smith's 1899 film *Kiss in the Tunnel*; the cutting to an unexpected point of view, such as occurs in W. R. Booth's 1899 film *Upside Down; or, the Human Flies*; and the splitting of the screen, as in James Williamson's 1901 film *Are You There?*, by which means the audience sees both halves of a telephone conversation simultaneously (a technique that was largely superseded by reaction shots and parallel action, although it made a recovery with the onset of deep-focus cinematography). Lewin Fitzhamon's 1905 film *Falsely Accused* offers an early use of a point-of-view shot as well as artificial lighting for dramatic effect. G. A. Smith's 1900 films *As Seen Through a Telescope* and *Grandma's Reading Glass* were possibly the first in which scenes were divided into a number of shots using masked and magnified inserts.

Now, while there may not be a recognizable science fiction film in sight amongst any of the earliest British-made films, each and every one of them renders time malleable, even if they do nothing more than abstract an instant from its real-time duration. To that extent, even the earliest actuality films countersign Paul's untimely patent for a filmic Time Machine, for a vernacular rendition of space-time relativity. We have explosives indeed.

### ACKNOWLEDGEMENTS

Much of the archival work for this chapter was funded by the Arts and Humanities Research Board (Award No. B/SG/AN2054/APN10258). We would like to thank staff at the National Film and Television Archive at the British Film Institute, London, particularly Simon Baker and Kathleen Dickson, and the Library of Congress, Washington DC. We are also grateful to Morag Bell, Phil Hubbard and Heather Norris Nicholson for insightful comments on earlier versions of the chapter.

## NOTES

1 Since there was no systematic recording of early films, the attribution of titles, directors, production companies, release dates, form and content remains a tentative affair. Several versions of a film were often released, exhibitors had considerable scope to edit, rework and recontextualize the films that they acquired, and plagiarism was rife. Most of the films produced in the 1890s and 1900s no longer survive, and those that do are often incomplete. Contemporary catalogue descriptions and film reviews are neither comprehensive nor entirely accurate, not least because of the variable conditions under which early films were produced, distributed and exhibited. It should also be borne in mind that a great many early films were coloured either in whole or in part and often accompanied by sound effects, music, song and narrative. Usai (1994) provides a helpful introduction to such considerations.

2 When referring to the English trade journals published in the 1890s and 1900s, the following abbreviations have been employed:

| | |
|---|---|
| B | *The Bioscope* |
| CBM | *Cinematography and Bioscope Magazine* |
| E | *The Era* |
| KLW | *The Kinematograph and Lantern Weekly* |
| OLCJ | *The Optical Lantern and Cinematograph Journal* |
| OLKJ | *The Optical Lantern and Kinematograph Journal* |
| OMLJPE | *The Optical Magic Lantern Journal and Photographic Enlarger* |
| PRR | *Photographic Review of Reviews: A Synopsis of Photographic Literature of the World* |
| WB | *The Westminster Budget* |

# 10

# WHAT WE CAN SAY ABOUT NATURE

## FAMILIAR GEOGRAPHIES, SCIENCE FICTION AND POPULAR PHYSICS

*Sheila Hones*

No matter how weird, new or unexpected, the spaces and places of science fiction are always realized through the conventional world-views of implied reader–writer communities. Off-world narrative adventures are always grounded in familiar geographies, just as those geographies are in turn always partly the product of familiar narratives, shared ways of describing, and rhetorical conventions. The tightness of this relationship between 'what we know', 'what we can say', and 'what we can imagine' is fundamental to science fiction, where writers create strange worlds by reference to familiar geographies and within the conventions of familiar narrative forms. The very narrative predictability of much science fiction actually facilitates its articulation of invented, unpredictable, idiosyncratic and destabilizing fictive worlds, as the strength of the reader's confidence in a familiar narrative form compensates for the unfamiliarity of the narrative content. The willing reader agrees to a self-contained reality within which the weird is unexceptional, and where the mundanity of recognizable narrative style renders the unimagined imaginable.

Like much science fiction, mass-market non-fiction works of popular science also routinely sell themselves as the textual articulation of the seriously weird. But where science fiction most commonly disguises its rhetorical connection to the reader's familiar world in the creation of what it presents as entirely self-contained textual realities, works of popular physics typically introduce themselves by reference to 'real world' genres such as travel writing and then work hard to draw direct explanatory parallels between their subject matter and the implied reader's taken-for-granted geographies. The problem with this rhetorical strategy is that many of the phenomena and events outlined by the science texts are not only practically unimaginable but, for the non-specialist at least, completely counter-intuitive, and this creates a clash between content and genre. In *Beyond the Quantum*, for example, a mass-market introduction to 'God, reality [and] consciousness in the new scientific revolution', Michael Talbot remarks that the implications of one important experiment 'are so profound they seem more science fiction than science fact', because its result 'assaults simple common sense' (Talbot 1987: 1, 2).

Perhaps if quantum physics seemed *more* like science fiction to the general reader, if popular texts presented themselves more explicitly as paraphrases of self-contained narratives, they would actually make better sense. After all, at least according to most popularizations, there are some interesting parallels between making science fiction and making physics. Two key elements involved in the reading or writing of science fiction – the suspension of disbelief and a reliance on self-contained narrative – seem to have interesting equivalents in the working practices of creative physicists. For the reader of science fiction, the suspension of disbelief is both contingent and contained, and in actual scientific practice a similar bracketing of common sense seems to function as a constructive willingness to outflank assumption. And where the science fiction writer creates a world of contingent sense in a self-contained narrative, the creative physicist seems also in some sense to 'create' a subatomic world through internally consistent description. In the study of this subatomic world, the point, according to the physicist Niels Bohr, is not 'how nature is' but rather 'what we can say about nature' (Gregory 1990: 95). And so, if we are to believe what we are told by most popularizations of modern physics, quantum physics and science fiction have at least this one thing in common: neither presents us with 'pictures of a world that is somehow independent of their descriptions' (Gregory 1990: 95).

Reflecting on the genres of science fiction and popular science, this chapter explores the idea that any rethinking of spatial common sense will demand conscious attention to 'what we can say about nature' and especially to the rhetorical foundations of how we say it. The chapter makes this exploration through a comparison of a group of popular science texts with one very well-known science fiction novel, looking particularly at the different ways in which these writings attempt to convey or create new understandings of space for the general reader. The science fiction text is Frank Herbert's hugely popular 1965 novel *Dune*. The scientific popularizations are mainly introductions to quantum physics from the period 1955–90, and include texts produced by both academic scientists and popular writers. In exploring the ways in which these two types of text approach the articulation of unfamiliar geographies (fictional and subatomic), the essay concentrates on the textual strategies they adopt, and assesses in particular their different uses of figurative language and rhetorical structure.

Like extreme forms of travel writing or spatial theory, science fiction and popular physics, at their best, are constantly faced with the challenge of subverting their own underlying spatial assumptions. As Michael Curry (1996) points out in his discussion of specifically geographical writing, *The Work in the World*, the problem for these kinds of writing is that their very instrument of reinvention or destabilization, the text, exists firmly within the familiar world, not only rhetorically but also literally. Addressing the work of Henri Lefebvre, Curry argues that despite the way it emphasized new conceptions of space it nonetheless inevitably 'appealed to a variety of spatial practices and conceptions' that Lefebvre would have been sure 'his reader understood and expected, and that are part and parcel of the system of written works' (Curry 1996: 11). As Curry points out, 'what we think about space and nature is not locked up in our minds . . . What we think is there to be seen, in the ways we write, argue, cite, publish' (Curry 1996: 13). For this reason, written attempts to rethink or reinvent common conceptions of space and nature are always forced to engage in some kind of struggle with rhetorical convention, as they try to contradict and also to exploit the implications of their own textual forms.

### THE CRUMBLING EDGE OF THOUGHT

If, like much science fiction, physics is simply an 'imaginative version of how the world might be put together', then it is not surprising that (as the physicist Frank Oppenheimer put it) there is always 'a groping for language' at the cutting edge of scientific discovery (Gregory 1990: 201; Cole 1984: 155). Among creative physicists there seems to be some general acknowledgement of the revolutionary powers of articulation and the extent to which language actually creates those things that it describes. Bruce Gregory, for example, insists that physics is not some thing explained in language, but actually 'is a language'. Gregory argues that when Einstein invented a new way of talking about space and time, 'as though they were a unity', this new articulation showed that 'both space and time are human inventions – ways of talking about the world' (Gregory 1990: 70). As journalist K. C. Cole (1984: 170) explains, in this sense mathematics 'is particularly useful jargon in that it allows you to describe things beautifully and accurately without even knowing what they are. You can forget about the problem of trying to imagine the unimaginable in everyday terms, because you don't need to.' Cole quotes Richard Feynman's famous remark that 'the glory of mathematics is that we do not have to say what we are talking about' (p. 170).

Science fiction writers, in the same way, never have to say, explicitly, what they are talking about. They accept no obligation to relate their material to a common-sense context, but simply talk their talk within the self-contained system that the talk creates. And this is the crux of the problem with quantum physics for non-specialists who have been led to expect that science 'fact' will connect to the 'real world'. The challenge to common sense in popular science seems neither contingent nor contained. The relationship between reality and language, between things and their descriptions, therefore becomes alarmingly problematic. Is a quark really a physical thing or is it some kind of metaphor? Is the whole of quantum physics just a kind of usable fiction? Struggling to describe by comparison with common-sense reality 'things' which are essentially abstract mathematical descriptions, popular physics frequently gets tangled up in a struggle with the distinction between invention and description.

As Gary Zukav admits in his overview of the new physics, trying to talk about quantum physics in non-mathematical, everyday language 'is like trying to

explain an LSD experience'. 'We try to use familiar concepts as points of departure', he writes, 'but beyond that, the familiar concepts do not fit the phenomena'
(Zukav 1979: 202). Zukav's reference to 'points of departure', with its implications of location and journey across conventionally mapped space, exemplifies the
very problem he is describing. Much popular physics is limited in this way by its
most hopeful textual strategies; its genre references and explanatory similes end
up trapping the reader in conventional space. Because, as Richard Feynman has
pointed out, when mathematical models get translated into 'metaphors drawn
from everyday experience', we inevitably 'get into trouble' (Cole 1984: 170).

We 'cannot visualize quantum mechanics', the physicist Victor Weisskopf
explains, because 'our imagination is just not up to it' (Cole 1984: 173). But
promotional materials for works of popular physics are nonetheless often
explicitly visual, presenting the reading experience as an exploration of new
territory, or a tour of exotic scenery. And the reliance on a comparison with real-
world travel immediately gets the reader into trouble, because while the back
covers promise guided expeditions, once into the text the metaphor collapses
relatively quickly. Because 'everybody likes adventure stories', as Paul Davies
explains in his book about the search for a 'grand unified theory of nature', the
characters in his *Superforce* are scientists venturing into 'the shadowy world of
fundamental physics', on a 'quest' for 'a prize of unimaginable value – nothing
less than the key to the universe' (Davies 1985: 5). Not only is this scenario of
spatial reinvention itself spatialized very conventionally, the reader expectations
created by defining a text as an 'adventure story' are likely to go unfulfilled.

The narrative conventions of adventure stories are well defined, and works of
popular physics that present themselves in the guise of such a story but fail to
achieve the narrative resolution implied within the genre demand of the reader a
major mid-stream readjustment. Readers who set out on a quest to find the key
to the universe but find themselves on the last page of the adventure lost in a fog
may feel somewhat frustrated. Nonetheless, this is a very common pattern.
Readers of K. C. Cole's (1984) *Sympathetic Vibrations* are told in the preliminary
promotional pages that they will 'read this fascinating book with emotions not
unlike those felt by Europeans of the Renaissance when they listened with awe to
travelers' tales of exotic scenes and wild adventures on strange continents'. The
back jacket of Werner Heisenberg's (1962) *Physics and Philosophy* presents it as a
'layperson's tour of [a] strange new world', and John Gribbin's (1986) *In Search
of the Big Bang* is advertised as 'an extraordinary journey across space and time to
find the ultimate cosmic truth'. Bruce Gregory's (1990) *Inventing Reality* 'makes
for smooth riding over the rough terrain of modern physics', Fred Alan Wolf's
(1988) *Parallel Universes* 'deftly guides the reader through the paradoxes of
today's physics to explore a realm of scientific speculation' and Anthony Zee's
(1986) *Fearful Symmetry* invites the reader to think of physics 'as a dynamic
journey to fathom the workings of the universe'. The 'world of leptons, hadrons,
gluons and quarks' may be 'baffling and seemingly lawless', like some ultimate
Wild West, but within the safe confines of the generic adventure story or

guidebook, these advertisements promise that the reader will remain unthreatened (Pagels 1984: back cover). Narrative rhetoric will hold them safe behind the wall separating the observer and the observed, despite the paradoxical fact that one of the key points of the universe they are being invited to explore is that this wall does not exist.

The collapse of the wall, the plunge into metaphors of fog, chaos and alarming unity, often happens quite dramatically inside the text, as for example in Banesh Hoffman's classic 1959 work *The Strange Story of the Quantum*. The work is at first presented 'as a guide to those who would explore the theories by which the scientist seeks to comprehend the mysterious world of the atom' (Hoffman 1959: ix). But the reinvention of its narrative structure that occurs midway through the text in a sudden 'Author's Warning to the Reader' is dramatic:

> If you have read thus far, there is no dignified way of escape left to you. You have paid your fare, and climbed to the highest peak of the roller coaster. You have therefore let yourself in for the inevitable consequences. It is no use trying to back out. You had warning in the preface of what to expect, and if contemplation of the heights there described now makes you giddy and apprehensive, I cannot accept responsibility. The going will be rough, but I can promise you excitement aplenty. So hold tight to your seat and hope for the best. We are about to push off into vertiginous space.
>
> (Hoffman 1959: 72)

'Stripped of mathematics', the back cover of Gary Zukav's overview promises, 'physics becomes pure enchantment.' But engagement with this enchanted world requires of the readers first that they 'stand at the edge of an abyss, still on the solid ground of Newtonian physics' but looking 'into the void', and then that they 'leap boldly' off it 'into the new physics'. John Barrow's work (Barrow 1990) is promoted as a 'rewarding journey to the limits of space and time', but readers are warned to expect 'a certain dizziness' when they reach those limits, 'at the crumbling edge of thought'. No matter that 'Barrow leads us to that extreme with wit and grace, making the journey an enjoyable one', we are still left at the end of the story on the crumbling edge of an abyss. Despite claims to the contrary, nobody 'tells the complete story of quantum mechanics, a truth far stranger than any fiction', which is what the back cover claims for John Gribbin's work, because it isn't a 'complete story' and there isn't 'a' truth. At the end of his narrative exploration, Anthony Zee explains that he has 'saved the discussion of time reversal invariance for the closing pages' because, he tells us, 'I do not understand it. Neither does anyone else' (Zee 1986: 178). This is not the kind of narrative closure we expect in a complete story. But as Fred Wolf explains at the end of *Taking the Quantum Leap*, we live in a 'world of paradox and utter confusion for human, limited intelligence'. Life as we know it, he admits, 'can only exist through the blessing of uncertainty, and security is a myth . . . We must accept the uncertainty of our positions' (Wolf 1981: 249–50). A central problem with many popularizations is that while it is one thing to accept the insecurity of our positions as revealed in a conventional scientific paper or a securely narrated adventure story, it is asking a lot of the reader to accept both cosmic and rhetorical insecurity at the same time.

## THE COMPLETE STORY

The 'uncertainty of our positions' that Wolf refers to is caused in some sense by the vertiginous loss of spatial confidence that quantum theory descriptions of nature so easily inspire: radical disorientation, or what Robert Nadeau terms 'a kind of death of ourselves' (Nadeau 1981: 13). The advantage that science fiction has over popular scientific explanation is that in its creation of self-contained alternative realities, 'topoi' inhabited by 'actants' in Carl Malmgren's terms, it routinely and conventionally asks its readers to reimagine familiar geographies and grasp the essence of new ways of existing in space without direct or metaphorical explanation (Malmgren 1991: 7). The other reality, taken for granted by the text's actants, is experienced vicariously by the story's readers, implied, lived in the text, and not explained. The troublesome distinction between observer and observed in some sense disappears, as the text and reader together create the unfamiliar reality, and the 'death of ourselves' is experienced not as 'bone-chilling terror' but as an essential aspect of the pleasurable defamiliarization of fantasy fiction.

Engaged in reading a well-constructed science fiction story, the reader takes that dissolution of the boundaries between self and world happily for granted. In a sense, the reading experience actually functions as a metaphor for what (apparently) the Copenhagen Interpretation of quantum mechanics seems to suggest is true of life in general: that 'physical theory deals only with an observed world . . . and [that] the observer has an uncontrollable and nonremovable effect on what is observed' as 'the observer and the observed form an integrated unit that cannot be broken down into independent components' (Jones 1983: 6). The role of consciousness in the world may be basically 'passive' and not 'active or creative', but it is nonetheless inextricably woven into it. In much the same way, reader and text form an integrated unit; any particular reader's imagination, experiences, memories, learned reading strategies, habits of concretization and expectations will have an uncontrollable and nonremovable effect on what is read.

The readiness of the implied readers to engage in limited and pleasurable defamiliarization means that they are not only prepared to experience disorientation as diversion, they are also prepared to take for granted such key points as the idea that the world is not independent of its description and that expression creates reality. Conventionally constructed science fiction narratives, like mathematics, work within a closed system and hence allow authors 'to describe things beautifully . . . without even knowing what they are'. In science fiction, again as in maths, 'we do not have to say what we are talking about'. We can create it by talking about it. The fog, the oneness, the drop off the edge – the alarming unity of observer and observed that causes so much trouble in popular physics – can be spread out and disentangled in the textual spatialization of narrative.

Paradoxically, the extremely tight and conventional narrative structure of much mass-market science fiction is precisely what permits this kind of reconceptualization. In his work *Physics As Metaphor*, Roger Jones argues that 'what we seek and enjoy most is the novelty of variation within prescribed limits', and this assessment of our need for spatialization (novelty creating a sense of time or difference within limits which allow for a sense of location) goes far to explain the potential the genre offers us for playing with our views of space (Jones 1983: 90). With its highly predictable narrative structures – unlike the disrupted adventure stories of the popular science texts discussed above – science fiction stories simultaneously reassure us with their re-inscriptions of familiar geographies and create opportunities to consider new ones. In their work on the impact of quantum theory and general relativity on literature since the 1920s, *Einstein As Myth and Muse* (Donley and Friedman 1985), Alan Friedman and Carol Donley argue that modern physics can be seen reflected in a shift from the kind of 'beginning–middle–end' narrative that is typical of conventional science fiction and that they associate with cause–effect determinism and Euclidean geometry, towards the more 'open' forms of surrealist or existentialist fiction. In discussing this move away from closed, linear and hierarchical forms they emphasize particularly the breakdown of the distinction between author and work or subject and object that can be found in 'serious' literature since the 1920s. 'Serious literature' has, according to this view, been engaging with new approaches to space through experimentation with narrative convention. Science fiction, in contrast, engages with the same problem precisely through its suppression of its own textuality, remaining a very 'closed' and at the same time spatialized, or 'spread out', text.

The advantage that science fiction has over scientific explanation is its ability to create a world in which the weird seems unexceptional. Where physicists talk in potentials – 'if we had eyes to see it' – science fiction can simulate for the reader some aspects of the experience of having such eyes: with Jessica's first experience with the spice drug in *Dune*, for example, the reader shares her sense of heightened awareness and connection with other 'life' and understands what she means when she explains 'I'm like a person whose hands were kept numb . . . until one day the ability to feel is forced into them' (Herbert 1965: 359). Jones explains how we use Newton's language of the calculus to 'help our poor eyes see what should have been perfectly clear from the outset'. 'A more visionary creature than a human being might not need the calculus', he speculates; 'that creature might simply see trajectory and acceleration as the same thing' (Jones 1983: 39). Space-time, too, might be imaginable to some other creature, and while we cannot imagine it, we can at least imagine that creature. 'The terrain of space-time, if we had eyes to see it', Robert Nadeau tells us, 'is mountainous in the region of large or massive bodies, like our sun, and evens out into something like a flat plain in those remote areas of space where matter does not exist in any great concentration' (Nadeau 1981: 48). Frank Herbert's novel provides us with eyes that can see this: the eyes of its hero Paul Atreides as he becomes increasingly immersed in his vision of a 'timeless stratum where he could view time . . . a trinocular vision that permitted him to see time-become-space' (Herbert 1965: 295).

## DUNE

Although the geographer I. G. Simmons has cited Herbert's Dune novels as outstanding examples of science fiction's characteristic attention to settings and surroundings worked out through the invention of a new but credible ecology, the novels are equally remarkable in their invention of a credible theatre of space-time (Simmons 1993: 97). This dimension to the novel's setting emerges gradually as Herbert expands Paul's awareness of his powers of understanding step by step. At first this theatre is presented in metaphors of terrain and landscape, with Paul orienting himself within his unfolding sense of space-time quite conventionally; the 'terrain' is relatively stable and presented as a kind of traversable landscape. Critically, the 'terrain' is metaphorical for the reader, but literal for the protagonist. Paul really exists in this multidimensional world, in which he climbs to a 'new level' and, 'clutching at a precarious hold', looks around (Herbert 1965: 193). The reader cannot say precisely how meta-phorical or how literal this description might be; the text does not have to say what it is talking about. 'It was as though he existed within a globe with avenues radiating away in all directions', the narrative explains (Herbert 1965: 193). Life is 'spreading outward like an expanding bubble' (Herbert 1965: 197). Whether that 'as if' and that 'like' are his or ours remains unclear. 'I have another kind of sight', Paul realizes. 'I see another kind of terrain' (Herbert 1965: 194). Gradually, he accustoms himself to a 'timeless stratum where he could view time', the past and the future become 'winds', and he develops a 'trinocular vision that permitted him to see time-become-space' (Herbert 1965: 295). As Paul becomes more and more immersed in this space-time, the land-scape begins to shift around him: his point of view is no longer fixed or separable from his surroundings. Early on, his vision appears to 'have shifted and approached him from a different angle while he remained motionless'; later it surrounds him in flow completely, like moving water, and he is no longer holding on to something and looking around, but completely caught up within it (Herbert 1965: 244–5). At a critical moment in the story he finds himself in a place that lies 'as a blurred nexus in his path . . . like a gigantic rock in the flood, creating maelstroms in the current around it' (Herbert 1965: 304). He begins to lose his ability to separate himself from his space-time surroundings, worrying his mother by speaking of the dead in the present tense, and clearly existing in the flood of some multidimensional flux. 'I need time now to consider the future that is a past within my mind', he says (Herbert 1965: 404). He himself becomes 'a theater of processes': 'he could not escape the fear that he had somehow overrun himself, lost his position in time' (Herbert 1965: 380).

Merging the rhetoric of science fiction and science fantasy in a half-mythic half-technological narrative, Herbert creates a 'realm' for his hero that can be expressed as 'alam al-mithal', the place 'where all limitations are removed' (Herbert 1965: 506). Paul comes gradually to this 'metaphysical realm', learning to survive within a subjectivity that allows, for example, for the sense that 'his entire future was becoming like a river hurtling towards a chasm – the violent nexus beyond which all was fog and clouds' (Herbert 1965: 388). A 'grey-cloud-future – with its feeling that the entire universe rolled towards a boiling nexus hung around him like a phantom world' (Herbert 1965: 436). By the end of the novel, through his heroic existence in this strange world, living out in 'normal' life the awareness that in his measurement or assessment of space-time 'a kind of Heisenberg indeterminacy intervened: the expenditure of energy that revealed what he saw, changed what he saw', Paul has confronted and overcome for us the fears that Robert Nadeau characterized as a 'death of ideas about substance and relation' that was 'a kind of death of ourselves' (Herbert 1965: 296; Nadeau 1981: 13). Paul fears this 'place' because 'removal of all limitations meant removal of all points of reference. In the landscape of myth he could not orient himself and say: "I am I because I am here"' (Herbert 1965: 382). This is the fear of what Roger Jones calls 'being swallowed up, dissolved, and blended with all other things in some primal uniform glob' (1983: 62). But just as we inevitably spatialize this fear of the loss of space – into those quantum leaps off crumbling edges, for example, that characterize works of popular physics – so the narrative of Paul's encounter with his fears spreads them out and disentangles them for us.

Crucial to this reassuring textual creation of familiar space is the way in which from the novel's first page the reader is placed in the story's own space and time, on Caladan, with Arrakis waiting both elsewhere and in the next chapter, located in the 72nd year of the Padishah Emperor, Shaddam IV, and at the same textual moment suspended in the 'ever-extended now' of the novel's hero, Paul Atreides. Reassured from the beginning by the narrative security of the novel's extensive textual apparatus – chapter headings that apparently come from other writings of the same world, a glossary, a map and four appendices – the reader is led gradually into a vicarious or concretized simulation of the experience of unified space-time. The careful creation of a fictitious context for the narrative – a kind of appeal to authority that has the effect of firmly placing the story in objective space and time – thus opens out the space within which the reader can experience the collapse of space and time into undifferentiated oneness without (as Richard Feynman puts it) going 'down the drain'. The framing of the narrative with quotations, maps and explanations has the effect of creating the kind of surrounding space that Michael Curry refers to in his discussion of the geographical *Work in the World*. In this case entirely invented, the apparatus nonetheless serves to place the reader safely within the very conventions of time and place it is questioning, in the same way that, as Curry explains, Lefebvre

questions a conventional understanding of space that he simultaneously reinscribes by writing 'as though the entire text exists as a whole in a textual present',
his rhetorical style having the effect that 'the text, from beginning to end is given
to the reader all at once' (Curry 1996: 182).

This rhetorical spreading out of textual time and space is consolidated in
*Dune* through the second very conventional rhetorical strategy of the omniscient
self-effacing narrator. The idea that the novel's hero, Paul, is 'the one who can be
many places at once' is created by an unmarked narrator who is inevitably, in the
text, the other one who can be all over the place at the same time. The narrator's
omniscient grasp of the thoughts and feelings of all the actants in this story works
just as critically as the text's apparatus to spatialize the dramatization of collapsed
space. Italics in the text mark both insertions from other texts and these
moments of simultaneous thought. '*Damn that Jessica!* The Reverend Mother
thought . . . Paul looked at his mother. *She told the truth* . . . Feyd-Rautha nod-
ded, thinking: *this is more like it*' (Herbert 1965: 6, 11, 18). Fritjof Capra, in *The
Tao of Physics*, quotes Bernard Lovell's version of what happens when we try to
imagine time and space before the 'big bang': 'we reach the great barrier of
thought', he explains, and 'I feel as though I've suddenly driven into a great fog
barrier where the familiar world has disappeared' (Capra 1983: 219). The advantage for the reader of *Dune* is that even when Paul disappears into such a fog
barrier, the narrator does not. The narrative's references to rituals of memory,
spice-drug experiences of other lives and times, and visions of past and future –
as well as the narrator's ability to dip in and out of the minds of the novel's
actants – suggest the implosion of time and space, ironically, by spreading it out.
When Paul finds himself crossing a time barrier into a fog, the narrative voice
and the reader with it, separated from him by the conventions of an omniscient
narrator unlocatable within the spaces of the text, remain outside it:

> Paul felt a kind of elation. In some recent instant, he had crossed a time
> barrier into more unknown territory. He could sense the darkness ahead,
> nothing revealed to his inner eye. It was as though some step he had taken
> had plunged him into a well . . . or into the trough of a wave where the
> future was invisible. The landscape had undergone a profound shifting.
> (Herbert 1965: 266)

In this way, the novel presents the experience of a unified space-time through the
strategy of a textual disentanglement: impossibly, we have the collapsed space of
oneness and the spread-out spaces of a distinct and omniscient point of view at
the same time. The novel's controlled and characteristically science fiction tensions between the unfamiliar and the familiar, chaos and place, suspense and
control in this way create for the reader a paradoxical context in which some
conceptualization of quantum non-locality becomes possible.

## CONCLUSION

Science fiction usefully draws our attention to the inventive, persuasive and even normative powers of shared narratives, reminding us of the power all story-tellers have to reinvent the obvious and redefine the natural. And while science fiction and 'real' physics are clearly vastly different endeavours, there is some point to a game of finding similarities. According to Niels Bohr, physics is not so much a search for the 'laws' of nature as a search for the most useful system: 'the laws of physics are our laws, not nature's' (Gregory 1990: 96). Modern science, in this sense, is aimed not so much at explaining things but at making tools, inventing ways of talking about the world that will render it less mysterious by making it more predictable. Introductions to popular science that set out to present modern physics more explicitly as the creative product of working scientists and less as a description of 'the way things are' – that presented it more directly as a form of narrative construction – might help the general reader to understand more clearly what physics really does.

According to Bruce Gregory, we have widely come to believe that Galileo was right in believing the universe to be a text 'written in the language of mathematics'. Gregory notes that the language of the mathematicians has been 'interpreted more and more as being the language in which nature is written' (Gregory 1990: 17–18). But as Niels Bohr's remark suggests, physicists are not, ultimately, communicating directly with the mathematically-pronouncing Voice of the Universe but are simply rendering an unimaginable nature into terms which can be productively manipulated. As Werner Heisenberg insisted, 'what we observe is not nature itself, but nature exposed to our method of questioning' (Heisenberg 1962: 58). This is something that science fiction can help us remember and that popular science ought to make clear. As K. C. Cole insists, science is not something beyond our everyday experience. 'People talk about traveling into *outer space*', she remarks, 'as if it were some strange and exotic landscape.' But it's an illusion: as she points out, in actuality 'we are living in outer space all the time' (Cole 1984: 23–4). The work of science fiction writers like Frank Herbert productively reminds us of the extent to which we participate in the construction of the spaces we inhabit and draws our attention to one liberating way of interpreting the constructions of modern physics: as Gary Zukav cheerfully insists, we are not 'Cogs in the Machine' at all, but 'Creators of the Universe' (Zukav 1979: 114).

# 11

## MURRAY BOOKCHIN ON MARS!

## THE PRODUCTION OF NATURE IN KIM STANLEY ROBINSON'S MARS TRILOGY

*Shaun Huston*

While science fiction most often conjures up images of technology and the so-called 'hard sciences', writers in the genre also address human social relations. One of the exemplars of this tradition is Kim Stanley Robinson. In his award-winning Mars trilogy, *Red, Green* and *Blue Mars*, Robinson uses the idea of transforming Mars into a habitable planet to explore the ethics and limits of the human ability to (re)produce nature. Philosophically and theoretically, Robinson's writing has particular relevance to the work of social ecologist Murray Bookchin.[1] The Mars trilogy provides a fruitful exploration of what Bookchin refers to as third or free nature, a synthesis of first (bio-physical) nature and second (human social) nature wherein humans 'co-operate' with first nature and directly participate in the evolution of life.

This chapter is divided into two main sections. The first sketches out Bookchin's 'dialectical naturalism' and considers a particular critique of the idea of third nature. The second section introduces Robinson's Mars trilogy and interprets those works as an exploration of free nature.

### BOOKCHIN'S PHILOSOPHY OF NATURE

Intellectually, Bookchin falls in the Western tradition of dialectical thought represented by Aristotle, Hegel, Marx and the Frankfurt School. Bookchin's relationship with Marx is largely oppositional; he rejects the centrality of class struggle, focusing on a more general struggle with hierarchy/domination (for example, 1971 and 1989; Purchase 1994: 57–70). At the same time, Bookchin clearly draws insights from Marx's analysis of capitalism (Kovel 1998: 37–48). His early work on cities, *The Limits of the City*, directly builds on Marx's observations regarding uneven development between city and country (1974: vi–xi, 4, 101). Similarly, Bookchin draws on Adorno and Horkheimer's critique of instrumental reason in developing his own critique of domination, both human on human and human on nature, but criticizes their work for reducing nature to a passive, crude object transcended by the human species (1982: 270–80). Bookchin develops his notion of 'eduction', or reasoning that draws out the developmental potential of things in nature, and nature itself, from Aristotle and Hegel, though he argues that their dialectics require a sense of natural evolution to be truly ecological, that is, a sense of nature as a 'flowing continuum' rather than a static 'ladder of Being' (1995: 124, also 119–33; Purchase 1994: 68–70). Perhaps the critical distinction between Bookchin and his influences, especially Marx and the Frankfurt School, is that Bookchin reasons that the domination of nature by the human species was preceded by, and emerged from, the domination of human by human (hierarchy), rather than in the reverse (Merchant 1994: 8–9; Bookchin 1990: 154).

Politically, Bookchin's closest predecessor, both historically and substantively, is the anarchist Peter Kropotkin. Kropotkin contributes several historical and theoretical themes to Bookchin's work, notably the rooting of co-operation (mutual aid) and ethics in nature, historical connections between cities and human freedom and the image of a free world made from regional confederations of cities and towns (which, in turn, are organized as grassroots confederations) (Macauley 1998; Purchase 1994: 57–70; also Bookchin 1990: 154 and 1992b: 152–3). It is out of this synthesis of an 'ecologized' dialectical tradition and anarchist communism that Bookchin develops his philosophy of nature.

As noted in the introduction, Bookchin conceives of nature as developing through three forms. Initially, there is first or bio-physical nature. In this form, nature strives for self-awareness, providing the basis for the emergence of the human species. With the human species comes second or social nature. In second nature, the development of life, as represented by the human species, and the interaction between life and its environments become self-conscious and self-directed, rather than instinctive and guided primarily by deep evolutionary memory. However, because human and non-human nature do not actually break from one another, but remain intertwined, it is necessary to bring social nature into conscious synthesis with first nature. Bookchin refers to this synthesis as third or 'free' nature. Here, human-defined second nature is integrated with first nature so that the human species actively participates in the differentiation and evolution of life.

Third nature is '*free* nature – that is, an ethical humanly scaled community that establishes a creative interaction with its natural environment' (Bookchin 1992b: xvii, italics in original). This integration of first and second nature heals the (illusory) split between 'the social' and 'the natural' that occurs in the elaboration of second nature. According to Bookchin:

Both are in a very real sense *natural*, and their naturalness finds its evolutionary realization in those remarkable primates we call human beings who, consciously responding to a sense of obligation to the ecological integrity of the planet, bring their rational, communicative, richly social,

imaginative, and aesthetic capacities to the service of the nonhuman world
as well as the human.

(1992b: xvii–xviii, italics in original)

Thus, in reaching third nature, humans realize their potential as 'nature rendered
self-conscious' (Bookchin 1982: 315–16). In second nature, humans emerge as a
species able to think and act in and for itself. This achievement lays the ground
for the human species to think and act in and for the world, or nature, at large
(see 1982, 1986, 1992b and 1995).

Bookchin's account of third nature is heavily weighted towards describing
human social relations and structures. His description of how first and second
nature can, and will, be integrated is much less developed. This leaves his work
open to the criticism that third nature is, at best, recklessly vague, and, at worst,
plays to human hubris regarding non-human nature. Eckersley (1992: 137)
argues that 'Bookchin's vision of stewardship does not qualify how and to what
extent our responsibility is to be discharged'. She proceeds to provide a list of
potentially disastrous human interventions into the evolution of life (wholesale
introductions of new species, the 'greening' of deserts, etc.), not to mention the
cumulative history of past and present human interventions. Furthermore, while
acknowledging that Bookchin's social ecology advances beyond a simple anthro-
pocentrism, one that justifies the use of non-human nature for strictly human
ends, she questions the extent to which Bookchin's world-view remains focused
on humanity to the potential detriment of other species. She asks whether 'we
now know enough about these processes [of natural evolution] to *foster and
accelerate* them' (Eckersley 1992: 142, italics in original). In other words, there
seem to be grave risks in moving humans to actively, and as a matter of course,
intervene in the evolution of non-human nature, especially with the intent of
promoting certain characteristics.

It can be argued, as Bookchin has (1992a), that critics such as Eckersley are
uncritical sceptics and unimaginative about the reconciliation of first and second
nature and the transcendence of inherited histories. Nonetheless, Bookchin's
discussions of third nature tend to be either highly abstract, advocating the use of
'eductive' reasoning to understand first nature (1995), or superficial and technical (see 1971, 1980 and 1982). Significantly, the technical innovations that
Bookchin writes about, renewable energy technologies and bioregional urban
design and architecture for example, do not directly address what human *participation* in the evolution of nature might be like. Such innovations may adapt
second nature to first, but, if anything, they are tools for minimizing, rather than
heightening, the impact of human development on non-human nature. If
Eckersley is too chained to the past or the world as it is, Bookchin appears too
confident in his own sense of the *process* of nature (see also Kovel 1998). At the
very least, the questions raised by Eckersley suggest a need for a more satisfactory
accounting of how third nature is to emerge and what it would mean for humans
to overcome their one-sided relationship with first nature.

There is also the issue of the relative specificity with which Bookchin addresses the two dimensions of third nature. While Bookchin's consideration of first nature in third nature tends to take the form of general principles with a smattering of specifics, his account of second nature and its revolutionary transformation is rife with detail (see 1980, 1990 and 1992b; Biehl 1998). Furthermore, in the 1990s, Bookchin turned much of his attention to beating back perceived misanthropic tendencies in the ecology movement, that is, tendencies which blame humans *per se* for ecological and environmental degradation, rather than social structures (see, for example, 1994). Bookchin's extensive effort to articulate the specific conditions for human freedom, while leaving the actual integration of first and second nature to the unfolding of 'the Dialectic', underscores the criticism that third nature is a hazy, if noble, idea fraught with potential difficulties if not disasters.

It is in addressing the criticism that his work fails to sufficiently elaborate on the content of third nature that Kim Stanley Robinson's Mars trilogy offers the greatest insight for Bookchin's social ecology.

### ROBINSON AND BOOKCHIN

Operating in the realm of social theory and philosophy, it is difficult for Bookchin to get around the largely negative history of human intervention into bio-physical nature and its environments, especially, though not exclusively, since the onset of the Industrial Revolution. Noting a lack of imagination in getting past that history on the part of critics such as Eckersley is not sufficient. By working in fiction, Robinson is able to take the question of third nature into new contexts for examination. Through the literal removal of humans from the bonds of the Earth, he presents the human species with a new beginning in its relationship with first nature.

In Mars, Robinson presents an environment that appears to require outside intervention for life to evolve (or, perhaps, to re-evolve). Mars possesses key elements necessary for life as humans know it, an atmosphere, albeit a thin one, and water, though locked up in ice and permafrost, but there are no signs of actual life or evolution. This puts a new perspective on possible human participation in the production of nature. The biological aspect of bio-physical first nature requires action out of second nature to exist, while second nature is extremely limited without completing first nature. Not surprisingly, in the trilogy, the issue of *whether* to use human technology and knowledge to release Mars's latent capacity for life, 'terraforming', quickly gives way to the question of *how* to transform the planet. The question thus becomes: will humans terraform Mars in order to reproduce an environment convenient to human activity, or will they choose to terraform in a manner that co-operates with the Martian environment and gives rise to a unique order of life? In more Bookchinist terms, will humans annex Mars to second nature, or will the species foster a third nature that transcends the legacy of human social nature on Earth?

The idea that moving humanity to another planet would be an opportunity to develop new social and physical environments is one that Robinson explicitly introduces in *Red Mars* through the character of Arkady Bogdanov, a space navigator and one of the First Hundred colonists.

> We have come to Mars for good. We are going to make not only our homes and our food, but also our water and the very air we breathe – all on a planet that has none of these things . . . This is an extraordinary ability, think of it! And yet some of us here can accept transforming the entire physical reality of this planet, without doing a single thing to change ourselves or the way we live . . . And so I say that among the many things we transform on Mars, ourselves and our social reality should be among them.
>
> (Robinson 1993: 89)

This statement captures the full sense of third nature: the freeing of humanity from a narrow second nature that fosters domination in both human and non-human nature, and a shift to a (more) fully self-conscious relationship to our own nature, the nature of others and the physical environments that tie all forms of nature together.

Through two devices, a longevity treatment and the benefits of living in a lower gravity environment, Robinson tracks the progress of the human project on Mars (and back on Earth) through a group of characters that live through large sections of the trilogy's 200-year-plus timespan. Two of the trilogy's central characters are physicist Saxifrage Russell (Sax) and geologist Ann Clayborne. The development of these two characters, more than others, captures the transition of Terran-Martian culture from a replicant of Earthly second nature to a unique third nature.

In *Red Mars*, both Sax and Ann are, in different ways, alienated from the Martian environment. Sax's alienation is more straightforward than Ann's. Sax is the archetypal master planner: an ivory tower scientist and technocrat. To Sax, Mars could be any place. What matters is that humanity, with its technology, its knowledge and the superiority of sentience and self-consciousness, has arrived. In one of the early exchanges about the human role on Mars, still on the transport from Earth, two proclamations sum up Sax's early relationship with the planet: 'We'll change it just by landing' and 'It's dead' (Robinson 1993: 40). Once humans arrive on Mars, the process of change will be underway, it will be irreversible and it will be for the better. Sax elaborates on these sentiments in a debate with Ann.

> Without the human presence it [Mars] is just a random collection of atoms, no different than any other random speck of matter in the universe. It's we who understand it, and we who give it meaning . . . Not the basalt and the oxides . . . If there are lakes, or forests, or glaciers, how does that

diminish Mars's beauty? I don't think it does. I think it only enhances it. It adds life, the most beautiful system of all . . . We can transform Mars and build it like you would build a cathedral, as a monument to humanity and the universe both.

(Robinson 1993: 177–8)

While Sax's sentiments are suggestive of third nature, the image of a cathedral or monument implies human control over the production of nature. For Sax, Mars in itself is irrelevant. What matters is the human ability to turn Mars into a habitable place.

In contrast with Sax, Ann is deeply attached to Mars, or, at least, to what it represents: billions of years of geologic history (apparently) uninterrupted by the chaos and disturbances of life. This attachment puts her in conflict. She wants to see Mars up close. She wants to touch and study it, but to do all that she must alter what makes Mars special to her. On a larger scale, the forces that make it possible for her to be on Mars will not allow the planet to remain as it was found. She lets these contradictions out in a conversation regarding how much time to spend on the surface in the face of radiation allowed in by the planet's thin atmosphere. Ann exclaims:

I look at this land and, and I *love* it. I want to be out on it travelling over it always, to study it, to live on it and learn it. But when I do that I change it – I destroy what it is, what I love in it . . . I'd rather die. Let the planet be, leave it wilderness and let radiation do what it will.

(Robinson 1993: 157, italics in original)

For Ann, there is an essential Mars to which humans, herself included, are anathema. To ease this contradiction, she seeks ways to minimize the human impact on Mars even as she realizes that the planet will never be the same now that humans have arrived, no matter how circumscribed their presence.

The early life of the First Hundred is observed by people back on Earth: a live-action soap opera and political thriller. Sax and Ann come to represent different sides of the terraforming debate, with the physicist representing a majority faction on both Mars and Earth that believes in terraforming Mars 'by all means possible, as fast as they could', and the geologist standing in for a smaller but committed 'hands-off attitude' (Robinson 1993: 169). In the face of overwhelming odds, Ann commits herself to slowing terraforming down, making the case that humans need to study and understand Mars before changing it.

Ann loses this argument and the human population on Mars grows. Many of the new arrivals possess distinct cultural and political identities and have different goals in mind for Mars: cultural autonomy for individual groups versus universal standards of rights and responsibilities, close ties to Earth versus Martian independence. In the end, the United Nations and corporate authorities that funded the Martian expedition assert their authority over the planet. Many of the First Hundred, identified with movements in favour of an independent Mars, are forced underground, including Sax and Ann. This change in circumstance sets the stage for *Green Mars*.

In *Green Mars*, Ann heads into the Martian outback. It is revealed to her that she has, reluctantly and, it seems, unknowingly, become a focal point and hero to a faction on Mars called the 'Reds', essentially a Martian Earth First! who practise ecotage against terraforming. Coyote, an unofficial member of the First Hundred who stowed away on the original transport, persuades her to meet with the Reds. Initially, Ann is sceptical about the efficacy of ecotage and is reluctant to involve herself in a political movement removed from scientific debate. Her turning point comes during a trek to the Red base of operations. Witnessing multiple signs of life and environmental transformation, she decides that she should meet with the Reds and arrives a hero. Ann's turn to the Reds is significant because it is a self-admission that her objections to terraforming are not grounded solely in science – too much has already changed for her arguments for further study of the native landscape to hold. Joining the Reds is an emotional and political decision.

> A bunch of radicals. Not really her type, Ann thought, feeling a residual sensation that her objection to terraforming was a rational scientific thing. Or at least a defensible ethical or aesthetic position. But then the anger burned through her again in a flash . . . Who was she to judge the ethics of the Reds? At least they expressed their anger, they had lashed out.
>
> (Robinson 1995: 129–30)

After witnessing the land 'melting' away from the unlocked water, she decides to lash out as well. At this moment, Ann does not perceive humans to be capable of transcending second nature, and, as a result, rejects the idea of a third nature on Mars.

Contributing to Ann's decision to join the Reds is her scepticism about human nature. She expresses the conviction that humans on Mars, whether they were born there or not, are 'human and human we remain'. A significant number of humans on Mars take as an article of faith that as humans terraform Mars, Mars 'areoforms' human nature. Areoforming is defined as a certain sense or spirit of place and life that is uniquely Martian. To Ann, the terraforming efforts in themselves, and the sameness of the colonists' tent cities, imply that areoforming is a bankrupt idea, one that serves to mask the destructive selfishness of human activity on Mars (see 1995: 365–6). This rejection of even the idea behind areoforming represents a rejection of third nature. For Ann, humans should withdraw from Mars as much as possible without leaving entirely. That is the only way to insulate the planet from a selfish and grasping human social nature.

Where Sax is concerned, *Green Mars* is a significant time of transition. Not satisfied with hiding out, he acquires a new identity and a new face.

Fundamentally a generalist, he transforms himself into a biologist and goes to
work for a biotech company designing plants for Mars's emerging environments.
Whereas, before, Sax was the master planner, working with macro-level design
and analysis of terraforming, in his new identity, Stephen Lindholm, he is
involved in the ground-level work of terraforming. His observations as a field-
worker have a profound affect on his awareness of the Martian influence on
human endeavours to change the planet and on the ability of life to develop in
unintended or unexpected ways.

In a key passage, Sax takes off on his own to explore a proto-alpine meadow.
Dotted with trees and grass, he observes that the trees, mainly white spruce and
lodgepole pine, are gnarled and stunted, and this is despite extensive engineering
for growth, hardiness and adaptation to Martian soil composition. Taking
delight in these trees and the few insects that had been released, he wishes for
'Some moles and voles, and marmots and minxes and foxes' (Robinson 1995:
180). His reasons are practical: many animals provide useful services to plant life
and vice versa, but he also begins to realize that not everyone is engaged in the
terraforming for the same reasons. He is especially disturbed by an arrangement
of solar mirrors and lenses being used to heat the surface and increase the melt of
ice and permafrost. This action not only destabilizes the surface, but increases
the amount of $CO_2$ in the atmosphere, intensifying and speeding up the warming of the planet, but making it uninhabitable for animal life. 'As if warming the
planet was the only goal! But warming was not the goal. Animals on the surface
was the goal' (Robinson 1995: 180). His commitment to life, articulated in *Red
Mars*, sharpens here. It is not only human life, but life in general that matters to
Sax. However, many of the more drastic, and apparently ascendant, terraforming
plans are centred on a heavy industrial model that would heat the surface and
thicken the atmosphere as fast as possible. This would make the planet eminently
exploitable, unveiling mineral ores and enabling activities on the surface otherwise inhibited by cold, but it would not support the introduction of life in
general, most likely only technologically or genetically enhanced humans.

This distinction in terraforming goals illustrates the practical and ethical differences between remaining in second nature and transitioning to third nature.
In the former, human knowledge and technology are employed to bend the Martian environment to serve human needs. In the latter, those same capabilities are
employed for the benefit of other species and, at some level, preserving the
integrity of the Martian landscape.

These differences also come into relief at an annual conference on terraforming. The push to heat and thaw the surface in all haste disturbs Sax. He begins to
doubt even his own initial plans for making a fast jump to a human habitable
surface. The extent to which terraforming now seemed to be driven by developing an environment exclusively convenient to human purposes and tastes, and by
the pursuit of profit, shakes Sax's faith in the political disinterest of science. He
becomes even more aware of the drastic changes to the Martian landscape
resulting from the terraforming. Significantly, he thinks:

All of this was as Ann had predicted to him, long ago. No doubt she was noting reports of all these changes with disgust, she and all the rest of the Reds. For them every collapse was a sign that things were going wrong rather than right. In the past, Sax would have shrugged them off; mass wasting exposed frozen soil to the sun, warming it and revealing potential nitrate sources and the like. Now he was not so sure . . . The collapse of landforms were considered no more than an opportunity, not only for terraforming which seemed to be considered the exclusive business of the transnats, but for mining.

(Robinson 1995: 217–18)

Sax comes to believe that the terraforming effort has become something other than a noble attempt to bring life to Mars, but a means for turning the planet into a raw materials colony for Earth.

Eventually, Sax's identity is uncovered by the Earth-based authorities on Mars. He is tortured and brain-damaged. After he is rescued by the underground, his mind and body are reconstructed, albeit not perfectly. He decides to take down one part of the solar mirror-lens arrangement to slow down the heating of the surface. His success leads to another exchange with Ann, a person that he has come to think about a lot. Until the end, this exchange is much like the others between the two of them. Sax defends the terraforming in principle. He reasserts a plan for a 'human-viable surface to a certain elevation' and a slower approach to transforming the surface and the atmosphere. Ann is curious about his decision to knock out the one portion of the heating device, but is still bitter about the terraforming and Sax's commitment. But this time Sax ends with this admission: 'I was wrong . . . We should have waited. A few decades of study of the primal state. It would have told us how to proceed. I didn't think things would change so fast.' Ann, non-plussed, simply responds: 'But now it's too late' (Robinson 1995: 415). This exchange, Ann in bitter alienation from Sax and what she believes he represents, and Sax expressing remorse and a desire to reach out to and understand Ann, sets the scene for *Blue Mars*. Ann continues to be uncomfortable with the idea of integrating the human species with the Martian environment, while Sax has undergone a significant transformation in consciousness, ethical awareness and judgement. No longer overwhelmingly enamoured of human capabilities, and freed from the belief that human second nature can freely bend other forms of nature to its will, Sax has moved to an understanding of the ethical and practical limits to human interventions into the production of nature. Most significantly, he has come to appreciate the value and role of the native Martian landscape in guiding the evolution of life on the planet.

Mars itself undergoes yet another revolution in *Green Mars*, only this time Mars breaks free from Earth. In *Blue Mars*, the independence movement must now address issues of Martian governance and what sort of relationship to establish with Earth. Both of these decisions shape the context for addressing Sax's and, especially, Ann's personal transformations and their respective relationships with the planet that has become their home. Indeed, in *Blue Mars*, Sax and Ann emerge as the trilogy's principal characters. Sax's focus in *Blue Mars* is on deepening his understanding of Ann's connection to Red Mars and finding an entry to persuade her that life on Mars is not a blight, but a beautiful and right thing.

It is clear in *Blue Mars* that Martian independence from Earth plays an important role in bringing Ann to an accommodation with the human presence on, and even transformation of, Mars. Most sections of the trilogy are introduced by the thoughts and descriptions of an unnamed observer. *Blue Mars* begins with one of these passages. The observer is describing a scene where Ann Clayborne is smiling, addressing a group of Reds. The heart of her message is recorded by the observer:

> *We came from Earth to Mars, and in that passage there was a certain purification. Things were easier to see, there was a freedom of action that we had not had before. A chance to express the best part of ourselves. So we acted. We are making a better way to live.*
>
> (Robinson 1997: 2, italics in original)

While still not persuaded that the terraforming is anything but a small-minded endeavour, it is significant that Ann would be talking not about restricting human action on Mars, but about the possibilities of making a better human life on the planet. The break with Earth distances Mars from what are, in Ann's estimation, the most selfish and grasping aspects of second nature.

There are several places in *Blue Mars* where Ann engages in close observation of human life on Mars. While these observations are not wholly positive, her curiosity about how humans are living on the planet is a crack in her shield against the idea of truly inhabiting, as opposed to simply studying, this new place. She finds herself concluding at one point 'People's faces, staring in concert; this ran the world' (Robinson 1997: 16). This thought indicates a recognition that humans have added value to Mars rather than simply taking value from it.

There is one particularly important moment in the book where Ann starts to make a turn away from her alienated relationship with humanity on Mars and the Martian environment. This moment is a conversation with Michel Duval, another of the First Hundred, who, at Sax's urging, has engaged her in conversation about possible suicidal tendencies. Perhaps because he has more distance from Ann, or perhaps because of his psychological training, Michel is able to talk to Ann in ways that Sax is not.

> [Michel:] *There is so much of Red Mars that remains. You should go out and look! Go out and empty your mind and just see what is out there. Go out at low altitude and walk free in the air, a simple dust mask only. It would be good for*

*you, good at the physiological level. Also it would be reaping a benefit of the terraforming. To experience the freedom it gives us – that we can walk on its surface naked and survive. It's amazing! It makes us part of an ecology. It deserves to be rethought, this process. You should go out to consider it, to study the process of areoformation.*

[Ann:] *That's just a word. We took this planet and plowed it under. It's melting under our feet.*

[Michel:] *Melting in native water. Not imported from Saturn or the like, it's been there from the beginning . . .*

(Robinson 1997: 252, italics in the original)

Ann resists Michel's arguments but this exchange does send her out on a trip around the planet, both in and out of human company. It is also evident that Michel has raised difficult questions about terraforming. The discussion about water is important because it questions Ann's assumptions about what is and what is not 'natural'. Her trip prompts further reflection on these lines.

The backdrop to Ann's rapprochement with Sax and with humanity on Mars is the changed political situation on Mars. Early in *Blue Mars*, a new, independent Martian government is established. This government exhibits many Bookchinist characteristics, including a confederal structure, common ownership of land, and a system of human and environmental ethics that is reflected in various institutions and limitations on strictly private enterprise (Robinson 1997: 153–8). This new government taps into Ann's hopes about building a better life, a better form of humanity on Mars.

The trilogy winds down with Sax devising a memory treatment to address one of the symptoms of the extreme old age made possible by the longevity treatments and Martian gravity. Many of the remaining First Hundred begin to die off, suffering a 'quick decline', with memory loss being one of the harbingers. Sax gathers together those who are left at their original settlement to undergo the treatment. Ann uses this as an opportunity to focus on Mars as it was before the terraforming, and emerges fully transformed from the experience. She and Sax sail on one of the inland seas, taking in the emerging Mars, one made blue as well as green and red by an earlier deal between them that resulted in Sax removing the final part of the solar heating arrangement.

As the final chapter begins, the reader is introduced to 'A new Ann. A fully Martian Ann at last' (Robinson 1997: 754). In a public way, this transformation is represented by Ann speaking in favor of allowing legal Terran immigration to Mars in order to avert a war that would destroy the still-developing, life-sustaining Mars. More privately, the closing paragraphs bring both Ann and, symbolically, humanity into a state of free nature with Mars.

Ann, Sax and a host of family and friends make a home out of the original settlement. On the beach, after bringing ice cream back for everyone and experiencing a brief, terrifying moment where she thinks she is experiencing quick decline, Ann is confronted by a child looking at the water, sky and passing pelicans. 'Innit pretty? Innit pretty? Innit pretty?' Eventually Ann answers 'Yes', but her reflection continues internally.

> Oh yes, very pretty! She admitted it and was allowed to live. Beat on, heart. And why not admit it. Nowhere on this world were people killing each other, nowhere were they desperate for shelter or food, nowhere were they scared for their kids. There was that to be said. The sand squeaked under-foot as she toed it. She looked more closely: dark grains of basalt, mixed with minute seashell fragments, and a variety of colorful pebbles, some of them no doubt brecciated fragments of the Hellas impact itself.
>
> (Robinson 1997: 761)

Mars is forever changed, but the Mars they inherited is still there, beneath her feet, mixed with what humans have, if not fully created, then set in motion. In the end, for both Sax and Ann, the desire to inhabit this particular place leads them to overcome their original states of alienation.

## CONCLUSION

By making Sax in particular struggle with the threat of Mars being terraformed into a tropical mining colony for Earth, Robinson does address the problematic history of human intervention into the production of (first) nature. Unlike Earth, Mars does not bear the full weight of this history. Mars represents the possibility of a different direction, one that is not marked by an attempt to subsume the rest of nature into the human fold. Sax and Ann, in their own ways, give up the idea that humans can dominate nature. Sax abandons the notion that humans can fully master the evolution of life or transformation of an environment, while Ann comes to accept that human intervention does not necessarily extinguish nature. By tracing the transformation of Sax and Ann, and speculating on the process of terraforming, the Mars trilogy opens a window on third nature, one that makes it possible to perceive the possibilities of a truly integrated relationship between human and non-human nature. Robinson creates a human culture where the central questions are: what does it mean to live in a place, and how can the human species use its abilities to enhance the life of that place? That these questions are difficult to answer is not in itself significant. What matters is that the questions are asked and the answers are meaningful and consequential. The struggle toward this type of social-cultural context is what Robinson elaborates in *Red, Green* and *Blue Mars*. It is also the struggle, and fundamental basis, for third nature.

## ACKNOWLEDGEMENTS

This chapter was prepared and edited with constant help and encouragement from Anne-Marie Deitering. Additional thanks to Rob Kitchin and James

Kneale for their efforts in putting the anthology together and helping me clarify the chapter.

## NOTE

1 The connection between Robinson and Bookchin is more than incidental. The Mars trilogy is peppered with explicit references to Bookchin's work. *Pacific Edge* (1990), one of the Three Californias books, is a slice-of-life story about a Bookchinesque municipality. Robinson's first post-Mars-trilogy book, *Antarctica* (1999), tackles social ecology themes such as what it means to inhabit a place, distinctions between radical, reformist and (arguably) misanthropic ecology, and the promises of collective self-management.

# 12

# IN THE BELLY OF THE MONSTER

## FRANKENSTEIN, FOOD, FACTISHES AND FICTION

*Nick Bingham*

It has become something of a cliché within SF criticism that the genre – despite the impression given by its conventions of displacement – is much less about the there and then and much more about the here and now. Science fiction geographies can be very close to home:

> It was a cold and windy, grey autumn morning in the peaceful environs of Kings Heath. As on every Saturday, cars crowded the road and Saturday shoppers went about their Saturday shopping . . . But in front of Sainsbury's, nothing was as it should be, for out of a huge Sainsbury's shopping bag there crawled the most hideous creature anyone this side of Birmingham had ever seen! The Gene-Beast reared its ugly head: part fish, part tomato, part turnip, part banana, it set out to prowl the street in search of its less sentient relatives. Little did it know that these were being carried around in tins and tubs and plastic wrappers: processed food products with gene soya, long-life tomatoes and herbicide resistant maize abound on our supermarket shelves. Luckily for this Saturday's shoppers, fearless Friends of the Earth campaigners battled valiantly to ban genetically modified food from our tables.
>
> (Friends of the Earth Birmingham 1998/99: 1)

Close to home, literally in my case, in that the supermarket in question is just around the corner from where I live, but also close to home more metaphorically for everyone in the sense that the GM food controversy signals so clearly 'the arrival of biotechnologies in the most intimate fabric of our everyday lives' (Whatmore 1999: 259). And with them – as the headline of this extract from a Birmingham Friends of the Earth briefing: '"Frankenstein Foods – No Thanks!" Say Sainsbury's Shoppers as "Gene Beast" Hits Birmingham Streets' makes clear – comes SF. Not just any SF either, but perhaps its ur-text, 'the first real novel of science fiction' (Aldiss and Wingrove 1986: 51). As Richard Kadrey and Larry McCaffery put it in their 'Cyberpunk 101' (in which *Frankenstein* is the first entry): 'The recycling of body parts, the creation of life (or monster making), murder, sex, revenge, the epic chase, the brilliant scientist working outside the law, a brooding romantic atmosphere – this book is a veritable sourcebook of SF motifs and clichés' (1991: 17). How and why this sourcebook might have fallen open again at the beginning of the twenty-first century is the subject of subsequent sections. Before setting down that particular road, however, I want to return to the scene outside the supermarket in order to make some brief arguments about SF in general, which are the starting point for much of what follows. For what we have in the displaying of the monster is nothing if not a demonstration. And what we are being shown, I want to claim, are (at least) three things.

The first is the materiality of science fiction. This point is well made by SF writer and critic Samuel Delany in his (non)definition of the field within which he works as – like 'all practices of writing, as are all genres, literary and paraliter-ary' – nothing more, nothing less, and nothing other than 'a way of reading' (1994: 273):

> the only meaningful things that we can say about SF *as* a genre tend to be about the way in which the way of reading which *is* SF differs from the way of reading that is poetry, say, or the way of reading that is naturalistic fiction, or the way of reading that is philosophy; or we can point out similarities shared between the way of reading that is SF and other ways of reading . . . [W]hat affects these ways of reading is specific and material: publishing policies, printing conventions, economic situations, socio-logical and historical events, readerly and writerly responses, educational contexts – as well as, of course, semantic conventions. Alerting people to the ways material forces contour the way of reading that is SF is a good deal of what my critical project – as far as it entails SF – has been about.
>
> (ibid.: 273–4, italics in original)

From this perspective (see also Kneale 1999), the thing we call SF only ever emerges from the meetings of authors, texts and readers, meetings which always take place in particular forms, at particular times, and under particular circum-stances. It is the outcome, then, of concrete practices. Including protesting in the suburbs of Birmingham.

The second thing we are being shown is the science fiction of materiality. Once again, Delany is helpful:

> Despite the many meaningful differences in the ways of reading that con-stitute the specifically literary modes, they are all characterized – now, today – by a priority of the subject, i.e. of the self, of human consciousness. To a greater or lesser extent, the subject can be read as the organizational centre of all the literary categories' many differing expectations . . .

Answering its own expectations as a paraliterary mode, science fiction is far more concerned with the organization (and reorganization) of the object, i.e., the world or the institutions through which we perceive it. It is concerned with the subject, certainly, but concerned with those aspects of it that are closer to the object: How is the subject excited, impinged on, contoured and constituted by the object?

(quoted in James 1996: xx)

As Ken James – in the introduction to a collection of Delany's criticism – expands,

By this rhetorical model, we can see that even the most conservatively inclined science fiction, if it is in any way sophisticated *as* science fiction, must keep a certain margin of imaginative space open for an apprehension of the historicity of objects, landscapes, and social institutions.

(1996: xx, emphasis in original)

SF is here considered then, as generically concerned with foregrounding the nonhuman, as drawing attention, to a degree that other ways of reading perhaps do not, to the 'objectivity' of the social. Objects like GM foods.

The third thing demonstrated is that SF matters. Far from being abstract 'mind-sets', to quote Delany once more (1994: 34), located safely (or otherwise) within the heads of a marginalized fandom, the 'expectations, conventions, and interpretative codes' (ibid.: 32) that constitute the genre have helped shape our contemporary surroundings in significant senses. To take but a single example, one only has to think of the role that William Gibson's seminal cyberpunk novel *Neuromancer* played in the 'becoming real' of the Internet. As David Tomas has written, Gibson's 'powerful vision' came – according to their own testimonies – to influence 'the way that virtual reality and cyberspace researchers [structured] their research agenda and problematics' (1991: 46). Sandy Stone underlines and emphasizes the point when she contends that by articulating a new 'techno-logical and social imaginary' and crystallizing a new research community from a number of disparate fields, *Neuromancer* acted as 'a massive intertextual presence not only in other literary productions of the 1980s, but in technical publica-tions, conference topics, hardware design, and scientific and technological dis-course in the large' (1991: 95, 99). We seem to be in a similar sort of position once again.

It is this position that I now – having set up some initial signposts – will proceed to explore for the remainder of the chapter, a chapter which is structured round the tale of two encounters.

## ENCOUNTER #1: *FRANKENSTEIN* MEETS THE
## GM CONTROVERSY

In the past decade or so, biotechnologies in general and genetic modification (hereafter GM) of food in particular, have superseded even the Internet to become established in the public consciousness as the latest in a long line of what I have referred to elsewhere as 'frontier technologies' (Bingham, Valentine and Holloway 1999). Represented as the materialized limit of human endeavour, these techniques are discursively mobilized across a whole range of contexts in order to act as a symbolic boundary between a 'here' of the present-as-past and a 'there' of the future-now. To put this another way, GM – like other technical developments before it, from the railroad, through the telephone network and electrification, to television, the space race, and latterly information and communication technologies (Nye 1994, 1998) – heralds access (at least for those who benefit from it) to a whole new world. This, for example, from the opening page of a recent book by long-time campaigner against the corporatization of biotechnology Jeremy Rifkin, gives a flavour of the rhetoric:

> There are many convergent forces coming together to create this powerful new social current. At the epicentre is a technology revolution unmatched in all of history in its power to remake ourselves, our institutions, and our world. Scientists are beginning to organise life at the genetic level. The new tools of biology are opening up opportunities for refashioning life on Earth while foreclosing options that have existed over the millennia of evolutionary history. Before our eyes lies an uncharted landscape whose contours are being shaped in thousands of biotechnology laboratories in universities, government agencies, and corporations around the world. If the claims already being made for the new science are only partially realised, the consequences for society and future generations are likely to be enormous.
>
> (1998: 1)

This literal and metaphorical 'uncharted landscape', as Rifkin puts it, is – at the time of writing – still very much up for grabs. As has become almost customary in the kinds of socio-technical imbroglios – from ozone holes to greenhouse effects to superbugs to mad cows – in the midst of which we seem to be finding ourselves with increasing regularity, everything has become controversial (Callon 1998). Of particular interest here, the heroic techno-scientific origin stories of their world-feeding GM crops propounded by Monsanto and the like, in all kinds of arenas from government regulatory committees to newspaper advertisements, have come to be challenged by anti-GM protesters who – determined to cast these innovations in a very different light – have brought into play a very different techno-scientific origin story all of their own. Like that of its corporate counterpart, the imagery of *Frankenstein* has been everywhere: from the pavements outside Sainsbury's to the streets of Seattle, from the front of the *Daily Mail* to the Greenpeace website.

Why the ubiquity of *Frankenstein*, though, in the debates around GM? Because, I want to suggest, the story offers a powerful resource for making sense of the controversy, for navigating a way through the unfamiliar territory that it announces. *Frankenstein* – as literary critic Chris Baldick has detailed (1987) – has, since its creation by Mary Shelley in 1818, taken on the status of a 'modern myth'. The myth which developed out of the novel 'turns repeatedly on [the] new problems of an age in which humanity seizes responsibility for re-creating the world, for violently reshaping its natural environment and its inherited social and political forms, for remaking itself' (Baldick 1987: 5), and today can be summarized by 'a skeleton story which requires only two sentences: (a) Franken-stein makes a living creature out of bits of corpses. (b) The creature turns against him and runs amok' (ibid.: 3). As Baldick notes, 'most myths, in literate societies at least, prolong their lives not by being retold at great length, but by being alluded to, thereby finding fresh contexts and applications' (ibid.: 3), and *Frank-enstein* is obviously no exception. In the encounter with GM, that fresh applica-tion has centred on a holding-up of the story as emblematic of the quality of hubris so often associated with modernity, a hubris exemplified by the desire to meddle with the workings of life itself:

> One of the phenomena which had particularly attracted my attention was the structure of the human frame, and, indeed, any animal endowed with life. Whence, I often asked myself, did the principle of life proceed? It was a bold question, and one which has ever been considered as a mystery; yet with how many things are we upon the brink of becoming acquainted, if cowardice or carelessness did not restrain our inquiries.
>
> (Shelley 1996 [1818]: 30)

The point here is not whether this hubris interpretation is 'correct' or not, for, as Baldick makes clear:

> The truth of a myth, as Lévi-Strauss rightly insists, is not to be established by authorising its earliest version, but by considering all its versions. The vitality of myths lies precisely in their capacity for change, their adapt-ability and openness to new combinations of meaning. That series of adaptations, allusions, accretions, analogues, parodies, and plain misread-ings which follows upon Mary Shelley's novel is not just a supplementary component of the myth; it *is* myth.
>
> (1987: 4)

And that myth works. It works because the myth is also a legend in the sense of the key to reading a map as well as in the sense of an old story with con-temporary relevance (Bingham and Thrift 2000). It works because the myth is also a figuration in the sense that feminist historian of science and technology Donna Haraway uses the term: 'Figurations are performative images that can be inhabited. Verbal or visual, figurations can be condensed maps of contestable worlds' (1997: 11). It works because making sense is always also making *sens* (Serres 1991), that is to say, finding directions. Once again, *Frankenstein* offers us a way of navigating through an unfamiliar landscape. Purchasing food from this shop rather than that one, putting in the basket the packet with this label rather than that one, pulling up the crops in this field rather than that one: this science fiction geography is a matter not of theory but practice.

And yet, however effective it has been in giving the biotechnology corporations a run for their money (and it has been effective), and however sympathetic I am to the motivations of the groups and individuals who have employed it to this end (and I am sympathetic), I find this science fiction geography a troubling one. Most notably I would agree with Haraway that the discourse of the purity of Nature and the transgression of God-given boundaries is problematic to say the least:

> I cannot but hear in the biotechnology debates the unintended tones of fear of the alien and suspicion of the mixed. In the appeal to intrinsic natures, I hear a mystification of kind and purity akin to the doctrines of white racial hegemony and US national integrity and purpose that so dominate North American culture and history. I know that this appeal to sustain other organisms' inviolable, intrinsic natures is intended to affirm their difference from humanity and their claim on lives lived on their own terms and not 'man's'. The appeal aims to limit turning all the world into a resource for human appropriation. But it is a problematic argument resting on unconvincing biology. History is erased, for other organisms as well as for humans, in the doctrine of types and intrinsic purposes, and a kind of timeless stasis in nature is piously narrated.
>
> (1997: 61)

Ironically then, despite its co-optation by radicals of various shades of green, the story that we are dealing with here is perhaps best described as a 'conservative parable of presumption' (Baldick 1987: 58). Is this as far as we can go with *Frankenstein*?

### ENCOUNTER #2: *FRANKENSTEIN* MEETS STS MEETS THE GM CONTROVERSY

No. Or certainly I want to make a case that *Frankenstein* can take us further, can help lead us along a genuinely progressive path re the GM controversy rather than down a blind alley, taking two steps back for every one forward. This assessment is based on the fact that there is more to both the novel and the issue than we have come across thus far. By introducing a third party to the encounter between *Frankenstein* and the GM controversy – namely some work from the field often summarized as science and technology studies (STS) – I

want to try and add back some of that 'more' and thereby suggest that a
shortcut story can become a story about shortcuts. A shortcut story because in
navigating according to the compass of something akin to the two-sentence
version outlined above, thereby reducing *Frankenstein* to a very simple spatial
narrative of origin, escape and return, the anti-GM protesters have too often
opted for the same sort of quick and easy route through the mess we are in as
did the biotechnology corporations whose actions got us here in the first place.
However, by following the twists and turns of the novel rather more carefully,
we find that *Frankenstein* also serves very effectively to flag up in advance these
'fabulous accelerations' (Latour 1999: 265), to warn us against taking the
tempting bypass of 'due process' (ibid.). At this stage, some examples are
overdue.

### Shortcut #1: the social and the technical

The first shortcut that *Frankenstein* warns us against taking is assuming a clear
distinction between the social and the technical such that the introduction of
the latter can provide a 'silver bullet' solution to the problems of the former.
So familiar has the story – or rather the myth – become that it is easy to forget
that the original intention of Victor's work was to be useful to humanity by
eliminating disease (Baldick 1987: 43). As he puts it himself,

> What glory would attend the discovery, if I could banish disease from the
> human frame, and render man invulnerable to anything but a violent
> death.
> [and later] I thought that if I could bestow animations upon lifeless matter,
> I might in the process of time (although I now found it impossible) renew
> life where death had apparently devoted the body to corruption.
>                                                  (Shelley 1996 [1818]: 22, 32)

Things, however, do not quite turn out this way in practice, and Victor
discovers that far from subtracting uncertainty from the world, making it a more
simple place, innovations are merely added to the world just like everything else.
The technical is social and the social is technical, a fact he is forced to confront
when Victor(ia) (the name which political theorist Timothy Kaufman-Osborn
gives to Frankenstein's creation in his wonderful reading) makes one of its
periodic returns:

> Acknowledgment of the responsibilities entailed in the project of making,
> Victor(ia) insists, should have been evident when s/he was first created. At
> that time, Victor should have considered how, if at all, this artifact might
> enter into, become part of, the larger company of made things. But it is too
> late for that now. Fashioned in a state of motherless abstraction, this being
> can find no place in the web of relations sustained by the world's artifacts.

To the extent that it remains without such a place, to the extent that it is by nature what Victor aspires to be by design, to that extent is its existence meaningless. Recognizing that it is only relatedness that enables some thing to mean some thing, Victor(ia) asserts a 'right' to a companion artifact, one that will link its biography 'to the chain of existence and events'.

(1997: 234, all quotations from the novel)

### Shortcut #2: the cultural and the scientific

The second shortcut that *Frankenstein* warns us against taking is assuming a clear distinction between the cultural and the scientific such that the objectivity, neutrality and truth of the latter is meant to be purified of the polluting illusion, ideology and opinion of the former. Victor's behaviour on reaching Ingolstadt where he will undertake the studies that will end in his unique act of creation demonstrates the supposed logic of the separation:

As an aspiring Cartesian dualist, he concludes that the achievement of autonomy demands wholesale detachment from this suffocating site [his father's household] of human relatedness. However, unlike Descartes, Victor recognizes that he need not shun the company of others to secure the soul's isolation. Granted he must extricate himself from the network of ascriptive ties into which he was of woman born, without choice and without reason. But, once freed from that, it matters not how many people surround him so long as he remains apart. Because the seclusion of his childhood years endowed him with an 'invincible repugnance to new countenances' as so rendered him 'totally unfitted for the company of strangers', Victor is confident that residence amongst his fellows at Ingolstadt will not compromise his solitude.

(Kaufman-Osborn 1997: 219, all quotations from the novel)

And remain apart he does, as he immerses himself in his work:

I knew well what would be my father's feelings; but I could not tear my thoughts from my employment, loathsome in itself, but which had taken an irresistible hold on my imagination. I wished, as it were, to procrastinate all that related to my feelings of affection until that great object, which swallowed up every habit of my nature, should be completed.

(Shelley 1996 [1818]: 33)

But at the very instant when this work reaches its fruition, Victor is reminded only too vividly of the hopelessness of this attempted cleansing, that, whether we like it or not, in practice – the practice of science just as the practice of anything else – there are always an entangled multiplicity of factors at play:

At this pivotal moment, the sense of Victor's world suffers wholesale dis-location, and the sense of that dislocation takes veiled shape as a night-mare. 'I thought I saw Elizabeth [his wife to be], in the bloom of health walking the streets of Ingolstadt. Delighted and surprised, I embraced her, but as I imprinted the first kiss on her lips, they became livid with death; her features began to change, and I thought that I held the corpse of my dead mother in my arms; a shroud enveloped her form, and I saw the graveworms crawling in the folds of the flannel.' To want the touch of Elizabeth's lips, to desire Elizabeth as a woman, is to be reminded of his emergence from the womb of another, of the fact that he ultimately owes his life to his mother.

(Kaufman-Osborn 1997: 224, all quotations from the novel)

### Shortcut #3: ourselves and our artefacts

The third shortcut that *Frankenstein* warns us against taking is assuming a clear distinction between ourselves and our artefacts such that we can imagine that the link between the former and the latter can be characterized in terms of omni-science and omnipotence. Certainly Victor believes at the beginning of his quest that the scientific method allows us access to the way things work and that in turn puts us firmly in control:

[W]ith the Baconian scientist and against the classical philosophers, Victor has learnt that one can know with certainty only that which one makes. At first, it is true, Victor's aim is not to fashion some palpable thing. His absorption of the aristocrat's prejudice against the labor of craftsmen is initially sufficient to deter him from such a grubby occupation. Yet only for the briefest of moments can he maintain that the discovery of the principle of life is 'the summit of my desires,' 'the most gratifying consummation of my toils . . . When I found so astonishing a power placed within my hands, I hesitated a long time concerning the manner in which I should employ it.' The fact that Victor's hesitation is eventually overcome by a compul-sion to 'employ' this principle as a means to some other end signals his exit from the world of classical contemplation and entry into that of modern utilitarianism. Driven by the unlovely logic of a bourgeois age, Victor sets out to create an artifact that will experimentally confirm what he already knows is true.

(Kaufman-Osborn 1997: 222, all quotations from the novel)

In practice – for a third time – everything happens differently to what had been expected. Refusing the roles to which they are assigned, our objects always seem to surprise us, exceed our intentions, confound our predictions, behave in ways we had never considered. They are more than we know:

What renders the thing especially vexing for Victor is its destabilization of virtually every one of the dualistic categories found within Descartes' conceptual tool kit. From the standpoint of those categories, this thing is unthinkable, an impossibility. Its existence violates the neat divisions Descartes erects between inside and outside . . . human and animal . . . life and death. Most fundamentally though, its existence violates the distinction between creator and creature, between this 'modern Prometheus' and the artifacts he makes. Victor must assume that he can touch without being touched, make without being made, project without suffering the consequences of artifactual reciprocation. But if the creature awakes and speaks, if this artifact proves able to participate in determining its own signification, if this being's capacity for agency dramatically reveals the ability of things to incarnate the sentient intelligence allegedly restricted to human beings, then Victor's conception of what counts as a subject and what counts as an object must fall apart.

(ibid.: 225, all quotations from the novel)

What I want to argue is that the exposure of the potential danger of taking any one of these three shortcuts is enough to severely undermine what Kaufman-Osborn refers to as 'the Cartesian paradigm of use'. This 'in a nutshell . . . affirms that human beings are so many discrete subjects whose autonomy is manifest in the choices they make concerning efficient use of the intrinsically neutral objects fashioned for their own convenience' (ibid.: 3). The pursuits of Victor Frankenstein are 'well understood as an effort to live the truth of Cartesian metaphysics', and his 'eventual failure to verify [the Cartesian paradigm of use] testifies, not to the weakness of his will, but to the impossibility of the project he seeks to make real. Relentlessly drawing him back to the world he seeks to escape, Victor's work mocks his pretensions' (ibid.: 217). Unlike most objects perhaps, whose 'internal stresses are present but subdued, the thing Victor makes loudly announces the unresolved tensions passing through the arms of its creator and into its body' (ibid.: 225). All the better for us, since the lesson remains that the relations, connections, interdependencies which it so eloquently speaks of have a wider applicability (which seems an opportune moment to acknowledge – if rather inadequately and belatedly – how indebted my analysis here is to the wealth of feminist scholarship on Frankenstein: for a selection see the pieces by Ellen Moers, Barbara Johnson, Gayatri Chakravorty Spivak, Anne Mellor, Susan Winnett and Marilyn Butler in the Norton Critical Edition of *Frankenstein* (1996), the text I have been quoting from throughout).

For, I want to argue further, considered together, the exposure of the potential danger of taking these shortcuts provides us with a fair plan of the workings of Modernity itself. For what else is the following but a portrait of Victor?

We can now sketch the ideal psychosocial type of the modern, the model of the critique. As an iconoclast, the modern breaks all the idols, all of them, always, fiercely. Then, protected by this gesture, in the silent practice opened up for him like a huge underground cavity, he can get his kicks, with all the juvenile enthusiasm of the inventor, from mixing up all sorts of hybrids without fearing any of the consequences. No fear, no past, only more and more combinations to try. But then, terrified by a sudden realisation of the consequences – how could a fact be just a fact with no history, no past, and no consequence, a 'bald' fact instead of a 'hairy' one? – he suddenly shifts from brave iconoclasm and youthful ardour to fits of guilt-ridden bad conscience: and this time he destroys himself, in endless ceremonies of atonement, looking everywhere for the broken fragments of his creative destruction, gathering them back into huge and fragile bundles.

(Latour 1999: 279)

The point here is not that we can find in *Frankenstein* (or in the work of anthropologist of science and technology Bruno Latour) a wholesale rejection of what has made us modern (far from it). Rather the point is that we can find in *Frankenstein* (and in the work of Latour) a recognition that there has always been much more going on in practice than we have led ourselves to believe. When, then, we hear Monsanto or another of the agricultural biotechnology companies telling us that GM crops will save the starving millions, are guided purely by scientific imperatives, or have passed laboratory safety tests, then we should (must) be suspicious of the 'poison of metaphor-free facticity', as Haraway so tellingly puts it (1994: 63). Suspicious not because these claims are made for a technique that in some way violates a putative sanctity of nature, but suspicious instead because we are no longer easily convinced of a Modernity without consequence and are thus willing to listen to, take seriously those contentions of the corporate line which suggest on the contrary that GM crops will exacerbate the inequities of global food distribution (Action Aid 1999), have benefited from some profoundly economic decisions (Busch *et al.* 1991), and have traits which can cross species barriers (Ho 1998).

All of which puts a rather different spin on Victor's folly:

'You're deceiving us Victor and have been deceiving us for a long time. You bewail your crimes, but you do this in order to hide another, bigger crime. Your sin is not that you fashioned the monster. You created it for its beauty, for its greatness, and you were right. Your crime does not come from the hubris of which you accuse yourself; it is not that you played the demiurge, that you wanted to repeat Prometheus' exploit. Your crime is that you abandoned your creation. Were you not the first person it saw when it opened its eyes? Did it not stammer your name? Did it not hold out those deformed limbs towards you? It was born good, like you, handsome like you, wise like you, since you were its creator. Why flee? Why leave it alone, ill adapted to a world that rejected it? . . . No, your sin is not that you took yourself to be God, for God never abandons his creatures, no matter how sinful. He follows them, sacrifices Himself for them, throws Himself at their feet, sends them His only son; He saves them. Continual, continuous creation . . . You are drawing the wrong lesson. It is not the creative power that we need to curtail; it is our love that we need to extend, even to our lesser brothers who did not ask us for life. We acquainted them with existence. We need to acquaint them with love.'

(Latour 1996: 248–9)

Which is emphatically not to suggest that we just need to learn to love GM. What I think it does is that if we are to indulge in that old science fiction staple, a bit of utopic thinking in order to solve the issues that it has raised, we should be seeking to base it less on a reliance of the rest of 'us' on the restraint of the producers of techno-science, and more on the invention of means of participation whereby the 'we' made to participate in the 'collective experiments' (Latour 1999) – of which GM is only one – have a chance not only to question the way ahead, not only to veto the shortcut, but also to examine the paths not travelled (Stengers 2000). In this sense at least, collective responsibility means becoming more and not less involved.

### CONCLUSION: GEOGRAPHIES OF THE FUTURE?

*Frankenstein* has been our worldly-wise travelling companion for nearly two hundred years: the GM controversy marks only the latest juncture where its guidance has been sought. Furnishing 'a testing ground for every possible mode of interpretation' (Lipking 1996: 313): why then have I sought here to add yet another? For two reasons. Firstly because myths 'are susceptible to closure, or to adaptations which constrain their further development into fixed channels' (Baldick 1987: 4), and I have been concerned to challenge (in however insignificant a fashion) the currently hegemonic *Frankenstein* which seems to threaten just such a reduction. But also secondly, and more positively, because *Frankenstein* – even if only by counselling us against taking the easy way out – also seems to point in the direction of a style of going on in the world which, while in many senses aiming towards the same goal as the anti-GM protesters described above, is more likely to take a detour rather than the shortcut.

And it is looking forward – by very briefly outlining a couple of possible elements of this style – that I want to close this chapter. For one thing, according to Bruno Latour, that is the only way to go, whatever populates the uncharted landscape we are faced with:

Reactionary is a dangerous and unstable word, but it might be understood as simply the wish to bring care and caution *back* into the fabrication of facts and to make the salutary 'Beware!' audible again in the depths of the laboratories – including those of the science students. In that sense, only the modernists want to drag us back to an earlier time and an earlier

settlement, and this nonmodern precaution appears commonsensical
enough, perhaps even progressive – if we accept that progress means step-
ping into an even more entangled future.

(1999: 289–90)

The only question, then, is how to go forward. Philosopher Michel Serres
(here summarized by Marcel Hénaff) has some ideas:

*Procedural*: this term has its origins in *procedo*, the act of walking, or rather
moving forwards, step by step. This also means to advance among the
particularity of sites and conditions. Can one define a way of thinking
based on such a model? Is it not precisely what proper philosophy
denounces as empiricism? Not even that, for at the end of its journey,
empiricism intends to rejoin the universal it did not posit at the beginning.
We are dealing here with something quite different – that is, taking seriously the particularities of the sites, the unpredictability of circumstances,
the uneven patterns of the landscape and the hazardous nature of becoming. In short, again: how to think the local? Which means: is there a science
of the particular?

(Hénaff 1997: 72)

If we take Latour and Serres and *Frankenstein* seriously, perhaps our science
fiction geographies could after all be about the there and then as well as the here
and now.

### ACKNOWLEDGEMENTS

Many thanks to Steve Hinchliffe and Doreen Massey for drawing my attention
to the worst excesses of my own shortcuts by their close and generous readings of
an earlier draft of this chapter.

# REFERENCES

Abel, R. (1994) *The Ciné Goes to Town: French Cinema, 1896–1914*. Berkeley: University of California Press.

Abu-Lughod, J. (1989) *Before European Hegemony: The World System A.D. 1250–1350*. New York: Oxford University Press.

Action Aid (1999) *Astra Zeneca and Its Genetic Research: Feeding the World or Fuelling Hunger?* London: Action Aid.

Adamson, J. (1999) England without Cromwell. In Ferguson, N. (ed.) *Virtual History*. New York: Basic Books, pp. 91–124.

Aitken, S. and Lukinbeal, C. (1998) Of heroes, fools and fisher kings: cinematic representations of street myths and hysterical males. In Fyfe, N. (ed.) *Images of the Street: Planning Identity and Control in Public Space*. London and New York: Routledge, pp. 141–59.

—— and Zonn, L. (1993) Weir(d) sex: representations of gender–environment relations in Peter Weir's *Picnic at Hanging Rock* and *Gallipoli. Environment and Planning D: Society and Space* 11: 191–212.

—— and —— (eds) (1994) *Place, Power, Situation and Spectacle: A Geography of Film*. Lanham, MD: Rowman & Littlefield.

Aldiss, B. (1982) *Helliconia Spring*. London: Triad Grafton.

—— (1983) *Helliconia Summer*. London: Triad Grafton.

—— (1985) *Helliconia Winter*. London: Triad Grafton.

—— and Wingrove, D. (1986) *Trillion Year Spree: The History of Science Fiction*. London: Gollancz.

Alkon, P. (1994) Alternate history and postmodern temporality. In Cleary, T. (ed.) *Time, Literature and the Arts: Essays in Honor of Samuel L. Macey*. Victoria, BC: University of Victoria Press, pp. 65–84.

Anderson, P. (1983) *Imagined Communities*. London: Verso.

Anzaldúa, G. (1987) *Borderlands/La Frontera: The New Mestiza*. San Francisco: Spinster.

Armitt, L. (ed.) (1991) *Where No Man Has Gone Before: Women and Science Fiction*. London and New York: Routledge.

—— (1996) *Theorising the Fantastic*. London: Arnold.

—— (2000) *Contemporary Women's Fiction and the Fantastic*. New York: St Martin's Press.

Austin, K. (2000) The wheels of H. G. Wells. *Cycle Touring and Campaigning* June/July: 34–5.

Bakhtin, M. (1984) *Rabelais and His World*. Trans. Iswolsky, H. Bloomington: Indiana University Press.

—— (1994) *The Dialogic Imagination*. Trans. Emerson, C. and Holquist, M. Austin: University of Texas Press.

Baldick, C. (1987) *In Frankenstein's Shadow: Myth, Monstrosity, and Nineteenth Century Writing*. Oxford: Clarendon Press.

Ballard, J. G. (1961) The overloaded man. In *The Voices of Time*. London: Indigo (1997).

—— (1962a) *The Drowned World*. New York: Carroll and Graf (1987).

—— (1962b) *The Wind from Nowhere*. New York: Berkley.

—— (1964) *The Terminal Beach*. London: Gollancz.

—— (1965) *The Drought*. London: Jonathan Cape.

—— (1966) *The Crystal World*. New York: Farrar, Straus & Giroux.

—— (1971) *Vermilion Sands*. London: Dent (1985).

—— (1973) *Crash*. New York: Farrar, Straus & Giroux.

—— (1974) *Concrete Island*. London: Jonathan Cape.

—— (1975) *High-Rise*. London: Jonathan Cape.

—— (1979) *The Atrocity Exhibition*. St Albans, UK: Triad Panther.

—— (1982) Myths of the near future. In *Myths of the Near Future*. London: Panther (1984), pp. 7–43.

—— (1984) *Empire of the Sun*. New York: Simon and Schuster.

—— (1991) A response to the invitation to respond. *Science-Fiction Studies* 18: 329.

—— (1993) *The Kindness of Women*. Orlando, FL: Harcourt Brace Jovanovich.

—— (1994) *Rushing to Paradise*, London: Flamingo.

—— (1996a) *Cocaine Nights*. London: Flamingo.

—— (1996b) *A User's Guide to the New Millennium*. New York: Picador.

Balsamo, A. (1996) *Technologies of the Gendered Body*. Durham, NC: Duke University Press.

Barber, X. T. (1993) The roots of travel cinema: John L. Stoddard, E. Burton Holmes and the nineteenth-century illustrated travel lecture. *Film History* 5(1): 68–84.

Barmé, G. and Minford, J. (1988) *Seeds of Fire: Voices of Chinese Conscience*. New York: Hill and Wang.

Barnes, J. (1976) *The Beginnings of the Cinema in England*. London: David and Charles.

—— (1983) *The Rise of the Cinema in Gt. Britain: The Beginnings of the Cinema in England 1894–1901*, Volume 2: *Jubilee Year 1897*. London: Bishopsgate.

Barnes, T. (1996) *Logics of Dislocation*. New York: Guilford.

—— and Duncan, J. (eds) (1992) *Writing Worlds: Discourse, Text and Metaphor in the Representation of Landscape*. London: Routledge.

Barr, C. (1997) Before *Blackmail*: silent British cinema. In Murphy, R. (ed.) *The British Cinema Book*. London: British Film Institute, pp. 5–16.

Barr, M. (1992) *Feminist Fabulation: Space/Postmodern Fiction*. Iowa City: University of Iowa Press.

Barrow, J. (1990) *The World Within the World*. Oxford: Oxford University Press.

Barry, I. (1972) *Let's Go to the Movies*. New York: Arno Press.

Bataille, G. (1985) *Visions of Excess: Selected Writings*. Minneapolis: University of Minnesota Press.

Baudrillard, J. (1983) *In the Shadow of the Silent Majorities*. Trans. Foss, P. *et al.* New York: Semiotext(e).

—— (1991a) Simulacra and science fiction. *Science-Fiction Studies* 18: 309–13.

—— (1991b) Ballard's *Crash*. *Science-Fiction Studies* 18: 313–20.

—— (1994) Simulacra and science fiction. In *Simulacra and Simulation*. Ann Arbor: University of Michigan Press, pp. 121–7.

—— (1999) *Fatal Strategies*. London: Pluto Press.

Bauman, Z. (1993) *Postmodern Ethics*. London: Routledge.

Benedikt, M. (1991) Introduction. In Benedikt, M. (ed.) *Cyberspace: First Steps*. Cambridge, MA: MIT Press.

Benford, G. and Greenberg, M. (eds) (1989a) *What Might Have Been*, Volume 1: *Alternate Empires*. New York: Bantam.

—— and —— (eds) (1989b) *What Might Have Been*, Volume 2: *Alternate Heroes*. New York: Bantam.

—— and —— (eds) (1991) *What Might Have Been*, Volume 3: *Alternate Wars*. New York: Bantam.

—— and —— (eds) (1998) *Hitler Victorious*. London: Bantam.

Benjamin, W. (1968) *Illuminations*. New York: Schocken.

—— (1969) The work of art in the age of mechanical reproduction. In *Illuminations*. New York: Schocken, pp. 217–51.

Bennett, J. (1974) Counterfactuals and possible worlds. *Canadian Journal of Philosophy* 4: 381–402.

Bergson, H. (1984) *Creative Evolution*. Lanham, MD: University Press of America.

Berman, M. (1970) *The Politics of Authenticity: Radical Individualism and the Emergence of Modern Society*. New York: Atheneum.

Bhabha, H. (1986) The Other question: difference, discrimination and the discourse of colonialism. In Barker, F. *et al.* (eds) *Literature, Politics, and Theory*. London: Methuen, 148–72.

Biehl, J. (1998) *The Politics of Social Ecology: Libertarian Municipalism*. Buffalo, NY and Montréal: Black Rose Books.

Bingham, N. and Thrift, N. (2000) Some new instructions for travellers: the geography of Bruno Latour and Michel Serres. In Crang, M. and Thrift, N. (eds) *Thinking Space*. London: Routledge, pp. 281–301.

——, Valentine, G. and Holloway, S. (1999) Where do you want to go tomorrow? Connecting children and the Internet. *Environment and Planning D: Society and Space* 17(6): 655–72.

Birkerts, S. (1994) *The Gutenberg Elegies: The Fate of Reading in an Electronic Age*. New York: Fawcett Columbine.

Blaut, J. (1993) *The Colonizer's Model of the World*. New York: Guilford.

Blaylock, J. P. (1988) *The Digging Leviathan*. London: Grafton.

Bookchin, M. (1971) *Post-Scarcity Anarchism*. Palo Alto, CA: Ramparts Press.

—— (1974) *The Limits of the City*. New York: Harper Colophon.

—— (1980) *Toward an Ecological Society*. Cheektowaga, NY, and Montréal: Black Rose Books.

—— (1982) *The Ecology of Freedom: The Emergence and Dissolution of Hierarchy*. Palo Alto, CA: Cheshire Books.

—— (1986) *The Modern Crisis*. Philadelphia: New Society Publishers.

—— (1989) New social movements: the anarchic dimension. In Goodway, D. (ed.) *For Anarchism: History, Theory, and Practice*. London and New York: Routledge, pp. 259–74.

—— (1990) *Remaking Society: Pathways to a Green Future*. Boston: South End Press.

—— (1992a) Recovering evolution: a reply to Eckersley and Fox. *Society and Nature* no. 2, September/December: 144–73.

—— (1992b) *Urbanization Without Cities: The Rise and Decline of Citizenship*. Cheektowaga, NY, and Montréal: Black Rose Books.

—— (1994) *Which Way for the Ecology Movement: Essays by Murray Bookchin*. San Francisco and Edinburgh: AK Press.

—— (1995) *The Philosophy of Social Ecology: Essays on Dialectical Naturalism*. Cheektowaga, NY, and Montréal: Black Rose Books.

Borges, J. L. (1970) The garden of forking paths. In Yates, D. and Irby, J. (eds) *Labyrinths: Selected Stories and Other Writings.* Harmondsworth, Middlesex: Penguin, pp. 27–41.

Bottomore, S. (1996) Nine days' wonder: early cinema and its sceptics. In Williams, C. (ed.) *Cinema: The Beginnings and the Future. Essays Marking the Centenary of the First Film Show Projected to a Paying Audience in Britain.* London: Routledge, pp. 135–49.

Bowser, E. (1990) *The Transformation of Cinema, 1907–1915.* Berkeley: University of California Press.

Brewster, B. and Jacobs, L. (1997) *Theatre to Cinema: Stage Pictorialism and the Early Feature Film.* Oxford: Oxford University Press.

Broderick, D. (1995) *Reading by Starlight: Postmodern Science Fiction.* London and New York: Routledge.

Brooke-Rose, C. (1981) *A Rhetoric of the Unreal: Studies in Narrative and Structure, Especially of the Fantastic.* Cambridge: Cambridge University Press.

Brosseau, M. (1994) Geography's literature. *Progress in Human Geography* 18: 333–53.

—— (1995) The city in textual form: *Manhattan Transfer*'s New York. *Ecumene* 2: 89–114.

Bruno, G. (1987) Ramble city: postmodernism and *Blade Runner. October* 41: 61–74.

Bukatman, S. (1993) *Terminal Identity.* Durham, NC: Duke University Press.

Burch, N. (1990) *Life to Those Shadows.* London: British Film Institute.

Burgess, J. (1987) Landscapes in the living-room: television and landscape research. *Landscape Research* 12(3): 1–7.

—— (1990) The production and consumption of environmental meanings in the mass media: a research agenda for the 1990s. *Transactions of the Institute of British Geographers,* New Series 15: 139–61.

—— and Gold, J. R. (eds) (1985) *Geography, the Media, and Popular Culture.* London: Croom Helm.

Burgin, V., Donald, J. and Kaplan, D. (eds) (1989) *Formations of Fantasy.* New York: Routledge.

Busch, L., Lacy, W., Burkhardt, J. and Lacy, L. (1991) *Plants, Power, and Profit: Social, Economic, and Ethical Consequences of the New Biotechnologies.* Oxford: Blackwell.

Butler, J. (1993) *Bodies That Matter: On the Discursive Limits of 'Sex'.* New York: Routledge.

—— (1997) *The Psychic Life of Power: Theories in Subjection.* Stanford, CA: Stanford University Press.

Callard, F. (2000) The difficulties of theorizing fear: phobia in the late nineteenth century. Paper presented at the annual meeting of the RGS/IBG, Brighton.

Callon, M. (1998) An essay on framing and overflowing: economic externalities revisited by sociology. In Callon, M. (ed.) *The Law of the Markets.* Oxford: Blackwell, pp. 244–69.

Capra, F. (1983) *The Tao of Physics: An Exploration of the Parallels Between Modern Physics and Eastern Mysticism,* second edition. London: Fontana Paperbacks.

Carr, E. (1961) *What Is History?* New York: Vintage.

Carter, P. (1987) *The Road to Botany Bay.* London: Faber.

Chakrabarty, D. (1992) Post-coloniality and the artifice of history: who speaks for 'Indian' pasts? *Representations* 37, Winter: 1–26.

Chanan, M. (1996) *The Dream That Kicks: The Pre-history and Early Years of Cinema in Britain,* second edition. London: Routledge.

Chirot, D. (1985) The rise of the West. *American Sociological Review* 50: 181–95.

Christ, C. T. and Jordon, J. O. (eds) (1995) *Victorian Literature and the Victorian Visual Imagination.* Berkeley: University of California Press.

Christie, I. (1994) *The Last Machine: Early Cinema and the Birth of the Modern World*. London: British Film Institute.

Clark, J. (1999) British America. In Ferguson, N. (ed.) *Virtual History*. New York: Basic Books.

Clarke, D. B. (ed.) (1997) *The Cinematic City*. London: Routledge.

Clover, C. (1989) Her body, himself: gender and the slasher film. In Donald, J. (ed.) *Fantasy and the Cinema*. London: British Film Institute, pp. 91–133.

Cohen, J. (1991) How to design an alien. *New Scientist* 21/28 December: 18–21.

Cole, K. C. (1984) *Sympathetic Vibrations: Reflections on Physics As a Way of Life*. Toronto: Bantam Books (1985).

Collingwood, R. (1965) The nature and aims of a philosophy of history. In Debbins, W. (ed.) *Essays in the Philosophy of History: R. G. Collingwood*. Austin: University of Texas Press, pp. 41–58.

Cowley, R. (ed.) (1999) *What If?* New York: G. P. Putnam.

Creed, B. (1986) Horror and the monstrous-feminine: an imaginary abjection. *Screen* 27 (1): 44–70.

—— (1993) *The Monstrous-Feminine: Film, Feminism, Psychoanalysis*. London and New York: Routledge.

Cresswell, T. (1993) Mobility as resistance: a geographical reading of Kerouac's *On the Road*. *Transactions of the Institute of British Geographers*, New Series 18: 249–62.

Csicsery-Ronay Jr, I. (1991) Editorial introduction: postmodernism's SF/SF's postmodernism. *Science-Fiction Studies* 18: 305–8.

Curry, M. R. (1996) *The Work in the World: Geographical Practice and the Written Word*. Minneapolis: University of Minnesota Press.

Daniels, S. and Rycroft, S. (1993) Mapping the modern city: Alan Sillitoe's Nottingham novels. *Transactions of the Institute of British Geographers*, New Series 18: 460–80.

Darby, C. (1948) The regional geography of Hardy's Wessex. *Geographical Review* 38: 426–43.

Davies, P. (1985) *Superforce: The Search for a Grand Unified Theory of Nature*. London: Unwin Paperbacks.

Davis, L. (1987) *Resisting Novels: Ideology and Fiction*. New York and London: Methuen.

Davis, M. (1990) *City of Quartz: Excavating the Future in Los Angeles*. New York: Verso.

—— (1992) *Beyond* Blade Runner*: Urban Control, the Ecology of Fear*. Open Magazine Pamphlet Series, no. 23. Westfield, NJ: Open Media.

Dear, M. and Flusty, S. (1998) Postmodern urbanism. *Annals of the Association of American Geographers* 88(1): 50–72.

Delany, S. (1994) *Silent Interviews: On Language, Race, Sex, Science Fiction, and Some Comics*. Hanover, NH: Wesleyan University Press.

De Lauretis, T. (1984) *Alice Doesn't: Feminism, Semiotics, Cinema*. London: Macmillan.

Demandt, A. (1993) *History That Never Happened*. Jefferson, NC: McFarland.

Derrida, J. (1987) *Of Grammatology*. Baltimore: Johns Hopkins University Press.

—— (1988) *Limited Inc*. Evanston, IL: Northwestern University Press.

Dick, P. K. (1962) *The Man in the High Castle*. New York: Bantam.

—— (1968) *Do Androids Dream of Electric Sheep?* New York: Ballantine Books.

Dirlik, A. (1994) *After the Revolution: Waking to Global Capitalism*. Hanover, NH: Wesleyan University Press.

—— (1997) *The Postcolonial Aura: Third World Criticism in the Age of Global Capitalism*. Boulder, CO: Westview.

Doane, M. (1982) Film and the masquerade: theorizing the female spectator. *Screen* 23 (3–4): 74–87.

Doane, M. (1991) *Femmes Fatales: Feminism, Film Theory, Psychoanalysis.* London: Routledge.

Dodge, M. and Kitchin, R. (2000) *Mapping Cyberspace.* London: Routledge.

Doel, M. A. (1999a) Occult Hollywood: unfolding the Americanization of world cinema. In Slater, D. and Taylor, P. J. (eds) *The American Century: Consensus and Coercion in the Projection of American Power.* London: Sage, pp. 243–60.

—— (1999b) *Poststructuralist Geographies: The Diabolical Art of Spatial Science.* New York: Rowman and Littlefield Publishers, Inc.

—— and Clarke, D. B. (1997) From ramble city to the screening of the eye: Blade Runner, death and symbolic exchange. In Clarke, D. B. (ed.) *The Cinematic City.* New York: Routledge, pp. 140–67.

Doherty, P. (1997) *Marge Piercy: An Annotated Bibliography.* Westport, CT: Greenwood Press.

Donley, A. J. and Friedman, C. C. (1985) *Einstein As Myth and Muse.* Cambridge, UK: Cambridge University Press (1989).

Douglass, P. (1999) Bergson and cinema: friends or foes? In Mullarkey, J. (ed.) *The New Bergson.* Manchester: Manchester University Press, pp. 209–27.

Dozois, G. and Schmidt, S. (eds) (1998) *Roads Not Taken.* New York: Ballantine.

Duncan, J. and Ley, D. (1982) Structural Marxism and human geography. *Annals of the Association of American Geographers* 72: 30–59.

—— and —— (eds) (1993) *Place/Culture/Representation.* London and New York: Routledge.

Duncan, N. and Sharp, J. (1993) Confronting representation(s). *Environment and Planning D: Society and Space* 11: 473–86.

Eckersley, R. (1992) Diving evolution: the ecological ethics of Murray Bookchin. *Society and Nature* no. 2, September/December: 120–43.

Ellul, J. (1964) *The Technological Society.* New York: Random House.

Elsaesser, T. with Barker, A. (eds) (1990) *Early Cinema: Space, Frame, Narrative.* London: British Film Institute.

Eyerman, R. and Lofgren, O. (1995) Romancing the road: road movies and images of mobility. *Theory, Culture and Society* 12: 53–79.

Fearon, J. (1991) Counterfactuals and hypothesis testing in political science. *World Politics* 43: 169–95.

Ferguson, N. (ed.) (1999) *Virtual History.* New York: Basic Books.

Fielding, R. (1983) Hale's Tours, ultra-realism in the pre-1910 motion picture. In Fell, J. L. (ed.) *Film Before Griffith.* Berkeley: University of California Press, pp. 116–31.

Flannigan, M. (1999) The *Alien* series and generic hybridity. In Cartmell, D., Hunter, I. Q., Kaye, H. and Whelehan, I. (eds) *Alien Identities: Exploring Differences in Film and Fiction.* London: Pluto Press.

Fogel, R. (1964) *Railways and American Economic Growth: Essays in Interpretative Econometric History.* Baltimore: Johns Hopkins University Press.

Foster, L. (1994) City primeval: high noon in Elmore Leonard's Detroit. In Preston, P. and Simpson-Housley, P. (eds) *Writing the City.* London and New York: Routledge, pp. 125–46.

Foucault, M. (1977) A preface to transgression. In Bouchard, D. (ed.) *Michel Foucault: Language, Counter-Memory, Practice: Selected Essays and Interviews.* Trans. Bouchard, D. and Simon, S. Ithaca, NY: Cornell University Press, pp. 29–52.

Freud, S. (1955) Medusa's head. In Strachey, J. (ed.), *Standard Edition of the Complete Psychological Works*, Volume 18. London: Hogarth Press, pp. 273–4.

Friends of the Earth Birmingham (1998/99) *Dec/Jan Action Briefing.* Birmingham: Friends of the Earth.

Fry, S. (1996) *Making History.* New York: Soho Press.

Fukuyama, F. (1992) *The End of History and the Last Man.* New York: Free Press.

Garreau, J. (1991) *Edge City: Life on the New Frontier.* New York: Doubleday.

Gertler, M. (1995) 'Being there': proximity, organisation and culture in the development and adoption of advanced manufacturing technologies. *Economic Geography* 71: 1–25.

Gibson, W. (1984) *Neuromancer.* New York: Bantam.

—— (1989) *Mona Lisa Overdrive.* New York: Bantam Books.

—— (1992) *Virtual Light.* London: Penguin.

—— (1996) *Idoru.* London: Penguin.

—— (1999) *All Tomorrow's Parties.* London: Penguin.

Gibson-Graham, J. K. (1996) *The End of Capitalism (As We Knew It).* London: Blackwell.

Giddens, A. (1981) *A Contemporary Critique of Historical Materialism.* Berkeley: University of California Press.

—— (1984) *The Constitution of Society.* Berkeley: University of California Press.

—— (1991) *Modernity and Self-Identity: Self and Society in the Late Modern Age.* Stanford, CA: Stanford University Press.

Gledhill, C. (1988) Pleasurable negotiations. In Pribram, E. D. (ed.) *Female Spectators: Looking at Film and Television.* London and New York: Verso.

Gober, P. (1997) Megalopolis: the future is now. In Hanson, S. (ed.) *Ten Geographic Ideas That Changed the World.* New Brunswick, NJ: Rutgers University Press, pp. 182–202.

Goddard, J. and Pringle, D. (1976) *J. G. Ballard: The First Twenty Years.* Slough, UK: Hollen Street Press Ltd.

Goldenweiser, A. (1913) The principle of limited possibilities in the development of culture. *Journal of American Folklore* 26: 259–90.

Golding, W. (1959) *Lord of the Flies.* New York: Capricorn Books.

Goodman, N. (1978) *Ways of Worldmaking.* Indianapolis: Hackett.

Gould, S. J. (1989) *Wonderful Life: The Burgess Shale and the Nature of History.* New York: Norton.

Grannovetter, M. (1985) Economic action and social structure: the problem of embeddedness. *American Journal of Sociology* 91: 481–510.

Gregory, B. (1990) *Inventing Reality: Physics As Language.* New York: John Wiley & Sons, Inc.

Gregory, D. (1976) Rethinking historical geography. *Area* 8: 295–9.

—— (1978) The discourse of the past: phenomenology, structuralism and historical geography. *Journal of Historical Geography* 4: 161–73.

—— (1981) Human agency and human geography. *Transactions of the Institute of British Geographers*, New Series 6: 1–18.

—— (1982) Action and structure in historical geography. In Baker, A. and Billinge, M. (eds) *Period and Place: Research Methods in Historical Geography.* Cambridge, UK: Cambridge University Press.

—— (1994) *Geographical Imaginations.* Oxford: Blackwell.

—— (1995) Imaginative geographies. *Progress in Human Geography* 19: 447–85.

Gribbin, J. (1986) *In Search of the Big Bang: Quantum Physics and Cosmology.* New York: Bantam Books.

Grosz, E. (1994) *Volatile Bodies: Toward a Corporeal Feminism.* Bloomington: Indiana University Press.

Guelke, L. (1977) The role of laws in human geography. *Progress in Human Geography* 1: 376–86.

Gunning, T. (1996) 'Now you see it, now you don't': the temporality of the cinema of attractions. In Abel, R. (ed.) *Silent Film.* London: Athlone, pp. 71–84.

Hall, S. (1991) Old and new identities; old and new ethnicities. In King, A. (ed.) *Culture, Globalization, and the World-System.* London: Macmillan, pp. 41–68.

Haraway, D. (1985) A manifesto for cyborgs: science, technology and socialist feminism in the 1980s. *Socialist Review* 15: 65–107.

—— (1989) *Simians, Cyborgs, and Women.* New York: Routledge.

—— (1994) A game of cat's cradle: science studies, feminist theory, cultural studies. *Configurations* 2(1): 59–71.

—— (1997) *Modest_Witness@SecondMillennium.FemaleMan©_Meets_OncoMouse™* London: Routledge.

Harris, R. (1992) *Fatherland.* New York: HarperCollins.

Harrison, H. (1998) *Stars and Stripes Forever.* New York: Bantam.

Harvey, D. (1989) *The Condition of Postmodernity.* Oxford: Blackwell.

—— (1990) Between space and time: reflections on the geographical imagination. *Annals of the Association of American Geographers* 80: 418–34.

Hawking, S. (1988) *A Brief History of Time,* tenth edition. New York: Bantam Books.

Hawthorn, G. (1991) *Plausible Worlds: Possibility and Understanding in History and the Social Sciences.* Cambridge, UK: Cambridge University Press.

Hayden, G. (1997) *Pacific Empire.* Bedford, IN: JoNa Books.

Hayles, K. (1999) *How We Became Posthuman: Virtual Bodies in Cybernetics, Literature and Informatics.* Chicago: University of Chicago Press.

Hearnshaw, F. (1929) *The 'Ifs' of History.* New York: George Newnes.

Heisenberg, W. (1962) *Physics and Philosophy: The Revolution in Modern Science.* London: Pelican Books (1989).

Hénaff, M. (1997) Of stones, angels, and humans: Michel Serres and the global city. *SubStance* 26(7): 59–80.

Hepworth, C. M. (1951) *Came the Dawn.* London: Phoenix House.

Herbert, F. (1965) *Dune.* New York: Penguin Putnam Inc. (1990).

Higson, A. (1987) The landscapes of television. *Landscape Research* 12(3): 8–13.

Ho, M.-W. (1998) *Genetic Engineering: Dream or Nightmare?* Bath: Gateway Books.

Hoffman, B. (1959) *The Strange Story of the Quantum,* second edition. New York: Dover Publications, Inc.

hooks, b. (1990) *Yearning: Race, Gender, and Cultural Politics.* Boston: South End Press.

Horkheimer, M. and Adorno, T. (1998) *Dialectic of Enlightenment.* New York: Continuum.

Huntingdon, J. (1989) *Rationalizing Genius: Ideological Strategies in the Classic American Science Fiction Short Story.* New Brunswick, NJ, and London: Rutgers University Press.

Hutcheon, L. (1988) *A Poetics of Postmodernism.* London: Routledge.

Jackson, R. (1981) *Fantasy: The Literature of Subversion.* London: Methuen.

James, K. (1996) Extensions: an introduction to the longer views of Samuel R. Delany. In Delany, S. (ed.) *Longer Views: Extended Essays.* Hanover, NH: Wesleyan University Press, pp. xiii–xl.

Jameson, F. (1991) *Postmodernism, or the Cultural Logic of Late Capitalism.* London: Verso.

—— (1992) *The Geopolitical Aesthetic.* Indiana and London: British Film Institute.

Jarry, A. (1969) *The Ubu Plays.* New York: Grove Press.

—— (1996) *Exploits and Opinions of Dr. Faustroll, Pataphysician.* Boston: Exact Change.

Jay, L. J. (1975) The Black Country of Francis Brett Young. *Transactions of the Institute of British Geographers* 66: 57–72.

Jay, M. (1994) *Downcast Eyes: The Denigration of Vision in Twentieth-Century French Thought.* Berkeley: University of California Press.

Jeffords, S. (1993) Can masculinity be terminated? In Cohen, S. and Clark, I. R. (eds). *Screening the Male.* London and New York: Routledge.

Jencks, C. (1993) *Heteropolis: Los Angeles, the Riots and the Strange Beauty of Hetero-Architecture.* London: Academy Editions.

Johnston, C. (1973) Women's cinema as counter-cinema. In Johnston, C. (ed.) *Notes on Women's Cinema.* London: Society for Education in Film and Television, pp. 24–31.

Johnston, R., Gregory, D. and Smith, D. (1994) *Dictionary of Human Geography*, third edition. Oxford: Blackwell.

Jones, J. and Hanham, R. (1995) Contingency, realism, and the expansion method. *Geographical Analysis* 27: 185–207.

Jones III, J. P. (1995) Making geography objectively: ocularity, representation, and the nature of geography. In Jones III, J. P., Natter, W. and Schatzki, T. (eds) *Objectivity and Its Other.* New York: Guilford, pp. 67–92.

Jones, R. (1983) *Physics As Metaphor.* London: Sphere Books Ltd/Abacus.

Juno, A. and Vale, V. (eds) (1984) *Re/Search: J. G. Ballard.* San Francisco: Re/Search Publishing.

Kadrey, R. and McCaffery, L. (1991) Cyberpunk 101. In McCaffery, L. (ed.) *Storming the Reality Studio.* Durham, NC: Duke.

Kaufman-Osborn, T. (1997) *Creatures of Prometheus: Gender and the Politics of Technology.* Lanham, MD: Rowman and Littlefield.

Kenney, J. (1995) Climate, race, and imperial authority: the symbolic landscape of the British hill station in India. *Annals of the Association of American Geographers* 85: 694–714.

Kern, S. (1983) *The Culture of Time and Space 1880–1918.* Cambridge, MA: Harvard University Press.

Kirby, K. (1996) *Indifferent Boundaries: Spatial Concepts of Human Subjectivity.* New York: Guilford.

Kitchin, R. (1998) *Cyberspace: The World in the Wires.* Chichester: Wiley.

—— and Kneale, J. (2001) Science fiction or future fact? Exploring imaginative geographies of the new millennium. *Progress in Human Geography* 25: 17–33.

Klein, M. N. (1991) Building *Blade Runner. Social Text* 28: 147–52.

Kneale, J. (1999) The virtual realities of technology and fiction: reading William Gibson's cyberspace. In Crang, M., Crang, P. and May, J. (eds) *Virtual Geographies.* London: Routledge, pp. 205–21.

Knowles, C. (2000) *Bedlam on the Streets.* London and New York: Routledge.

Kovel, J. (1998) Negating Bookchin. In Light, A. (ed.) *Social Ecology After Bookchin.* New York: Guilford, pp. 27–57.

Kristeva, J. (1982) *Power of Horrors.* New York: Columbia University Press.

Kuhn, A. (1984) Women's genres: melodrama, soap opera and theory. *Screen* 25(1): 18–28.

—— (1990) Repressions. In Kuhn, A. (ed.) *Alien Zone: Cultural Theory and Contemporary Science Fiction Cinema.* London and New York: Verso, pp. 91–5.

Kvart, I. (1986) *A Theory of Counterfactuals.* Indianapolis: University of Indiana Press.

Lanham, R. (1993) The electronic word: literary study and the digital revolution. In *The Electronic Word: Democracy, Technology and the Arts.* Chicago: University of Chicago Press, p. 228.

Lant, A. (1995) Haptical cinema. *October* 74: 45–73.

Lapham, L. (1999) Furor Teutonicus: the Teutoburg forest, A.D. 9. In Cowley, R. (ed.) *What If?* New York: G. P. Putnam, pp. 57–70.

Laplanche, J. and Pontalis, J.-B. (1973) *The Language of Psycho-Analysis.* Trans. Nicholson-Smith, D. New York: Norton.

—— and —— (1986 [1964]) Fantasy and the origins of sexuality. In Burgin, V., Donald, J. and Kaplan, C. (eds) *Formations of Fantasy.* London and New York: Routledge, pp. 5–34.

Latour, B. (1996) *Aramis, or the Love of Technology.* London: Harvard University Press.

—— (1997) *On Actor-Network Theory: A Few Clarifications.* [Internet] Centre for Social Theory and Technology (CSTT), Keele University, UK. Available from http://www.keele.ac.uk/depts/stt/ant/latour.htm (accessed 10 November 1998).

—— (1999) *Pandora's Hope: Essays on the Reality of Science Studies.* London: Harvard University Press.

Laurel, B. (1993) *Computers As Theatre.* Glenview, IL: Addison-Wesley Publishing.

Lefanu, S. (1988) *In the Chinks of the World Machine: Feminism and Science Fiction.* London: The Women's Press.

Lefebvre, H. (1991) *The Production of Space.* Trans. Nicholson-Smith, D. Oxford: Blackwell.

Lem, S. (1987) *Solaris.* Trans. Kilmartin, J. and Cox, S. London: Harcourt Brace Jovanovich.

Lewis, D. (1973) *Counterfactuals.* Oxford: Blackwell.

—— (1986) *On the Plurality of Worlds.* Oxford: Blackwell.

Lewis, L. and Wigen, K. (1997) *The Myth of Continents.* Berkeley: University of California Press.

Lewontin, R. C. (1994) The dream of the human genome. In Bender, G. and Drucker, T. (eds) *Culture on the Brink: Ideologies of Technology.* Seattle: Bay Books, pp. 107–27.

Lipking, L. (1996) Frankenstein the true story: or Rousseau judges Jean–Jacques. In Shelley, M. *Frankenstein.* New York: Norton Critical Editions, pp. 313–31.

Lipset, S. (1990) *Continental Divide: The Values and Institutions of the United States and Canada.* New York: Routledge.

Livingstone, D. (1992) *The Geographical Tradition: Episodes in the History of a Contested Enterprise.* Oxford: Blackwell.

Lu, H. (1999) *Beyond the Neon Lights: Everyday Shanghai in the Early Twentieth Century.* Berkeley: University of California Press.

Luckhurst, R. (1994) Petition, repetition, and 'autobiography': J. G. Ballard's *'Empire of the Sun'* and *'The Kindness of Women'. Contemporary Literature* 35: 688–709.

Lynch, K. (1960) *The Image of the City.* Cambridge, MA: MIT Press.

Lyotard, J. F. (1979) *The Postmodern Condition.* Trans. Bennington, G. and Massumi, B. Minneapolis: University of Minnesota Press.

—— (1984) *The Postmodern Condition: A Report on Knowledge.* Minneapolis: University of Minnesota Press.

Macauley, D. (1998) Evolution and revolution: the ecological anarchism of Kropotkin and Bookchin. In Light, A. (ed.) *Social Ecology After Bookchin.* New York: Guilford, pp. 298–342.

McCaffery, L. (ed.) (1991) *Storming the Reality Studio.* Durham, NC: Duke University Press.

McCole, J. (1993) *Walter Benjamin and the Antinomies of Tradition.* London: Cornell University Press.

Macksey, K. (ed.) (1995) *The Hitler Options: Alternate Decisions of World War II.* London: Greenhill Books.

Malmgren, C. D. (1991) *Worlds Apart: Narratology of Science Fiction.* Bloomington: Indiana University Press.

—— (1993) Self and Other in SF: alien encounters. *Science-Fiction Studies* 20: 15–33.

Mann, M. (1986) *The Sources of Social Power*. Cambridge, UK: Cambridge University Press.

Meinig, D. (1993) *The Shaping of America: A Geographical Perspective on 500 Years of History,* Volume 2: *Continental America, 1800–1867*. New Haven: Yale University Press.

Merchant, C. (1994) Introduction. In Merchant, C. (ed.) *Key Concepts in Critical Theory: Ecology*. Atlantic Highlands, NJ: Humanities Press, pp. 1–25.

Moorcock, M. (1993) Introduction. In Wells, H. G. *The Time Machine*. London: Everyman, pp. xxix–xli.

Moore, W. (1953) *Bring the Jubilee*. New York: Bantam.

Moretti, F. (1998) *Atlas of the European Novel, 1800–1900*. London: Verso.

Morris, M. (1992) Great moment in social climbing: King Kong and the Human Fly. In Colomina, B. (ed.) *Sexuality and Space*. Princeton, NJ: Princeton Architectural Press, pp. 1–51.

Moulthrop, S. (1994). Rhizome and resistance: hypertext and the dreams of a new culture. In Landow, G. P. (ed.) *Hyper/Text/Theory*. Baltimore: Johns Hopkins University Press, pp. 299–319.

Mulvey, L. (1975) Visual pleasure and narrative cinema. *Screen* 16(3): 6–18.

Nadeau, R. (1981) *Readings from the New Book of Nature: Physics and Metaphysics in the Modern Novel*. Amherst: University of Massachusetts Press.

Nast, H. (2000) Mapping the 'unconscious': racism and the Oedipal family. *Annals of the Association of American Geographers* 90(2): 215–55.

Natter, W. (1994) The city as cinematic space: Modernism and place. In Aitken, S. and Zonn, L. (eds) *Place, Power, Situation and Spectacle: A Geography of Film*. Lanham, MD: Rowman and Littlefield, pp. 203–27.

—— and Jones, J. P. (1997) Identity, space, and other uncertainties. In Benko, G. and Strohmayer, U. (eds) *Space and Social Theory: Interpreting Modernity and Postmodernity*. Oxford: Blackwell, pp. 141–61.

Neale, S. (1990a) Questions of genre. *Screen* 31: 45–66.

—— (1990b) 'You've got to be fucking kidding!' Knowledge, belief and judgement in science fiction. In Kuhn, A. (ed.) *Alien Zone*. London and New York: Verso, pp. 160–8.

Nisbet, R. (1980) *History of the Idea of Progress*. New York: Basic Books.

Nozick, R. (1981) *Philosophical Explanations*. Cambridge, MA: Harvard University Press.

Nute, D. (1975) Counterfactuals and the similarity of worlds. *Journal of Philosophy* 72: 773–8.

Nye, D. (1994) *American Technological Sublime*. Cambridge, MA: MIT.

—— (1998) *Narratives and Spaces*. Exeter: University of Exeter Press.

Oakeshott, M. (1933) *Experience and Its Modes*. Cambridge, UK: Cambridge University Press.

Oettermann, S. (1997) *The Panorama: History of a Mass Medium*. New York: Zone Books.

Pagels, H. R. (1984 [1982]) *The Cosmic Code: Quantum Physics As the Language of Nature*. Harmondsworth, Middlesex: Pelican Books.

Pearson, R. E. (1992) *Eloquent Gestures: The Transformation of Performance Style in the Griffith and Biograph Films*. Berkeley: University of California Press.

—— (1996) The attractions of cinema, or, how I learned to start worrying about loving early film. In Williams, C. (ed.) *Cinema: The Beginnings and the Future. Essays Marking the Centenary of the First Film Show Projected to a Paying Audience in Britain*. London: Routledge, pp. 150–7.

Penley, C. (1990) Time travel, primal scene and the critical dystopia. In Kuhn, A. (ed.) *Alien Zone*. London and New York: Verso, pp. 128–44.

Phillips, R. (1997) *Mapping Men and Empire: A Geography of Adventure*. London and New York: Routledge.

Piercy, M. (1991) *He, She and It*. New York: Ballantine Books.

Pile, S. (1996) *The Body and the City*. London and New York: Routledge.

—— and Thrift, N. (1995) *Mapping the Subject: Geographies of Cultural Transformation*. London: Routledge.

Pocock, D. (1979) The novelist's image of the North. *Transactions of the Institute of British Geographers*, New Series 4: 62–76.

—— (ed.) (1981) *Humanistic Geography and Literature: Essays on the Experience of Place*. London: Croom Helm.

Porush, D. (1996) Hacking the brainstem: postmodern metaphysics and Stephenson's *Snow Crash*. In Markley, R. (ed.) *Virtual Realities and Their Discontents*. Baltimore: Johns Hopkins University Press, pp. 107–41.

Prakash, G. (1992) Postcolonial criticism and Indian historiography. *Social Text* 31/32: 8–19.

Pratt, G. (1998) Geographic metaphors in feminist theory. In Aiken, S. H., Brigham, A., Marston, S. A. and Waterstone, P. (eds) *Making Worlds: Gender, Metaphor and Materiality*. Tucson: University of Arizona Press, pp. 13–30.

Pred, A. (1990) *Making Histories and Constructing Human Geographies*. Boulder, CO: Westview Press.

Price, D. (2000) *History Made, History Imagined: Contemporary Literature, Poiesis, and the Past*. Champaign-Urbana: University of Illinois Press.

Prignogine, I. (1996) *The End of Certainty: Time, Chaos, and the New Laws of Nature*. New York: Free Press.

Pringle, D. (1979) *Earth Is the Alien Planet*. San Bernardino, CA: The Borgo Press.

—— (1984) *J. G. Ballard: A Primary and Secondary Bibliography*. Boston: G. K. Hall & Co.

Purchase, G. (1994) *Anarchism and Environmental Survival*. Tucson, AZ: Sharp Press.

Putnam, H. (1987) *The Many Faces of Realism*. LaSalle, IL: Open Court Publishing.

Rawlence, C. (1990) *The Missing Reel*. London: Collins.

Resnick, M. (ed.) (1992) *Alternate Presidents*. New York: Tor Publishing.

—— (ed.) (1993) *Alternate Warriors*. New York: Tor Publishing.

—— (ed.) (1994) *Alternate Outlaws*. New York: Tor Publishing.

—— (ed.) (1997) *Alternate Tyrants*. New York: Tor Publishing.

Richards, J. (1999) *Things to Come* and science fiction in the 1930s. In Hunter, I. Q. (ed.) *British Science Fiction Cinema*. London: Routledge, pp. 16–32.

Rifkin, J. (1998) *The Biotech Century*. London: Phoenix.

Roberts, R. (1993) *A New Species: Gender and Science in Science Fiction*. Urbana: University of Illinois Press.

Robinson, D. (1996) *From Peep Show to Palace: The Birth of American Film*. New York: Columbia University Press.

Robinson, K. S. (1990) *Pacific Edge*. New York: Tom Doherty Associates Inc./A Tor Book.

—— (1993) *Red Mars*. New York: Bantam Books/Spectra.

—— (1995) *Green Mars*. New York: Bantam Books/Spectra.

—— (1997) *Blue Mars*. New York: Bantam Books/Spectra.

—— (1999) *Antarctica*. New York: Bantam Books.

Rogers, A. (1992) The boundaries of reason: the world, the homeland, and Edward Said. *Environment and Planning D: Society and Space* 10: 511–26.

Rose, G. (1993) *Feminism and Geography*. Minneapolis: University of Minnesota Press.

Ross, A. (1991) *Strange Weather: Culture, Science and Technology in the Age of Limits*. London: Verso.

Ruddick, N. (1992) Ballard/*Crash*/Baudrillard. *Science-Fiction Studies* 19: 354–60.

Russ, J. (1975) *The Female Man.* New York: Bantam Press.

Said, E. (1978) *Orientalism.* New York: Vintage.

Samuelson, D. N. (1993) Modes of extrapolation: the formulas of hard SF. *Science-Fiction Studies* 20: 191–232.

Sanders, B. (1995) *A Is for Ox: The Rise of Violence and the Decline of Literacy in the Electronic Age.* New York: Vintage Books.

Sargent, P. (1998) *Climb the Wind.* New York: HarperCollins.

Sayer, A. (1992) *Method in Social Science: A Realist Approach.* London: Routledge.

Schivelbusch, W. (1988) *Disenchanted Night: The Industrialisation of Light in the Nineteenth Century.* Oxford: Berg.

Schmid, D. (1995) Imagining safe urban space: the contribution of detective fiction to radical geography. *Antipode* 27: 242–69.

Schmidt, A. (1983) *History and Structure.* Cambridge, MA: MIT Press.

Schwartz, V. R. (1998) *Spectacular Realities: Early Mass Culture in Fin-de-Siècle Paris.* Berkeley: University of California Press.

Serres, M. (1991) *Rome: The Book of Foundations.* Stanford, CA: Stanford University Press.

Sharp, J. (1994) A topology of 'post' nationality: (re)mapping identity in *The Satanic Verses. Ecumene* 1: 65–76.

Shelley, M. (1996 [1818]) *Frankenstein.* New York: Norton Critical Editions.

Shippey, T. (1991) Preface: learning to read SF. In Shippey, T. (ed.) *Fictional Space.* Oxford: Basil Blackwell Ltd, pp. 1–33.

Short, J. R. (1991) *Imagined Country: Environment, Culture and Society.* London: Routledge.

Short, R. (1980) *Dada and Surrealism.* Secaucus, NJ: Chartwell Books.

Sibley, D. (1995) *Geographies of Exclusion: Society and Difference in the West.* London: Routledge.

Silverman, K. (1992) *Male Subjectivity at the Margins.* London and New York: Routledge.

Simmons, I. G. (1993) *Interpreting Nature: Cultural Constructions of the Environment.* London: Routledge.

Simon, D. (1998) Rethinking (post) Modernism, postcolonialism and posttraditionalism: South–North perspectives. *Environment and Planning D: Society and Space* 16: 219–45.

Smith, J. (1996) Geographical rhetoric: modes and tropes of appeal. *Annals of the Association of American Geographers* 86: 1–20.

Smith, S. (1972) The image of women in film: some suggestions for future research. *Women and Film* 1: 13–21.

Smoler, F. (1999) Past tense. *American Heritage* September: 45–9.

Snowman, D. (ed.) (1979) *If I Had Been . . . Ten Historical Fantasies.* London: Bantam.

Sobchack, V. (1987) *Screening Space: The American Science Fiction Film,* second edition. New York: Ungar.

Sobel, R. (1973) *For Want of a Nail . . . If Burgoyne Had Won at Saratoga.* New York: Macmillan.

Soja, E. (1989) *Postmodern Geographies: The Reassertion of Space in Critical Social Theory.* London: Verso.

—— (1993) Postmodern geographies and the critique of historicism. In Jones, J., Natter, W. and Schatzki, T. (eds) *Postmodern Contentions.* New York: Guilford.

—— (1996) *Thirdspace: Journeys to Los Angeles and Other Real-and-Imagined Places.* Oxford: Blackwell.

Solove, A. J. (1995) Monstrosity and male birthing in Mary Shelley's *Frankenstein* and Marge Piercy's *He, She and It.* MA thesis, Montclair State University, Montclair, CA.

Sontag, S. (1965) The imagination of disaster. In Mast, G. and Cohen, M. (eds) *Film Theory and Criticism: Introductory Readings*, third edition (1985). Oxford: Oxford University Press, pp. 451–65.

Spivak, G. C. (1988) Can the subaltern speak? In Nelson, C. and Grossberg, L. (eds) *Marxism and the Interpretation of Culture*. London: Macmillan, pp. 207–20.

Squire, J. (1931) *If It Had Happened Otherwise: Lapses into Imaginary History*. New York: Longmans, Green.

Stengers, I. (2000) *The Invention of Modern Science*. Minneapolis: University of Minnesota Press.

Stephenson, N. (1992) *Snow Crash*. New York: Bantam Books.

—— (1993) In the kingdom of Mao Bell, or destroy the users on the waiting list! *Wired* 2.02, online version: http://www.wired.com/wired/archive/2.02/mao.bell.html.

—— (1995) *The Diamond Age*. New York: Bantam.

—— (1996a) *The Diamond Age*. New York: Spectra Books.

—— (1996b) Hotwired online chat with Neal Stephenson (17 December): http://hotwired.lycos.com/talk/club/special/transcripts/96-12-17-stephenson.html.

Sterling, B. (1988) Preface. In Gibson, W. *Burning Chrome*. London: Grafton, pp. 9–13.

—— and Gibson, W. (1991) *The Difference Engine*. New York: Bantam.

Stone, A. (1991) Will the real body please stand up?: boundary stories about virtual cultures. In Benedikt, M. (ed.) *Cyberspace: First Steps*. Cambridge, MA: MIT Press, pp. 81–118.

Storper, M. (1988) Big structures, small events, and large processes in economic geography. *Environment and Planning A* 20: 165–85.

—— (1997) *The Regional World: Territorial Development in a Global Economy*. New York: Guilford.

Strauss, B. (1999) The Dark Ages made lighter. In Cowley, R. (ed.) *What If?* New York: G. P. Putnam, pp. 71–92.

Su, X. and Wang, L. (1991) *Deathsong of the River: A Reader's Guide to the Chinese TV Series Heshang*. Ithaca, NY: Cornell University.

Suvin, D. (1979) *Metamorphoses of Science Fiction: On the Poetics and History of a Literary Genre*. New Haven, CT: Yale University Press.

Talbot, M. (1987) *Beyond the Quantum*. Toronto: Bantam Books (1988).

Telotte, J. P. (1999) *A Distant Technology: Science Fiction Film and the Machine Age*. Hanover, NH: Wesleyan University Press.

Tetlock, P. and Belkin, A. (eds) (1996) *Counterfactual Thought Experiments in World Politics: Logical, Methodological, and Psychological Perspectives*. Princeton, NJ: Princeton University Press.

Thompson, E. (1966) *The Making of the English Working Class*. New York: Vintage Books.

—— (1976) Time, work-discipline and industrial capitalism. *Past and Present* 38: 56–97.

—— (1978) *The Poverty of Theory*. London: Merlin.

Thornham, S. (1999) *Feminist Film Theory*. Edinburgh: Edinburgh University Press.

Thrift, N. (1978) Landscape and literature. *Environment and Planning A* 10: 347–9.

—— (1981) Owners' time and own time: the making of a capitalist time consciousness, 1300–1880. *Lund Studies in Geography Series B*, no. 48. Lund University, Sweden.

—— (1983) On the determination of social action in space and time. *Environment and Planning D: Society and Space* 1: 23–57.

Todorov, T. (1973) *The Fantastic: A Structural Approach to a Literary Genre*. Ithaca, NY: Cornell University Press.

Tomas, D. (1991) Old rituals for a new space: rites de passage and William Gibson's cultural model of cyberspace. In Benedikt, M. (ed.) *Cyberspace: First Steps*. Cambridge, MA: MIT Press, pp. 31–47.

Touraine, A. (1995) *Critique of Modernity*. Trans. Macey, D. Oxford: Blackwell.

Tsouras, P. (1994) *Disaster at D-Day: The Germans Defeat the Allies, June 1944*. London: Bantam.

Tuan, Y. (1976) Literature, experience and environmental knowing. In Moore, G. and Golledge, R. (eds) *Environmental Knowing*. Stroudsberg, PA: Dowden, Hutchinson and Ross, pp. 260–72.

—— (1978) Literature and geography: implications for geographical research. In Ley, D. and Samuels, M. (eds) *Humanistic Geography: Prospects and Problems*. Chicago: Maaroufa Press, pp. 194–206.

Turtledove, H. (1992) *The Guns of the South*. New York: Ballantine.

—— (1997) *How Few Remain*. New York: Ballantine.

—— (1998a) *The Great War: American Front*. New York: Ballantine.

—— (ed.) (1998b) *Alternate Generals*. New York: Baen.

Usai, P. C. (1994) *Burning Passions: An Introduction to the Study of Silent Cinema*. London: British Film Institute.

Vale, V. and Juno, A. (1983) *Re/Search #6/7: Industrial Culture Handbook*. San Francisco: Re/ Search Publications.

Virilio, P. (1989) The last vehicle. In Kamper, D. and Wulf, C. (eds) *Looking Back on the End of the World*. New York: Semiotext(e), pp. 106–19.

Wagar, W. (1991) J. G. Ballard and the transvaluation of utopia. *Science-Fiction Studies* 18: 53–70.

Warf, B. (1993) Post-modernism and the localities debate: ontological questions and epistemological implications. *Tijdschrift voor Economische en Sociale Geografie* 84: 162–8.

Wendt, A. (1987) The agent–structure problem in international relations theory. *International Organization* 41: 335–70.

Westfahl, G. (1993) 'The closely reasoned technological story': the critical history of hard science fiction. *Science-Fiction Studies* 20: 157–75.

Whatmore, S. (1999) Editorial: geography's place in the life-science era? *Transactions of the Institute of British Geographers* 24: 259–60.

White, H. (1973) *Metahistory: The Historical Imagination in Nineteenth-Century Europe*. Baltimore: Johns Hopkins University Press.

—— (1987) *The Content of the Form: Narrative Discourse and Historical Representation*. Baltimore: Johns Hopkins University Press.

—— (1999) *Figural Realism: Studies in the Mimesis Effect*. Baltimore: Johns Hopkins University Press.

Williams, L. (1991) Film bodies: gender, genre and excess. *Film Quarterly* 44(4): 2–13.

Winnicott, D. W. (1971) *Playing and Reality*. London: Tavistock.

Wolf, F. A. (1981) *Taking the Quantum Leap: The New Physics for Non-Scientists*. New York: Harper & Row, Perennial Library (1988).

—— (1988) *Parallel Universes: The Search for Other Worlds*. New York: Touchstone (1990).

Wollen, P. (1972) *Signs and Meanings in the Cinema*. London: Secker and Warburg, Cinema One Series.

Wolmark, J. (1993) *Aliens and Others: Science Fiction, Feminism and Postmodernism*. Hemel Hempstead: Harvester Wheatsheaf.

Wood, D. (1992) *The Power of Maps*. New York: Guilford.

Young, I. M. (1990) *Justice and the Politics of Difference*. Princeton, NJ: Princeton University Press.

Youngbear-Tibbetts, H. (1998) Making sense of the world. In Aiken, S. H., Brigham, A.,

Marston, S. A. and Waterstone, P. (eds) *Making Worlds: Gender, Metaphor and Materiality.* Tucson: University of Arizona Press, pp. 31–44.

Zee, A. (1986) *Fearful Symmetry: The Search for Beauty in Modern Physics.* New York: Collier Books.

Zukav, G. (1979) *The Dancing Wu Li Masters: An Overview of the New Physics.* Toronto: Bantam Books (1980).

# INDEX